SOCIETY FOR NEW TESTAMENT STUDIES

MONOGRAPH SERIES

GENERAL EDITOR

MATTHEW BLACK, D.D., F.B.A.

1

THE TEMPLE AND THE COMMUNITY IN QUMRAN AND THE NEW TESTAMENT

THE TEMPLE AND THE COMMUNITY IN QUMRAN AND THE NEW TESTAMENT

A COMPARATIVE STUDY IN THE TEMPLE
SYMBOLISM OF THE QUMRAN TEXTS AND
THE NEW TESTAMENT

BY

BERTIL GÄRTNER

CAMBRIDGE
AT THE UNIVERSITY PRESS
1965

PUBLISHED BY
THE SYNDICS OF THE CAMBRIDGE UNIVERSITY PRESS

Bentley House, 200 Euston Road, London, N.W. 1
American Branch: 32 East 57th Street, New York 22, N.Y.
West African Office: P.O. Box 33, Ibadan, Nigeria

©

CAMBRIDGE UNIVERSITY PRESS

1965

Printed in Great Britain at the University Printing House, Cambridge
(Brooke Crutchley, University Printer)

CONTENTS

CONTENTS

LIST OF ABBREVIATIONS

Abh. Theol. A.u.N.T.	*Abhandlungen zur Theologie des Alten und Neuen Testaments*
Anal. Bibl.	*Analecta Biblica*
B.A.S.O.R.	*Bulletin of the American Schools of Oriental Research*
Beitr. z. Förd. christl. Theol.	*Beiträge zur Förderung christlicher Theologie*
Bibl. Research	*Biblical Research*
B.J.R.L.	*Bulletin of the John Rylands Library*
Bonner Bibl. Beitr.	*Bonner biblische Beiträge*
B.Z.	*Biblische Zeitschrift*
C.B.Q.	*Catholic Biblical Quarterly*
Ephem. Theol. Lov.	*Ephemerides Theologicae Lovanienses*
E.T.	*The Expository Times*
F.R.L.A.N.T.(N.F.)	*Forschungen zur Religion und Literatur des Alten und Neuen Testaments*
H.T.R.	*Harvard Theological Review*
I.E.J.	*Israel Exploration Journal*
J.B.L.	*Journal of Biblical Literature*
J.J.S.	*Journal of Jewish Studies*
J.Q.R.	*Jewish Quarterly Review*
J.S.S.	*Journal of Semitic Studies*
J.T.S.	*Journal of Theological Studies*
Nouv. Rev. Théol.	*Nouvelle Revue Théologique*
N.T.S.	*New Testament Studies*
R.A.C.	*Reallexikon für Antike und Christentum*
R.B.	*Revue Biblique*
Rech. S.R.	*Recherches de Science Religieuse*
Rev. S.R.	*Revue des Sciences Religieuses*
Rev. Thom.	*Revue Thomiste*
R.G.G.	*Die Religion in Geschichte und Gegenwart*
R.Q.	*Revue de Qumrân*

R.S.P.T.	*Revue des Sciences Philosophiques et Théologiques*
S.J.Th.	*Scottish Journal of Theology*
Stud. Theol.	*Studia Theologica*
Sv. Exeg. Årsbok	*Svensk Exegetisk Årsbok*
Theol. Zeitsch.	*Theologische Zeitschrift*
Th.St.	*Theological Studies*
T.L.Z.	*Theologische Literaturzeitung*
T.W.B.	*Theologisches Wörterbuch zum Neuen Testament*
V.T.	*Vetus Testamentum*
Wiss. Unters. z. N.T.	*Wissenschaftliche Untersuchungen zum Neuen Testament*
Z.A.T.W.	*Zeitschrift für die alttestamentliche Wissenschaft*
Z.N.T.W.	*Zeitschrift für die neutestamentliche Wissenschaft*
Z.Th.K.	*Zeitschrift für Theologie und Kirche*

INTRODUCTION

THE origins of the concept of the Church, and its development in the earliest Christian community, are subjects which have taxed the resources of many scholars; the literature on the subject is consequently very extensive. In the realm of New Testament studies few concepts have aroused such controversy as that of the Church. The literature of the last hundred years reveals a many-sided development—a development which is still in progress, giving cause for constant revision of accepted views and leading to much fruitful pioneer work.[1] This development is, however, to some extent dependent upon currents within New Testament scholarship as a whole; the concept of the Church is not one which can be dealt with in isolation, since it stands in intimate relationship to such vital questions as the person and the self-consciousness of Jesus, the desire and capacity of the early Church for the creation of new theological ideas, and the influence of Hellenistic civilization on the Christian thought-world.

A number of the basic characteristics and presuppositions of the early Christian concept of the Church are nowadays generally accepted. For example, the principle that the origins of the concept of the Church are to be sought in the Messianic expectations of the group around Jesus and in the early Church's understanding of the person of Jesus. Nor can it well be denied that the Messianic consciousness of Jesus was such as to tend in the direction of the creation of a Church. Further, there is the fact of the solidarity of the early Church with the people of God, Israel, and the history of that nation. It is evident that the Christian congregation believed itself to have inherited the promises of God recorded in the Scriptures: in other words, to be the ideal Israel, as opposed to the Israel of history. This relationship to the people of God forms one of the most important sources of the concept of the Church.[2]

[1] See O. Linton, *Das Problem der Urkirche in der neueren Forschung* (1932); K. Stendahl, Art. 'Kirche', *R.G.G.* III³ (1959), cols. 1303f.; R. Schnackenburg, *La théologie du Nouveau Testament* (1961), pp. 105f.; and their bibliographies.

[2] N. A. Dahl, *Das Volk Gottes. Eine Untersuchung zum Kirchenbewußtsein des Urchristentums* (1941); R. Bultmann, *Theologie des Neuen Testaments* (1953), pp. 95ff.; Stendahl, *op. cit.* cols. 1297ff.

A most important source of supplementary information about those controversial New Testament texts in which the Church is mentioned has in recent years been provided by the Dead Sea Scrolls. There is no doubt that here we have a collection of early Jewish source-material giving us an insight into a milieu which had a great deal in common with that of the early Church. Both the Qumran community and the early Church owe their existence to a 'founder', whose interpretation of the Scriptures is regarded as being decisive. Both may be said to live in a Messianic atmosphere: in fact both believed themselves to be living in the last days. Both claim to be the true Israel, and claim that the promises of God apply to them. Both set strict limits to their membership.[1] The list could be extended. It follows that an attempt to illustrate the New Testament concept of the Church from the Dead Sea Scrolls should ideally compare all these points separately, in order to obtain an over-all view of the relation between the two communities. But this task is too extensive to be undertaken here; much more detailed research must be undertaken before an overall view can be expected to emerge. There is however one idea which, recurring in the thought of both communities, fulfils a most important function and can illustrate the New Testament concept of the Church at a decisive point: that is the symbolism surrounding the temple. I consider this symbolism to be of great value for the understanding of important aspects of the Qumran congregation's self-estimation; further, it provides an essential background to the understanding of the New Testament concept of the Church, particularly in its necessary connexion with Christology. New light is also cast on those elements of the New Testament concept of the Church which have hitherto been regarded as part of the Hellenistic heritage, and more adequate justice is done to the Palestinian background.

This study does not claim to consider in detail all the Qumran and New Testament texts which deal with the symbolism surrounding the temple. Nor is it possible to consider the comparative Jewish material in its entirety. This would lead far beyond the bounds of our present task. Instead we shall

---

[1] But at the same time each theme contains a difference of principle; see e.g. R. Schnackenburg, *Die Kirche im Neuen Testament* (1961), pp. 107ff.; P. Benoit, 'Qumrân et le Nouveau Testament', *N.T.S.* VII (1960–1), 276ff.

attempt to bring together the most important texts from Qumran and the New Testament respectively, showing how the two communities observed the same principle in respect of the temple and its cultus. Further, we shall try and demonstrate that certain details are to be found in both groups of texts, and that the manner of their occurrence is such as to witness to some kind of connexion between the Qumran traditions and the early Church. And finally, we shall bring forward a hypothesis explaining the nature of the link between the two communities: this remains no more than a hypothesis, since we know so little about the actual relations between the Qumran community and the early Church.

A suitable point of departure for the understanding of the Qumran statements about the temple and its priests is provided by the examination of relevant material from other Jewish sources.

AUTHOR'S NOTE

The Biblical quotations are for the most part according to the Revised Standard Version. There are details, however, in several Old Testament and New Testament texts, where the translation is closer to the Hebrew or Greek wording in order to bring out the parallel between the Biblical and Qumran texts.

CHAPTER I

THE PRIESTHOOD AND THE JERUSALEM TEMPLE

JUDAISM was rich in groups and factions. There were the groups which gathered around judges, prophets and popular leaders of various kinds; there were groups connected with the organization of the army; and many more: all were inter-related and played an important role in the social and religious life of the people. The most important of these groups during the periods when the Jerusalem temple provided a national focus were the Levites and priests. Another group which took over the spiritual leadership of the nation during the last period of the temple was the company of the scribes. But although the scribes became spiritual leaders and were respon-sible for the education of the people, the priests retained their position of prominence, for reasons connected with their necessary offices in the temple.[1] It was characteristic of the priests that they formed a closed group, membership of which was determined by heredity: they were proud to be of the family of Aaron. Priests were born, not made. Priestly marriage was also hedged about by a multitude of restrictions, for the same reason, the preservation of priestly exclusiveness.[2]

The priests thus formed a holy company distinct from the common people. Their task was to preserve the holiness and purity of Israel, and their holiness was directly derived from that which flowed forth from the temple. The temple was a focus of holiness, an idea which was stressed frequently in the days of the last temple. Yahweh himself dwelt there: there were his *kabod* and *šem*; hence Jerusalem could be called the holy city and Israel the holy people.[3] Yahweh caused his

[1] See e.g. L. Rost, 'Gruppenbildungen im Alten Testament', *T.L.Z.* LXXX (1955), 1 ff.; G. von Rad, *Theologie des Alten Testaments*, I (1957), 243 ff.; R. de Vaux, *Les institutions de l'Ancien Testament*, II (1960), 195 ff., 254 ff.

[2] Cf. E. Schürer, *Geschichte des jüdischen Volkes im Zeitalter Jesu Christi*, II (1907), 280 ff.; J. Jeremias, *Jerusalem zur Zeit Jesu*, III (1958), 77 ff.

[3] Cf. von Rad, *op. cit.* pp. 235 ff.; de Vaux, *op. cit.* pp. 166 ff.

presence, his *Shekinah*, to rest upon the 'Holy of holies' in the temple, from whence holiness spread as it were in growing concentric circles with diminishing intensity.[1] Those who would meet the Holy One in the service of the temple must therefore themselves possess a standard of holiness far exceeding that of the majority; hence the life and duties of the priest were circumscribed by laws intended to preserve his ceremonial purity.

When a priest was appointed to the service of the temple he was brought into this sphere of holiness. In the days of the last temple he was first placed on probation; he was then examined by the Sanhedrin, and if found satisfactory, was consecrated to his office in a special ceremony.[2] A priest officiating in the temple had to wear the appropriate garments, which might not be profaned;[3] he must be without physical blemish, since his duty was to offer a perfect sacrifice, and he must therefore be perfect himself. This was laid down in Lev. xxi. 17 ff.: 'For no one who has a blemish shall draw near, a man blind or lame, or one who has a mutilated face or a limb too long.... He may eat the bread of his God, both of the most holy and of the holy things, but he shall not come near the veil or approach the altar, because he has a blemish, that he may not profane my sanctuaries; for I am the Lord who sanctify them.' Those of the priestly caste who were excluded from office in this way were allowed to eat the consecrated bread, but not to approach the altar. The priests thus had to be pure both in service and in life; compared with the common people, they were required to show 'double purity'.[4] They had to be careful not to touch anything which might pollute them, and before officiating in the temple had to take a 'ritual bath', washing their hands and feet with the utmost care. At the end of a day in the temple

[1] J. Pedersen, *Israel. Its Life and Culture*, III–IV (1940), 275 ff.; J. Bonsirven, *Le Judaïsme Palestinien au temps de Jésus-Christ*, II (1935), 111 ff. This concept of holiness proceeding with diminishing intensity from the 'Holy of holies' in the temple also had its equivalent in the synagogue; see Dahl, *Das Volk Gottes*, p. 70.

[2] Schürer, *Geschichte*, II, 28 f. This act implied 'consecration' to the service of Yahweh; see further de Vaux, *Les institutions*, pp. 198 f.

[3] Josephus, *Antiq.* III, 7, 1 ff.

[4] Josephus, *Antiq.* III, 12, 2, *Bell.* V, 5, 7; I Macc. iv. 42. Cf. Schürer, *Geschichte*, II, 284.

they took off the holy white garments (of linen) and repeated their ceremonial lustrations.[1]

Each priest had his place in a strict hierarchy, and was responsible for certain definite tasks. All belonged to a main group and a further sub-group. Lots were cast when special tasks were to be allocated.[2] Evidence of the closed nature of the priestly group is provided by the ceremonial meals, to which only priests were admitted; sacral in character, they were made up of sacrificial food, which had been in contact with 'the holy'.[3] The 'bread of the Presence', too, could only be eaten by the priests. Some scholars have suggested that bread and wine were eaten at this meal in the temple.[4]

[1] Schürer, *Geschichte*, II, 340, 565. Cf. Test. Levi vii.

[2] Schürer, *op. cit.* pp. 352 f.

[3] Cf. K. G. Kuhn, 'The Lord's Supper and the Communal Meal at Qumran', in Stendahl, *The Scrolls and the New Testament* (1957), pp. 68 and 260.

[4] M. Black, *The Scrolls and Christian Origins* (1961), pp. 108 f. The difficulty with the theory of wine as part of the meal is that the priests were forbidden to drink wine while in service; see Schürer, *Geschichte*, II, 340.

CHAPTER II

THE TEMPLE PRIESTS AND QUMRAN

THE theology of the Qumran community was largely concentrated on establishing that degree of holiness which was
accounted necessary for winning God's favour in the last days.
This they believed could be attained by the detailed observance
of the rules and regulations of the Law.[1] By this means they
won a renewal of the covenant, and stood out as the pure and
holy Israel, the elect out of the 'official' Israel. This concentration on sanctification, expressed in a multitude of regulations
for ceremonial purity and an intense exclusiveness, was not
merely an expression of personal piety, but is to be seen
against the background of the priestly office as we have described it. There is a striking correspondence between the rules
binding the priests in their holy office and the methods used
by the Qumran community in order to build up their organization and preserve their holiness.[2]

The Qumran community was made up of priests and laymen, the former having considerably greater authority. These
were known as the 'sons of Zadok' or the 'sons of Aaron'. The
latter seems to have been a fairly common priestly title, setting
the priests apart from 'Israel', the community; the expression
'the sons of Zadok, the priests', on the other hand, has polemical
overtones, and implies the superiority of the class from which
the high priest was drawn. In the history of the Qumran community it was told that the Teacher of Righteousness, who was
of the priestly line, entered into conflict with a certain man who
carried out the duties of a priest without belonging to the
family of Zadok.[3] It was believed that the 'true' priests were
to be found in Qumran. Further, the community applied the

---

[1] B. Gärtner, 'Bakgrunden till Qumranförsamlingens krig', *Religion och
Bibel*, XIX (1960), 47 ff.

[2] On the general subject of the connexion between the Qumran texts
and the so-called priestly traditions, see E. Stauffer, 'Probleme der Priestertradition', *T.L.Z.*, LXXXI (1956), 135 ff.

[3] J. T. Milik, *Ten Years of Discovery in the Wilderness of Judaea* (1959), pp. 77 ff.

tradition, recorded in Ezekiel, that only the sons of Zadok might serve in the new Temple (Ezek. xliv. 15, xl. 46). There is an exposition of Ezek. xliv. 15 in C.D. iv. 1 ff., in which the expression 'the sons of Zadok' is made to apply to the whole community, and not only to the priests: the same interpretation is found in C.D. v. 5.[1] This may however have to do with the play on words between בני צדוק, 'the sons of Zadok', and בני צדק, 'the sons of righteousness', referring to the whole community (1QS iii. 20, 22; ix. 14). The texts so far discovered often have הכוהנים, 'the priests', qualifying 'the sons of Zadok' (1QS v. 2, 9; 1QSa i. 2, 24; ii. 3; 1QSb iii. 22).[2] These are the group of those whose task it is to guard the life of the community in faithfulness to the Law, שומרי הברית.[3]

A number of the characteristics of the temple priests which distinguished them from the common people are stressed in the Qumran texts, but here they are applied to the whole community. This is not to say that the entire community was made up of priests, but certain aspects of the priests' ideal of sanctification were elevated into general conditions of membership of the community—a phenomenon also to be found in Pharisaism.[4] It is laid down on a number of occasions that

[1] Cf. P. Wernberg-Møller, *The Manual of Discipline* (1957), pp. 90ff.; O. Betz, 'Le ministère cultuel dans la secte de Qumrân et dans le Christianisme primitif', in *La secte de Qumrân et les origines du Christianisme* (1959), pp. 166ff.; Fitzmyer, 'The Use of Explicit Old Testament Quotations in Qumran Literature', *N.T.S.* VII (1960–1), 318f.

[2] A third group, the Levites, are also mentioned in a number of texts. They stand in the same relationship to the priests here as they do in temple services: i.e. they have an inferior position (1QS ii. 20ff., 1QSa ii. 1, C.D. xiv. 3f.) with less important tasks. On occasion a Levite may, if he is prominent as a scholar of the Law, be given precedence over a less well-qualified priest (C.D. xiii. 3f.).

[3] The verb שמר, 'preserve', 'watch over', is used in 1QS v. 2f. to describe the task of the priests, while the 'multitude' is characterized by חזק, 'hold fast to'. This distinction between the functions of the priests or the 'inner council', שמר (1QS v. 9, viii. 3, 1QSa i. 3, C.D. iv. 1, with the exception of 1QpHab v. 5, 1QH xvi. 13, 17), and the members as a whole, חזק, seems to hold good (C.D. iii. 12, 20, viii. 2, 1QS v. 1). The priests and Levites seem also to have had the traditional task of preserving and transmitting the Torah tradition; see B. Gerhardsson, *Memory and Manuscript* (1961), p. 86.

[4] See e.g. J. Jeremias, 'Der Gedanke des "Heiligen Restes" im Spätjudentum und in der Verkündigung Jesu', *Z.N.T.W.* xlii (1949), 185f.

members must observe Levitical purity.[1] There was a catalogue of physical blemishes which excluded a priest from serving in the temple,[2] and the same demand was made of ordinary members of the Qumran community. There are texts from Qumran which specify which were the physical blemishes which excluded a man from full membership:

> But none of those who are afflicted by any human uncleanness may enter into the congregation of God. And any one who is afflicted so as to be unable to fulfil any function in the congregation, likewise any one who has a bodily affliction, mutilated in his feet or hands, lame or blind or deaf or dumb or afflicted by any bodily imperfection, which can be seen by the eyes, or an old man who stumbles so that he cannot control himself in the midst of the congregation of the renowned men, for holy angels are [in] their [congreg]ation....
>
> (1QSa ii. 3 ff.)

But those who were unable to present themselves without blemish were not thereby excluded from the community. 1QSa i. 21 f. indicates that a 'weak' person could be allocated certain tasks without being made a full member of the community; these were evidently menial tasks. If a person in this category had anything to say to the community at large, he might convey his wish to a member of the 'council', who would pass it on to the community; but he had no right to enter the 'council' himself, and speak, 'for he is indeed afflicted' (ii. 10). There is a certain parallel here to the regulations governing such temple priests as were not without blemish: these too were allocated duties outside the sacred office.[3]

Other texts which take up the question of physical qualifications for membership of the community, such as C.D. xv. 15–17 and 4QFlor. i. 3 f., show how important the question of 'perfection' was thought to be, since it was this which determined the holiness and purity of the group as a whole.[4] The link with the

---

[1] J. Maier, 'Zum Begriff יחד in den Texten von Qumran', *Z.A.T.W.* LXXII (1960), 152.

[2] Schürer, *Geschichte*, II, 284, gives a list of 142 physical blemishes which excluded a priest from serving in the temple.

[3] Schürer, *op. cit.* p. 284, n. 20.

[4] For other texts, see Gärtner, 'Bakgrunden till Qumranförsamlingens krig', pp. 66f. Note that the demand for physical perfection was not confined to the eschatological community. Although there is a certain eschatological air about 4QFlor. and 1QSa, the C.D. texts apply to the community

regulations for the temple priests is emphasized by the motivation which accompanies all texts of this type: 'for the holy
angels are in their community'. The demand for holiness was
thus subject to the demands of the cultus, a situation reminiscent of the Jerusalem temple priests, where Yahweh was
believed to be present.[1] The temple priests had to be 'perfect'
before the face of Yahweh: the members of the Qumran community were commanded to be 'perfect' in the exercise of their
cultic functions.

We know very little about the age-limits imposed on the
priests who served in the temple. It is commonly supposed that
they were the same as for the Levites, on which we have a
certain amount of information in the Torah texts. The difficulty
here is that different ages are given for entry into the offices of
priest and Levite. According to Ezra iii. 8 the Levite had to
be twenty years old before he might serve in the temple;[2] the
figure in Num. viii. 23 ff. is twenty-five, and in Num. iv. 3
thirty.[3] The upper age-limit for these specific offices is said to
be fifty (Num. viii. 23 ff.). It is interesting to note that similar
age-limits were imposed in Qumran. 1QSa mentions in this
connexion the ages twenty, twenty-five and thirty. At the age
of twenty a man might enter the community and be allocated
his particular task (i. 8 ff.). The age-limit for entry to the
'council' was however twenty-five (i. 8 ff.), and no one under
the age of thirty was entitled to sit in judgement. An upper
age-limit is mentioned, but no specific age is given. When a
member becomes so old that he is no longer able to do his
appointed work and there is a risk that he may cause 'defilement' in the community, he is, like any other who might be
unclean in any way, excluded from being a full member
(1QSa ii. 7 f.).[4] The upper age-limit need not necessarily have

as it existed. The characteristics which it was believed would distinguish
the community of the future must be sought after here and now, particularly
since the purity of the community provided the conditions on which victory
would be won in the final war and the eschatological community established.
[1] Cf. F. Nötscher, 'Heiligkeit in den Qumranschriften', *R.Q.* II (1959–60),
pp. 167 f.　　[2] Cf. I Chron. xxiii. 24, 27; II Chron. xxxi. 17.
[3] Cf. Num. iv. 23, 30, 35, 39, 43, 47; I Chron. xxiii. 3.
[4] C.D. x. 6 f. gives twenty-five years as the lowest age at which a man
might belong to a court of ten, and sixty as the upper age-limit, after which
he is debarred from service. F. F. Hvidberg, *Menigheden af den nye Pagt i*

anything to do with that imposed on the temple priests,[1] but it forms an interesting addition to the resemblances between the temple priests and the Qumran community.

The strict hierarchy of the Qumran community resembles so closely the system observed among the temple priests that it is tempting to regard it as a reminiscence of the group which once broke away from the Jerusalem temple. This is particularly true of 1QSa, in which every priest, Levite and member has his own place and his own particular task (i. 16ff., 23, ii. 14, 21). In 1QS ii. 22 we read that 'every one in Israel must know his place, בית מעמדו', the reference being to his position in the hierarchy of priests, Levites and 'people'. Promotion is achieved on the basis of the individual's knowledge of the Law and 'revelation', his good works and the quality of his life; it may be withheld if these are not evident (1QS v. 23f., vi. 26).[2] The positions to be occupied by the individual members of the community were reviewed each year, lots being cast in order to avoid being led astray by appearances, and in order to secure the seal of divine approval. As in the temple, we find rings of holiness widening and diminishing according to their proximity to the 'Holy of holies' of the inner group.

Particular difficulties are connected with the passage 1QM ii. 1ff., which deals with the division of the priestly class in the temple,[3] the allocation of tasks, the celebration of the

Damascus (1928), p. 141, points out that according to Lev. xxvii. 7 a man's worth becomes less once he has passed the age of sixty. C. Rabin, *The Zadokite Documents* (1954), p. 50, refers to a passage in pseudo-Hieronymus, which reads *ab anno sexagesimo et levitae ministrare et milites pugnare desinebant.* The age-limits in 1QM vi. 13ff., vii. 1ff. seem also to be connected with the hierarchical structure of the community, but are more difficult to interpret, cf. J. Carmignac, *La Règle de la Guerre* (1958), pp. 29f.

[1] P. Borgen, '"At the Age of Twenty" in 1QSa', *R.Q.* III (1960–1), 267ff., considers the reference to 'the age of twenty' to have to do with property and coming of age. Cf. the discussions between S. Hoenig and J. M. Baumgarten in *J.Q.R.* 1958 and 1959.

[2] Cf. the order of seniority of the Rabbinic colleges, Gerhardsson, *Memory and Manuscript*, pp. 245ff.

[3] Here twenty-six sub-groups are mentioned, as against twenty-four in the temple. The Qumran figure of twenty-six may be connected with the community's having its own festival calendar based on the solar year. Cf. Sh. Talmon, 'The Calendar Reckoning of the Sect from the Judaean Desert', *Scripta Hierosolymitana*, IV (1958), 168ff.

festivals and the offering of the sacrifices. We do not know whether it refers to temple worship at some future date when the community will have conquered all its enemies and rebuilt and purified the temple, or whether it is a symbolic and 'spiritual' description of the actual cultus of the community itself.[1] The 'War Scroll' contains widely divergent material, and it is not easy to interpret the various sections. But that the congregation is of priestly origin[2] is evident from the interest shown in the divisions and hierarchy of the priesthood, in the allocation of their duties in the temple and in their dress.[3] This is also to some extent true of the fragmentary texts of *Mišmarôt* which give the rota of the priestly families' service in the temple,[4] texts closely linked with the liturgy of the Jerusalem temple and similar material.[5]

These texts were however mainly the concern of the priests in the community. We have seen how certain aspects of the life and organization of the priestly caste came to influence the entire community; other aspects remained restricted to the priests within the community. Those members of the Qumran

[1] Interpretation depends on such difficult questions as that of the attitude of the community to the Jerusalem sacrifices of their time; see e.g. Carmignac, *La Règle de la Guerre*, pp. 27 ff., and 'L'utilité ou l'inutilité des sacrifices sanglants dans la "Règle de la Communauté" de Qumrân', *R.B.* LXIII (1956), 525 ff. On the symbolical exposition see below, pp. 44 ff.

[2] Nielsen–Otzen, *Dødehavsteksterne* (1959), p. 157, mention, in connexion with 1QM ii. 1 ff., that the Qumran community was organized as a parallel to the Jerusalem priesthood.

[3] The description of the garments of the priests in 1QM vii. 10 f. corresponds exactly to those worn by the temple priests in the performance of their duties, מכנסים, כתות, אבנט and מגבעה. Cf. Schürer, *Geschichte*, II, 338 f.

[4] Interest in families and descent, which is such a marked feature of the temple priests, can also be seen in 1QM iii. 4. Cf. the term אבות העדה in 1QSa i. 16, 24 f., ii. 16, which may have to do with a classification of the serving priests' divisions and sub-groups, בתי אבות, Schürer, *op. cit.* pp. 286 ff.

[5] M. Baillet, in a report on Cave 6, *R.B.* LXIII (1956), 55; Milik, *Ten Years of Discovery in the Wilderness of Judaea*, pp. 41 f.; Baillet, 'Fragments araméens de Qumrân 2', *R.B.* LXII (1955), 222 ff., and 'Un recueil liturgique de Qumrân, grotte 4: "Les paroles des luminaires"', *R.B.* LXVIII (1961), 198 ff. See also K. H. Rengstorf, *Hirbet Qumrân und die Bibliothek vom Toten Meer* (1960), pp. 25 ff., who claims that the description of temple worship in these texts refers to the actual temple in Jerusalem, and not to an eschatological temple (cf. pp. 68 ff.).

community who were of priestly descent evidently continued to exercise priestly functions, though now within the framework of the community. These included priestly and Levitical blessings, cursings and proclamations—according to 1QS i. 18–ii. 25 on the festival of the renewal of the covenant. These passages contain a number of reminiscences of the temple liturgy.[1]

Other tasks carried out by the Qumran priests included taking care of the common property of the community (1QS ix. 7f.) and the administration of justice.[2] The custom of having common property, as practised in the community, was more than a mere expression of ascetic piety; it probably had to do with an ideal of cultic purity and may have originated in the distribution among the various priests of the temple income, which took place within the temple itself.[3] The priestly administration of justice (C.D. x. 5ff.) can be clearly traced back to the Old Testament, and in particular to Ezekiel's description (in xliv. 24) of the ideal priest.[4] A further prominent function of the priests was their role in battle, according to the 'War Scroll'. The whole of the battle described there was in fact led by the priests, blowing blasts on their trumpets.[5]

A comparison between the milieu of the temple priests and that of the Qumran community must also take into account the table fellowship which was such an important element in the lives of the two groups. At the centre of the Qumran fellowship there was a meal which was purely sacral in character, and which consisted of bread and wine (1QS vi. 2–8 and 1QSa ii. 11–22). There has been a great deal of discussion about the implications and ritual form of this meal, and widely

[1] J. Baumgarten, 'Sacrifice and Worship among the Jewish Sectarians of the Dead Sea (Qumrân) Scrolls', *H.T.R.* XLVI (1953), 158f.; M. Weise, *Kultzeiten und kultischer Bundesschluß in der 'Ordensregel' vom Toten Meer* (1961), pp. 61ff., appears not to be interested in the liturgy of the temple in this context.

[2] 1QS v. 3 lays down that it is the priests and the people who are to decide; in ix. 7f. the priests are regarded as of more importance. Cf. Wernberg-Møller, *The Manual of Discipline*, p. 134.

[3] Cf. Rost, 'Gruppenbildungen im Alten Testament', *T.L.Z.* LXXX (1955), 6f. [4] Hvidberg, *Menigheden*, p. 140.

[5] Here too I consider that we have a reminiscence of temple worship in Jerusalem, which was accompanied by flourishes on the trumpet. Trumpets were of course cultic instruments, as well as instruments used in wartime.

divergent conclusions have been reached.[1] Significant for our purpose is the possibility that it may have embodied reminiscences of the closed table fellowship enjoyed by the temple priests. We are reminded of the meals held in the temple, at which the priests ate the 'holy things', pieces of the offerings.[2] It has also been suggested that there may be some connexion between the priests partaking of the 'bread of the Presence', and the sacral meal of the Qumran community. The Meeting hall, the 'Hall of the Covenant' in the Qumran monastery, it is said, may have contained a table reminiscent of that on which the 'bread of the Presence' was exhibited in the temple.[3] Only those who were 'pure', that is, full members of the community, might attend the meals in the Meeting hall.[4]

This meal, which differed from the normal meals of the community in that it was sacral in character, was presided over by a priest, who blessed the elements and was the first to partake of them. It was hedged about with detailed regulations ensuring the purity of those taking part, and was eaten in strict conformity with the hierarchical order of the community. An Aramaic fragment from Qumran is said to describe the sacral meal in the heavenly temple, a meal in which the sons of Zadok were to take part.[5] The inference seems to be that the community's sacral meal was understood as being an anticipation of the perfected ritual of the heavenly temple.[6] Philo's description of the Therapeutae, which in many ways resembles what we know of the Qumran community without, however, permitting an identification of the two, contains reminiscences of the priest's

Cf. Friedrich, art. σάλπιγξ, *T.W.B.* vii, 82. The cultic function of the trumpet is also mentioned in C.D. xi. 22, cf. Hvidberg, *op. cit.* pp. 158 ff., and Baumgarten, 'Sacrifice and Worship', pp. 146 f.

[1] See e.g. J. van der Ploeg, 'The Meals of the Essenes', *J.S.S.* ii (1957), 163 ff.; J. Gnilka, 'Das Gemeinschaftsmahl der Essener', *B.Z.* 5 (1961), 39 ff.

[2] K. G. Kuhn, 'The Lord's Supper and the Communal Meal at Qumran', in Stendahl, *The Scrolls and the New Testament* (1957), pp. 68 f. Cf. Maier, 'Zum Begriff יחד in den Texten vom Qumran', *Z.A.T.W.* lxxii (1960), 158 f.

[3] M. Black, *The Scrolls and Christian Origins* (1961), pp. 108 f.

[4] See Gnilka, *op. cit.* pp. 45 f.

[5] M. Baillet, 'Fragments araméens de Qumrân 2', *R.B.* lxii (1955), 228, 243 f.

[6] Black, *op. cit.* pp. 110 f.

offering of the 'bread of the Presence' in the temple, again in the context of a cultic meal (*De vita contemplativa*, IX, 69ff.). Similar details are to be found in Josephus' account of the Essenes, pointing to the temple as the place of origin of their cultic meal.[1]

Inseparable from the sacral meal were rites of purification, indicative of the high degree of holiness surrounding the ritual actions. Archaeology confirms that facilities for carrying out the ceremonies of purification were provided around the Meeting hall. Water was piped from the main conduit to one end of the hall, evidence that large amounts were required for the needs of washing and purification.

The Meeting hall is the largest of the rooms belonging to the Qumran monastery which have been excavated, and it is probable that it served as an assembly hall for the inner circle of the community, those who had achieved purity and holiness. It was here too that the normal meals were eaten by the 'pure', to judge from the discovery of a large number of plates and cups in a smaller room beyond the hall.[2] This accords well with Josephus' description of the Essenes' sacral meals, and provides further support for the theory of their priestly origin.[3] Josephus mentions the rites of purification observed by the Essenes before partaking of the meal, the putting on of special garments of white linen, the strictly private character of the meal (excluding all who did not possess the requisite degree of holiness), the conclusion of the meal with new purifications and the taking off of the white garments, *Bell.* II, 8, 5.[4] Opinions differ as to

[1] Kuhn, 'The Lord's Supper', pp. 68ff.; Betz, *Le ministère cultuel dans la secte de Qumrân*, pp. 163f.

[2] R. de Vaux, *L'archéologie et les manuscrits de la Mer Morte* (1961), pp. 8ff.; H. Bardtke, *Die Handschriftenfunde am Toten Meer*, II (1958), 53ff.

[3] Baumgarten, 'Sacrifice and Worship', pp. 155–7. Betz, *Le ministère cultuel dans la secte de Qumrân*, pp. 184f., attempts to connect the measurements of the Meeting hall with those of the upper room in the second temple (above the 'Holy place' and 'Holy of holies') in Jerusalem.

[4] These garments, worn only on the occasion of the Essenes' cultic meal, are reminiscent of the temple priests' linen garments, which might be used only in the service, and which might only be put on or taken off with purificatory rites. These were also white, a colour which symbolized purity, see Middot v. 4c. Josephus, *Bell.* v, 5, 7, writes that 'defective' priests were compelled to wear ordinary clothes, ταῖς γε μὴν ἐσθήσεσιν ἰδιωτικαῖς ἐχρῶντο, the holy garments being limited to priests in service. On the

whether the Essenes' cultic meal had the character of a sacrifice, and it is not possible to advance this as a further parallel between the temple priests and the Qumran community. Discoveries of pots containing fragments of bone, which might *per se* indicate a sacrificial meal, have not as yet been placed in their proper context.[1] I believe that this aspect of table fellowship can also be traced to the conditions of the priests' duties in the temple. The Qumran sacral meal may have been intended to replace the custom of the temple priests' eating the flesh of the sacrificial animals: the holy oblation must be eaten by the sanctified in a consecrated room—a situation emphasized by the rites of purification in connexion with the meal. These rites may also have included the taking of a ritual bath, a condition likewise imposed on the temple priests.[2]

It thus seems that there was a certain amount in common between the Qumran community, the Therapeutae as described by Philo and the Essenes as described by Josephus; this common ground included reminiscences of the temple priests and worship in the temple. Faced with these resemblances, it is impossible to escape the thought that the attitude of the Qumran community was not dictated solely by an intensified search for sanctification and a desire for absolute purity. Their attempt to re-establish the true Israel by means of perfect submission to the Law was, as they saw it, aimed at the creation of those conditions on which Israel might be raised from humiliation and set on the road to final victory. But this ideal of sanctification and purity drew its inspiration very largely from the temple in Jerusalem and the priests who served there. The centre of Israel was the temple; there dwelt Yahweh, thence poured holiness. Should the congregation be compelled

---

subject of clothes, see A. Büchler, *Die Priester und der Cultus im letzten Jahr-zehnt des Jerusalemischen Tempels* (1895), pp. 136f. Cf. also 1QM vii. 11, which lays down that the priests' 'field clothes' are not to be used in the 'sanctuary'.

[1] Fr. M. Cross, *The Ancient Library of Qumrân* (1958), pp. 51f., calls these bones 'the remains of the sacramental meals of the community', and concludes that the community offered its own sacrifices (p. 76). A more cautious approach to the problem is made by de Vaux, *L'archéologie*, pp. 10f. and van der Ploeg, *The Meals of the Essenes*, pp. 172f.

[2] Betz, *Le ministère cultuel*, pp. 179f.; Gnilka, *Das Gemeinschaftsmahl*, p. 43.

to abandon this centre, it was of the utmost importance that a new centre should be created: this idea, too, was characteristic of the ideology of the community.

There seems to have been a purely historical reason for this interest in the temple and its priests.[1] The evidence seems to suggest that the founders of the Qumran community came from the temple and from the company of the temple priests.[2] They believed themselves to represent the true priestly line—the sons of Zadok—and believed that the cultus and the holiness it required had become degenerate. Their critical attitude to the 'profanation' of the office of high priest by the Maccabees had driven them out from the official cultus of Israel and from its spiritual centre. It seems likely that the existence of the community was the product of very many causes.[3] But an important element in the profanation of the temple was that a family other than that from which the high priest could traditionally be drawn had taken over the office, thereby 'defiling' the cultus.[4] A related question was which calendar should be followed in temple worship; it is common knowledge that the Jerusalem authorities had been severely criticized for observing the festivals and the hours at the wrong times.[5] The Qumran community now attempted to set itself up as the true Israel, and it is probably true to say that the leaders of the community were temple priests who had settled down by the shores of the Dead Sea in the hope of creating a new spiritual centre to replace the desecrated temple until the day when God would finally reveal himself and confirm Israel's victory. The coming Messiah, of the line of Aaron, would be of their

[1] J. L. Teicher, 'Priests and Sacrifices in the Dead Sea Scrolls', *J.J.S.* v (1954), 93 ff., denies that there is any connexion between the temple priests and Qumran, saying that when the texts speak of the temple, the priests and the sacrifice they are merely making use of metaphors. His argument is however unconvincing.

[2] Here we may compare in particular C.D. iv and its interpretation of Ezek., 4QpPs xxxvii. 11. 15 and its description of the Teacher of Righteousness, [הכוהן מורה ה[צדק], and 1QpHab ii. 7 ff.

[3] Cf. Gärtner, 'Bakgrunden till Qumranförsamlingens krig', pp. 44 f.

[4] See e.g. Milik, *Ten Years of Discovery in the Wilderness of Judaea*, pp. 66 ff.; de Vaux, *L'archéologie*, pp. 90 ff. Cf. Jeremias, *Jerusalem*, III, 49 f.

[5] de Vaux, *op. cit.* p. 96, 'cette adoption d'un calendrier spécial est un trait essentiel de la communauté et a été l'une des causes—peut-être la cause principale—de sa séparation du Judaïsme officiel'.

number, and would precede the royal Messiah of the house of David.[1]

It is thus possible to trace a connexion between the Qumran community and the temple and its priesthood, a connexion which existed from the very first; hence the resemblances we have noted between the rules and ideals of the community and those of the temple priests. This explains the sense in which the Dead Sea texts claim that the community constituted a new temple. Once the focus of holiness in Israel had ceased to be the temple, it was necessary to provide a new focus. This focus was the community, which called itself 'the Holy place' and 'the Holy of holies'.

[1] See Kuhn, 'Die beiden Messias Aarons und Israels', *N.T.S.* I (1954-5), 170 ff.; J. Liver, 'The Doctrine of the Two Messiahs in Sectarian Literature in the Time of the Second Commonwealth', *H.T.R.* LII (1959), 180 ff.; F. F. Bruce, *Biblical Exegesis in the Qumran Texts* (1959), pp. 37 ff.

CHAPTER III

THE 'NEW TEMPLE' IN QUMRAN

ONE of the fundamental elements in the temple symbolism of the Qumran community was a conviction that the 'presence' of God, the Spirit of God, was no longer bound to the temple in Jerusalem but to the true and pure Israel represented by the community. The Jerusalem temple had been defiled by 'the wicked priest' and his people. The fathers of the community therefore left 'the holy city and placed their trust in God in those days when Israel sinned and made the temple unclean' (C.D. xx. 22 f.). But the fact of the disruption did not mean that it was impossible to replace in some way the Divine presence and the cultus of the temple. Thus it was that the community came to replace the temple of Jerusalem; they themselves were the 'new temple'. This symbolism was of course not wholly due to the fact that they traced their descent to the company of the temple priests and that certain of their number were priests; we must reckon with the belief, common among the Jews at that time, that the temple would be restored and re-established in the last days. The old temple would be replaced by a new one, of quite new dimensions.

As far back as the traditions of Ezekiel and Haggai we find the idea of the coming aeon, under the rule of God, when a new temple would be given to the people to replace the one which had been destroyed. The temple would be a sign that God had come to dwell among the people eternally (Ezek. xxxvii. 26 ff., xl. 1 ff.), and its glory a manifestation of the entire fulfilment of the promises of God: 'The latter splendour of this house shall be greater than the former...' (Hagg. ii. 9). At this time, when the exiles dreamed of the restoration of Israel, the image was of an earthly temple, built on Mount Zion, in which faultless worship would be celebrated. This 'earthly' aspect recurs in the dreams of the Maccabaean age. Having experienced the desecration of the temple under the Seleucids, they comforted themselves with the thought of a new temple of glory in Jerusalem, built by men for God.

It is this idea which forms the background of, for example, the legend of Jeremiah and his concealment of the Tabernacle and the Ark in expectation of the coming temple (II Macc. ii. 4ff.), and which is behind the words of the Book of Tobit about the two temples, one temporary, existing only to the end of the present age, and one permanent: 'and the house of God shall be built in it (Jerusalem) for all generations in the (coming) age to be a glorious building as the prophets have said' (xiv. 5).

But there was another view, according to which the coming temple was to be the work of God himself and of heavenly dimensions (I En. xc. 28f., Jub. i. 28f.).[1] Although an attempt was being made to describe heavenly realities, the temple had become such a centre for the people and such a symbol of Israel that it was impossible to visualize even the age to come without its temple.[2] This temple was to come down from heaven, and would be eternal.[3] It was sometimes believed that the coming Messiah would himself build the new temple, distinguished from its predecessors by its absolute perfection.[4] This we might perhaps call a 'spiritual' version of what tended otherwise to be a worldly and—at least partly—politically inspired hope. It is of course not always easy to distinguish these two aspects of Israel's hope of a new temple; they often went hand in hand.[5]

This brings us to the complex problem of how to interpret the relationship between, on the one hand, the temple and its cultus and, on the other, the Law and its fulfilment. Wenschkewitz, who is one of the leading authorities in this field,[6] has

---

[1] Bonsirven, *Le Judaïsme Palestinien*, I, 431 f.; Volz, *Die Eschatologie der jüdischen Gemeinde*, pp. 373 ff.; Strack–Billerbeck, *Kommentar*, IV, 884 f.; Vielhauer, *Oikodome. Das Bild vom Bau in der christlichen Literatur vom Neuen Testament bis Clemens Alexandrinus* (1940), pp. 20f.; Jeremias, *Jesus als Weltvollender*, Beitr. z. Förd. christl. Theol. XXXIII (1930), 35 ff.; G. Schrenk, art. ἱερός, *T.W.B.* III, 239f.; Dahl, *Das Volk Gottes*, pp. 88f.; H. Riesenfeld, *Jésus transfiguré* (1947), pp. 52, 182 ff.

[2] Cf. Strack–Billerbeck, *op. cit.* IV, 884f.

[3] See e.g. F. Weber, *Jüdische Theologie* (1897), pp. 375 ff.

[4] K. L. Schmidt, 'Jerusalem als Urbild und Abbild', *Eranos*, XVIII (1950), 221 ff.; Congar, *Le mystère du temple*, pp. 119 ff.

[5] See e.g. Wenschkewitz, *Die Spiritualisierung der Kultusbegriffe*, Angelos-Beiheft IV (1932), 22f.

[6] See previous note.

17

suggested that the religious life of the Jews between the Maccabaean period and the time of the Rabbis after A.D. 70 had two
foci: the worship of the temple and the Law. The Law came
gradually to occupy a more prominent position, resulting in a
diminution of the influence of the priests and the emergence of
the scribes as the leaders of the people. This alteration in the
balance of power provides one of the reasons why the destruction of the temple proved less of a catastrophe for Jewish
religion than might have been expected: the scribes—the
expositors of the Torah—were thereby given the chance of
developing and extending their influence. This development
from the Maccabaean age down to the Rabbinic period was
closely followed by a spiritualizing of the temple and the terms
of the cultus.

If we compare this development with the ideology of the
Qumran community, we see at once that the latter was also
dominated by the same two factors, the Law and the temple
cultus, and that the Law, its exposition and fulfilment, occupies
the place of honour. This dominance of the Law was of course
largely due to the critical attitude of the founders of the community to the cultus as performed by the Maccabees and the
temple priests. The historical explanation of the community's
characteristic criticism of the temple is to be found in the
struggle between the 'wicked priest' and the Teacher of
Righteousness. But the community's concentration on the
Law[1] must not be allowed to obscure the importance of
the ideology connected with the temple and the cultus. For the
community did not consider itself to have broken with the
temple and the cultus in all its forms; instead they transferred
the whole complex of ideas from the Jerusalem temple to the
community. This undoubtedly meant that some measure of
'spiritualization' had taken place, since the idea of the temple
was now linked with the community, and since the temple
worship was now performed through the community's observance of the Law and through its own liturgy and cultus. The
use of the word 'spiritualization' must not be taken to mean
that the 'temple' which was the community was thought of any
less realistically than the Jerusalem temple, or that the community's life of obedience to the Law was considered to be any

[1] See Gärtner, 'Bakgrunden till Qumranförsamlingens krig'.

less real than the blood sacrifices. The word is used to indicate the transference of the concrete entity, the temple building, to a more 'spiritual' realm in the living community, and of the sacrifices to deeds in the life lived according to the Law.[1] At the same time we find traces of the idea that the victory to be won at some time in the future by the true Israel (the community) would usher in a new temple era.[2] This vision of the restoration of the temple and the re-establishment of the cultus represents one side of the demand for perfection in the life of Israel made by the Messianic epoch. The other was made up of the consummate power of the Law among a righteous people. The Law and the temple thus belong to the same complex of ideas.[3]

If what we have said about the view of the Qumran community on the relation between the Law and the temple be correct, it is not surprising that we encounter texts which on the one hand criticize sharply the institution of the temple, and on the other have a great deal of positive comment to make on the sacrificial office and the temple cultus. We thus find expressions of considerable interest in what took place in the temple and its cultus; further, we find a positive attitude to the temple priests in Jerusalem in the midst of all the criticism.[4] Mention is also made of the various kinds of sacrifice which belonged in the context of temple worship. But at the same time serious accusations are made against those who served in the temple (C.D. iv. 18ff., 1QpHab ix. 4f., xi. 12ff.), to the effect that they profaned the temple (1QpHab xii. 9, cf. Ps. Sol. viii. 10ff.), and failed to observe the Law and its regulations for service in the temple (C.D. v. 6f., vi. 12f.). There were many in those days who brought forward objections (of varying force) to the temple. Their reasons for doing so differed.[5] Few however directed such bitter accusations against

---

[1] See below, pp. 44ff.   [2] See above, pp. 8f.
[3] This also applies to the Rabbinic ideology, in which the Law is otherwise the dominant factor. Cf. Weber, *Jüdische Theologie*, pp. 376ff.
[4] Cf. M. Burrows, *More Light on the Dead Sea Scrolls* (1958), pp. 363ff.; Ringgren, *Tro och liv enligt Döda-havsrullarna* (1961), pp. 169f.
[5] See e.g. Gärtner, *The Areopagus Speech and Natural Revelation* (1955), pp. 205ff.; Cullmann, 'L'opposition contre le temple de Jérusalem, motif commun de la théologie johannique et du monde ambiant', *N.T.S.* v (1958–9), 164ff.

the temple as those we find in the Qumran texts.[1] They refused even to send their offering to the temple, because the altar had been polluted, and would in turn pollute the sacrifice (xi. 19f.).[2] This is not an objection to the principle of blood sacrifice—at least not according to some texts—but at the same time they regarded the sacrifices offered in the temple as unclean. But at the end of the evil age through which the world was then passing, the temple cultus would once more be set up in all its majesty; then the precepts of the Law would be followed, and the sacrifice would be pure and pleasing to God. It is this kind of positive attitude which, it has been suggested, forms the background to texts like C.D. xvi. 13, 1QS ix. 4f., 1QM ii. 5–6 and the Aramaic fragment from Cave 2 which is said to describe the heavenly Jerusalem.[3] But when the cultus of the Jerusalem temple could no longer be accepted, a substitute was found in the community itself: the temple, its worship, 'abodâ, and its sacrifices were made to apply to the community per se, its life of obedience to the Law and its liturgy. This process may

[1] Similar ideas are to be found in documents closely related to the ideology of Qumran: e.g. Test. Levi xiv–xvi, the Assumption of Moses, the Psalms of Solomon, etc. See Betz, Le ministère cultuel dans la secte de Qumrân, pp. 171f.

[2] Some consider that this is tantamount to an order forbidding the members of the community to send sacrificial gifts to the temple; this seems to be the most likely interpretation, see Hvidberg, Menigheden, pp. 156ff.; Baumgarten, 'Sacrifice and Worship', pp. 143ff. The text can however be interpreted as laying great emphasis on purity, without expressly forbidding blood sacrifices, cf. Carmignac, 'L'utilité ou l'inutilité des sacrifices sanglants', R.B. LXIII (1956), 524ff. (Milik supports him.) This seems to fit what Josephus tells us of the Essenes and their attitude to the temple and its sacrifices (see Black, The Scrolls and Christian Origins, pp. 41f.); according to one interpretation of Josephus' statements, the Essenes sent sacrifices to the temple, but took care to avoid having their gifts contaminated by contact with 'unclean' sacrifices. But the Josephus text in question (Antiq. XVIII, 1, 5) can also be interpreted so as to support the contention that the Essenes declined to take part in the temple sacrifices; this again provides a point of contact (though based on a diametrically opposed interpretation) between the Essenes, in Josephus' account, and the Qumran community; e.g. Flusser, 'The Dead Sea Sect and Pre-Pauline Christianity', Scripta Hierosolymitana, IV (1958), 230; D. H. Wallace, 'The Essenes and Temple Sacrifice', Theol. Zeitsch. XIII (1957), 335ff. On the discussion see Strugnell, 'Flavius Josephus and the Essenes', J.B.L. LXXVII (1958), 113ff., and H. H. Rowley, 'The Qumran Sect and Christian Origins', B.J.R.L. XLIV (1961), 131f.   [3] Cf. Carmignac, op. cit. 524ff.

have been further facilitated by the idea, found elsewhere in late Judaism, that the works of the Law were sufficient to make atonement for sins.[1]

This complex of ideas seems to have applied only to the interim period preceding the final re-establishment by God of the temple and its cult, once all his enemies had been overcome. The reason why the community, though isolated from Jerusalem, did not wholly abandon the temple ideal seems to have been that the entire fulfilment of the Law—the condition on which victory in the final conflict depended—demanded the fulfilment of the Law in respect of the temple as well. This was rendered possible by a transfer of meaning, from the carrying out of blood sacrifice to the living of a life according to the precepts of the Law, thus making a sacrifice of deeds and of lips. Note, however, that the Qumran texts contain eschatological passages which make no mention of the future restoration of the Jerusalem temple, but represent the 'new' temple of the future entirely in 'spiritual' terms, referring to the community and its life according to the Law.[2]

The transference of this complex of ideas from the temple to the community may have been facilitated by the fact that even in the Old Testament Israel was sometimes spoken of as 'the house of God'.[3] The people are described as a 'house', thus providing a parallel to the ideology of the Qumran community in speaking of itself as 'the house of God', the true temple. The word 'house' has of course a double meaning: on the one hand 'building', on the other 'family', 'dynasty'. In its former meaning it is often used to refer to the temple.[4] This 'house' symbolism seems to have been primary; the symbolism of the 'temple' developed later in response to the demands of a particular situation, in which there was a strong element of temple criticism.[5] There is clear evidence of both these exegetical traditions in the Qumran texts, and also in the New

---

[1] Cf. E. Lohse, *Märtyrer und Gottesknecht*, F.R.L.A.N.T.(N.F.) XLVI (1955), 24 ff. [2] See below, pp. 30 ff., on 4QFlor.

[3] Cf. Vielhauer, *Oikodome*, p. 10.

[4] Cf. Congar, *Le mystère du temple*, pp. 44, 190. On the temple as 'house' see p. 104, and Michel, art. οἶκος, *T.W.B.* v, 123 f., Schlier, *Der Brief an die Epheser* (1957), p. 141.

[5] Michel, *op. cit.* p. 129, considers that the 'house' symbolism has developed out of the image of the temple.

Testament.[1] They are often so interwoven as to be inseparable from each other: compare C.D. iii. 19 f., 'And he built for them in Israel a firmly established house, the like of which has not existed from ancient times until this day. They that hold fast unto it are (destined) for life eternal. . . '[2] and 1QpHab viii. 1 f., where the use of the terms 'the house of Judah' and 'the house of judgement' witnesses to the widespread use of the metaphor.

A. 1QS V. 5 ff., VIII. 4 ff., IX. 3 ff.

There are a number of Qumran texts which illustrate the way in which the symbolism of the temple was expressed, and provide clear evidence of the idea of the community as a replacement for the official temple. The members of the community were to separate themselves from the 'godless' and live a life of perfect obedience to the Law; in this way they could create the conditions for the fulfilment of the promises of God in the true Israel, and at the same time win the blessing of God, bringing victory over all the enemies of the people.[3] A further consequence is the re-establishment of the people, the country and the Law. The people and the temple had been abandoned by God (C.D. i. 3 ff.), but now God could once more intervene, choosing a new elect and coming to dwell among them. This means that even the official cultus in Jerusalem was replaced, since the community had become the new temple, ' . . . to lay a foundation of truth for Israel, for the community, יחד,[4] of the eternal covenant, to make atonement for all those who of their own free will have dedicated themselves to (be) a sanctuary in Aaron and a house of truth in Israel, and for those who join them for a community, יחד, and an accusation and a judgement, declaring the guilt of all those who transgress the

---

[1] Cf. Betz, 'Felsenmann und Felsengemeinde', *Z.N.T.W.* XLVIII (1957), 52 ff., and Michel, *op. cit.* pp. 128 ff.

[2] On the subject of the relationship between the 'house' and the 'kingdom', and the way in which the term 'house' is taken to mean the future Israel, see S. Aalen, '"Reign" and "House" in the Kingdom of God in the Gospels', *N.T.S.* VIII (1961–2), 234 ff.

[3] Gärtner, 'Bakgrunden till Qumranförsamlingens krig', pp. 47 ff.

[4] For a discussion of the meaning of this obscure word, see Maier, 'Zum Begriff יחד in den Texten von Qumran', *Z.A.T.W.* LXXII (1960), 148 ff. It is of particular interest to note that the term יחד is closely connected with temple symbolism, pp. 161 f.

fixed (commandments of God)...' (1QS v. 5ff.). This division
of the community into the two groups, Aaron and Israel, is
commonly seen in those texts which deal with the organization
and rules of the community:[1] it corresponds to priests and laity
(people).[2] In the passage quoted above the expressions 'a
foundation of truth', מוסד אמת, 'a sanctuary in Aaron', קודש
באהרון, and 'a house of truth', בית האמת, seem to be parallel,
all describing the Qumran community. The community is the
bearer of truth; and more, for it is itself an expression of the
truth. The community knows the will of God, possesses his
revelations, and may therefore be called the 'foundation of
truth'; this foundation can never be disturbed, since it is an
expression of what is eternal, the true revelations of God.[3] The
foundation of the community established it as 'the house of
truth in Israel'. Here we sense that an attempt is being made
to represent the community as opposed to Jerusalem and the
temple, the centre of Israel. The name of God was linked with
the holy city and its temple: God himself 'dwelt' there; thence
proceeded the word of God, the Torah and its exposition. There
was the 'city of truth', and every dream of the future centred
on the temple and its springs of salvation. From Zion, too,
judgement was to be pronounced on the nations (Zech. viii. 3,
Isa. ii. 3, Ezek. xlvii. 1, Ecclus. xxiv. 10ff., etc.).[4]

The community occupied the same position in the eyes of
its members as did Jerusalem and the temple in the eyes of
Judaism as a whole. It is thus only natural that the Qumran
texts should emphasize so strongly that it is the community
that is now the foundation of truth, the house of truth and the

---

[1] 1QS v. 6, viii. 6, 9, ix. 6, 7, 1QSa i. 16, 23, ii. 13, C.D. i. 7, v. 18, x. 5,
etc.

[2] For the term 'sons of Zadok', see above, pp. 4f. On the dichotomy
of Aaron and Israel, see Kuhn, 'Die beiden Messias Aarons und Israels',
N.T.S. 1 (1954-5), 174ff.

[3] The word 'truth' as an expression describing the correct interpretation
of the holy scriptures—the special revelation possessed by the community
through the Teacher of Righteousness—is strongly reminiscent of the use
of the word ἀλήθεια in the Fourth Gospel. It is Jesus who transmits truth
to the people of God, and who in person represents eternal Divine truth.
This idea is also expressed in other books of the N.T. (e.g. the Pastoral
Epistles), see below, pp. 68f.

[4] See Gerhardsson, *Memory and Manuscript*, pp. 214f.

true temple, and not the temple in Jerusalem.[1] We meet a
similar idea in 1Q14, the commentary on Micah, which contains an exposition of Mic. i. 5: 'What is the transgression of
Jacob? Is it not Samaria? And what are the high places of
Judah? Is it not Jerusalem?' The commentary states: 'Its
interpretation is by the Preacher of Lies, [he who leads astray]
the simple. "And what are the high places of Judah? [Is it
not Jerusalem?" Its interpretation is by] the Teacher of
Righteousness who...and all those who of their own free will
offer themselves to be received into the elect [of God]...in
the council of the community....'[2] In this passage 'the high
places of Judah' and 'Jerusalem' are interpreted as referring
to the Teacher of Righteousness and the community he
founded. We sense that this is a further expression of the
community's critical attitude to the official Jerusalem which,
having been led astray by the Preacher of Lies, is now to be
compared with Samaria, which is to be destroyed by the wrath
of God. The community, on the other hand, is the true Jerusalem, the interim replacement for the holy city, at present
the spiritual focus of Israel. Jerusalem had not been perman-
ently replaced; once the victory had been won, Jerusalem
might well be restored to its position as the centre of the world
and the dwelling place of God.[3]

We may also note the use in 1QS v. 5 ff. of the term 'foundation', יסד, which the Rabbis often used to denote the firm
foundation of the Law, but which may also refer to the 'foundation' of the altar, the basis of the temple, the object of wide
speculation.[4] But at the same time the community is expressly
stated to be a 'sanctuary', meaning that the community has
replaced the Jerusalem temple and its functions. One of these

[1] Note the importance of the concepts of 'truth' and 'justice' in those
O.T. texts which speak of the Zion of the future: e.g. Zech. viii.

[2] *Discoveries in the Judaean Desert*, ed. D. Barthélemy and J. T. Milik (1955),
i, 78.

[3] See Baillet, 'Un recueil liturgique de Qumrân, grotte 4: "Les paroles
des luminaires"', *R.B.* LXVIII (1961), 207, col. IV. 9 ff.

[4] See Levy, *Wörterbuch über die Talmudim und Midraschim*, II, 248. On the
subject of the speculations surrounding the 'foundation' of the altar and
the sanctity of the temple rock, see Jeremias, *Golgotha*, Angelos-Beiheft I
(1926), 51 ff. For a discussion of the concept of the 'foundation' in Qumran,
see Betz, 'Felsenmann und Felsengemeinde', *Z.N.T.W.* XLVIII (1957),
57 ff.

is mentioned in the text: the community is said, owing to its life of obedience to the will of God (the Law), to make atonement for its members. Elsewhere this idea is developed in more detail, the inference being that the life of the community makes atonement, after the fashion of a 'sacrifice', for those who belong to its number; in the same way the sacrifice made in the temple was in some cases regarded as making a similar atonement.[1] This text, 1QS v. 5ff., does not however contain a pure 'temple' symbolism; the symbolism of the temple is here combined with a more general 'house' symbolism. The image of the 'house' is based in this context on the idea of a permanent and protective building. Consequently, certain ideas can be connected with the 'new' temple only in part, since their true milieu is that of the permanent building.[2] It is often difficult to distinguish the two areas of imagery—the 'house' and the 'temple'—and this is true of most of the texts in which the symbolism of the temple is dealt with.[3]

The idea of the community as the temple recurs in a number of passages in the same document, 1QS, though with the emphasis placed on a different aspect of the image. The first part of column VIII speaks of the 'council of the community', עצת יחד, which is to consist of 'twelve men and three priests', which is in possession of the 'truth' and whose responsibility it is to care for the life of the community. Certain aspects of the 'new' temple are connected with this 'council'.[4] 'When

---

[1] See below, pp. 44ff.

[2] The concept of the firmly established building may have to do with expectation of the holy Jerusalem of the future, the city whose walls and fortifications should be immovable. See Lohse, art. Σιών, *T.W.B.* VII, 324ff.

[3] See Betz, 'Felsenmann und Felsengemeinde', pp. 52ff.

[4] It is difficult to decide whether this 'council' was a separate group within the community, or whether the term refers to the entire community. The expression עצת יחד is to be found some twenty times in the texts so far published; only a few of these point to the necessity of a special council in the community: 1QpHab xii. 4, 1QS viii. 1, 1QSa i. 26f. In the other texts the expression stands for the whole community (1QS vi. 10, 14, 16, vii. 2, 22, etc.). I consider it quite possible that there may have been a council in the community, with special functions, but this is of little importance for the symbolism used here. It is not the council that represents the temple; it is the community as a whole. The ambiguity of the texts on this point may be due to the use of the two rooms in the temple, the 'Holy place'

these (things) come to pass in Israel,[1] the council of the community shall stand fast (be firmly based) on the truth, as an eternal plantation, a holy house for Israel and a most holy foundation (or council)[2] for Aaron, witnesses of truth unto judgement and chosen by (God's) pleasure, bringing atonement to the land and retribution upon the evildoers. It is the tested wall, the precious corner-stone. Its foundations (יסוד) shall not be shaken and shall not be removed from their place, a most holy dwelling place (מעון)[3] for Aaron with eternal knowledge of the covenant of justice and the bringing forth of the sweet smell of sacrifice and a house of justice and truth in Israel, upholding the covenant according to the eternal laws. And they shall be well pleasing, making atonement for the land and passing judgement on the evil one. When these (the members of the council) stand fast (are firmly based) for two years on the foundation (יסוד) of the community in a perfect life and without turning aside, they shall separate themselves (and become)[4] a sanctuary in the midst of the men of the council of the community...' (1QS viii. 4ff.).

There are a number of themes in this passage which are connected in some way with the symbolism of the temple. The two groups in the community, Aaron and Israel, here represent the two most important rooms in the Temple, the 'Holy place'

and the 'Holy of holies', to symbolize the two groups, Aaron and Israel (in 1QS v. 5ff., viii. 5ff., ix. 3ff. and elsewhere, see below, pp. 42f.). This means that although it is the whole community that is called the 'temple', a division is quite possible. Cf. 1QpHab xii. 3ff., '"Lebanon" stands here for the council of the community, and the "beasts" for the simple-minded in Judah, who carry out the Law...'. On this problem, see Wernberg-Møller, *The Manual of Discipline*, pp. 122f., and E. F. Sutcliffe, *The Monks of Qumran* (1960), pp. 254f.

[1] Cf. Gärtner, 'Bakgrunden till Qumranförsamlingens Krig', pp. 50f.

[2] וסוד or יסוד. The latter reading fits in best with the temple symbolism generally, and can be accounted for by the importance given to the 'foundation' in those three texts in 1QS which speak of the community as a temple (v. 5ff., viii. 4ff. and ix. 3ff.). The reading יסוד is favoured by, e.g., Nielsen–Otzen, *Dødehavsteksterne*, p. 81.

[3] In certain O.T. texts the word refers to the temple, the 'temple place', see Gesenius, *Handwörterbuch*, p. 443.

[4] The meaning of the expressions 'a holy house for Israel' and 'for Aaron' is that both groups comprise, become, the temple. See Wernberg-Møller, *Manual*, p. 124.

and the 'Holy of holies'. The 'new' temple is the community; the firm and secure foundation of this temple is the 'truth', that is, the exposition of the Law and the revelations to which the community owes its existence. Here is offered the perfect sacrifice, 'the bringing forth of the sweet smell of sacrifice', which provides the conditions on which atonement can be made, an atonement which does not apply merely to the one group (1QS v. 6) but to the whole 'country'—Israel. Justice and judgement also proceed from this 'new' sanctuary, for it is here that the 'eternal laws' are kept. To the same complex of ideas surrounding the temple belong such images as 'the precious corner-stone', 'the tested wall' and the foundations which 'shall not be shaken and shall not be removed from their place'; these form an exegesis of Isa. xxviii. 16[1] and belong to the imagery with which late Judaism surrounded the 'stone' on which the Ark of the Covenant rested in the 'Holy of holies'.[2] The way in which the foundations of the community are referred to here, and the references to the 'wall' and 'corner-stone', bear ample witness to the self-consciousness so typical of the members of the community. Taking certain aspects of the ideology of the holy city, the temple and the temple rock, they reinterpreted them so as to apply to themselves and their own situation.[3]

An image connected here (in 1QS viii. 5) and elsewhere in

---

[1] חומה, 'the wall', here replaces אבן, 'the stone' (Isa. xxviii. 16). The term 'wall' is occasionally used in the texts in connexion with a description of the community as a fortified and impregnable city. 1QH iii. 37 calls God a strong wall, חומת עוז. 1QSb v. 23 calls the 'prince of the community' a 'strong tower upon a high wall, חומה נשגבה', an expression for the power and permanence which defeats the enemy. 1QH vi. 25ff. (see below, pp. 76f.) speaks of the building to which the wall belongs, as a structure which cannot be shaken (cf. 1QH vii. 8f.). This quality in the community, built upon the unshakable faithfulness of God, seems to have dominated the exposition of Isa. xxviii. 16; thus 'stone' has been replaced by 'wall'. This is probably a reason why חומה has been introduced into 1QS viii. Cf. Betz, 'Felsenmann und Felsengemeinde', pp. 61ff. Wernberg-Møller, *Manual*, p. 126, thinks that the change took place because the community (a collective) is meant; they 'naturally wanted a word for something consisting of more than one stone'—an interpretation relevant for I Pet. ii, where 'living stone' and 'living stones' are mentioned. See below, pp. 75ff.

[2] Cf. Jeremias, *Golgotha*, 51ff.   [3] Cf. below, pp. 76ff.

the Qumran texts with those of the house and the temple is that of the 'plantation'. The community is called 'an eternal plantation, a holy house for Israel'. The combination seems however to have come about merely by chance, and appears to lack special motivation. The author may simply have adopted another expression for the election and blessing by God of the community: a 'plantation' set by God. But the combination of the two images 'to build up' and 'to plant' is found in the Old Testament, for example in Jer. i. 10, xviii. 9, xxiv. 6, xxxi. 28 and xlv. 4. If we examine later Jewish exposition on the subject of the holy rock of the temple we find a link between this rock and the ideas of Paradise, the water which gives the world life and fertility and the tree of life.[1] We know that there are references in a number of Qumran texts to the garden of Paradise, to the water of life, and to the trees planted by the springs of the water of life, with their roots in the 'primeval waters'; and all are connected with the foundation and the eternal future of the community (1QH vi. 15 ff., viii. 4 ff.; 1QS xi. 3 ff.).[2] In two of these texts we find related images drawn from the holy building, the house of God (1QH vi and 1QS xi). It thus seems likely that the combination of temple and 'plantation' in the Qumran texts is to be traced back to Jewish speculations on the subject of the rock of the temple and Paradise. A fragmentary text from Cave 4,[3] which deals with the liturgy of the Sabbath sacrifice, contains a description of the throne of God and the heavenly temple which closely resembles the visions of the temple and Paradise recorded in Ezekiel, and which makes mention of 'streams' flowing from the holy place, evidence that the Qumran community, following Ezekiel, was not unfamiliar with those traditions dealing with the temple and its life-giving streams of water. Further, we find that in I Enoch, which shows a number of affinities with Qumran,[4] the images of Paradise and the 'plantation' are similarly combined with the 'temple' complex.

[1] Cf. Jeremias, *Golgotha*, 52 ff.

[2] Gärtner, *Die rätselhaften Termini Nazoräer und Iskariot*, pp. 21 ff.; Betz, 'Felsenmann und Felsengemeinde', pp. 51 f.; Ringgren, 'The Branch and the Plantation in the *Hodayot*', *Bibl. Research*, VI (1961), 3–9.

[3] J. Strugnell, 'The Angelic Liturgy at Qumran—4Q serek šîrôt 'ôlat haššabāt', *V.T., Suppl.* VII (1960), 335 ff.

[4] Gärtner, *Die rätselhaften Termini*, pp. 35 ff.

Chapters xxiv–xxvi speak of the tree of life, the throne of God, the temple, and the holy mountain from which the streams of life are to flow; we also read that the tree of life is to be planted in the holy place, in the temple of the Lord (xxv. 5 ff.).[1]

The same combination of ideas connected with the two rooms of the temple and the sacrificial office is to be found in 1QS ix. 3 ff.—a passage which it is extremely difficult to translate satisfactorily: 'When these (things) come to pass in Israel according to all these laws, it is for (or in order to establish) the foundation (יסוד) of the holy spirit, for eternal truth, for the atonement of the guilt of sin and misdeeds, and for the well-being of the land by means of[2] the flesh of burnt offerings and the fat of sacrifices, (that is) the right offerings of the lips as a righteous sweet savour and a perfect way of life as a free-will offering, pleasing (to God). In those days the men of the community shall separate themselves (and become) a holy house for Aaron, so that they are joined together (and become) a Holy of holies and a house of community, בית יחד, for Israel, those who walk in perfection.' In this text the community is spoken of as a temple, in which there are the two rooms, the 'Holy place' and the 'Holy of holies', corresponding to the priests and the laymen, Aaron and Israel, in the community.[3] Characteristic of the temple here, as in the texts we have dealt with above, is that its foundation is 'truth', defined as 'eternal' and transmitted by the holy spirit (cf. 'the spirit of truth' in 1QS iv. 21). It is the spirit who has purified the members of the community, giving them an insight into the mysteries of

---

[1] See below, pp. 31 f., on Exod. xv. 17–18, where a similar complex of ideas is found. Cf. Strack–Billerbeck, *Kommentar*, IV, 933 ff.

[2] On the discussion surrounding this translation, see Carmignac, 'L'utilité ou l'inutilité des sacrifices sanglants', *R.B.* LXIII (1956), 524 ff. Irrespective of which translation ('through' or 'more than the flesh of burnt offerings') is preferred, it seems to me that the text is saying that blood sacrifices have been replaced indefinitely by 'spiritual sacrifices'. See above, pp. 20 f.

[3] The two rooms in the temple are also expounded in the Epistle to the Hebrews and in Philo. Here, however, the symbolism differs from that of Qumran. The subject is the archetypal temple in heaven, in which Jesus is high priest (Heb.) or an image of the universe (Philo). Cf. Spicq, *L'Épître aux Hébreux* (1952), I, 72 ff., and II (1953), 234 f., and A. Cody, *Heavenly Sanctuary and Liturgy in the Epistle to the Hebrews* (1960).

God (1QH ix. 32, xii. 11ff.; C.D. ii. 12f.).[1] The sacrificial office in this 'new' temple is described thus: that the burnt offerings and sacrifices of the Jerusalem temple have been replaced by prayers and the perfect life according to the Law. These 'spiritual' sacrifices have the effect of making atonement for the people, and are well pleasing in the sight of God. Once more we see how it was believed that the promises of God with respect to the temple and the cultus had been revived through the founding of the community. The temple in Jerusalem has been superseded; its cult is unclean and the expression of untruth.

If we compare this with 1QS v. 5ff. and viii. 4ff. we cannot help noticing the close resemblance there is between them; this indicates the presence of a definite tradition of temple symbolism in the community, the object of which was to clarify its attitude to the Jerusalem temple and the sacrifices offered there (cf. 1QS xi. 8). This tradition served at the same time to underline the audacious idea that this little company, separated as it was from the 'official' Israel, was the true house of God, in whom all God's promises were to be fulfilled. The overall picture is not affected by the discrepancy in the texts between the community and its 'council' as objects of comparison with the temple. These are two ways of saying the same thing: 'the council of the congregation' in 1QS viii represents the entire community, as its nucleus and foundation. In both texts the point is that the holiness of Israel has become concentrated in the community, which thereby becomes a substitute for the Jerusalem temple.[2]

B. 4Q FLORILEGIUM

The concept of the community as the true temple in which is offered the perfect sacrifice, may be expressed differently. The fragmentary text known as 4QFlor. has an exposition of the community as the eschatological temple, in which particular emphasis is placed upon the holiness, purity and eternal quality

---

[1] Cf. Nötscher, 'Geist und Geister in den Texten von Qumran', in *Mélanges bibliques André Robert* (1957), pp. 307ff.

[2] A text which closely resembles these three from 1QS is 1QH vi. 25ff., which we discuss below, pp. 76ff.

of the 'new' temple.[1] The first part of the text is an exposition
(of *pesher* type) of II Sam. vii. 10–14, part of Nathan's prophecy to David on the building of a house. This prophecy uses
the word 'house' in two senses, first as the 'dwelling place' of
God, that is, the temple, and secondly with the meaning of
'dynasty', ruling house. This dichotomy fits in well with the
4QFlor. exposition of the term 'house' as referring to the community and its Messianic teacher and leader.[2] The starting-
point for the text is provided by Yahweh's words, spoken by the
prophet Nathan, that the Israel of the future is to have a
'secure place' and need no longer be troubled. There is to be
no more persecution from unrighteous men: '"And from the
days that (2) [I commanded judges] to be over my people
Israel" (II Sam. vii. 10f.)—that is the house that [he will
build] for [you at the] end of the days as it is written (3) in
the book [of Moses]: "[The sanctuary, O Lord,] which thy
hands have [established.] Yahweh will reign for ever and
ever" (Exod. xv. 17–18).'[3] This exposition recalls the song of
praise sung by Moses and the children of Israel in Exod. xv.
17–18, the terminology of which is close to the symbolism used
in 1QS viii and ix with its combination of the 'plantation',
the mountain of the Lord and the temple: 'Thou wilt bring
them in, and plant them on thy own mountain, the place, O
Yahweh, which thou hast made for thy abode, the sanctuary,
O Lord, which thy hands have established. Yahweh will reign
for ever and ever.'[4]

The Old Testament texts quoted in 4QFlor. are interpreted
as referring to the 'house' (that is temple) which Yahweh is to
establish in the last days; this is none other than the community

---

[1] 4QFlor. is in fact not so much a florilegium as a *pesher* or *midrash*, in
which a number of O.T. texts are expounded. See W. R. Lane, 'A New
Commentary Structure in 4QFlorilegium', *J.B.L.* LXXVIII (1959), 343 ff.

[2] On the subject of 'house' and 'kingdom' in II Sam. vii and its parallel
text I Chron. xvii, see Aalen, '"Reign" and "House" in the Kingdom of
God in the Gospels', *N.T.S.* VIII (1961–2), 233 ff.

[3] For the restoration of the text, see J. M. Allegro, 'Fragments of a
Qumran Scroll of Eschatological *Midrāšim*', *J.B.L.* LXXVII (1958), 351 ff.,
and Y. Yadin, 'A Midrash on II Sam. vii and Ps. i–ii (4QFlorilegium)',
I.E.J. IX (1959), 95 ff.

[4] See above, pp. 28 f. Targum Jonathan on Exod. xv. 17–18 also speaks
of the presence of God, שכינה, in the temple of God.

itself.[1] Just as the quotation from II Sam. vii. 10–11 was taken to refer to the last days and their temple, so the exposition of Exod. xv. 17–18 continues: 'That is the house where there shall not enter (4) [anyone whose flesh has a] permanent [blemish] or an Ammonite or a Moabite or a bastard or an alien or a stranger[2] for ever, for his holy ones are there (5) [for ever].' The congregation which is to be established in the last days—and a start was made when the Qumran community was founded—is that company of the pure in Israel who now fulfil the prophecy of Nathan. The eschatological 'house of God' is to be built up by a process of exclusiveness, by the avoidance of contact with the unclean and the preservation of ritual purity within the community.[3] The prophecies of the Old Testament are thus taken to refer not to the Jerusalem temple but to a group of holy persons who constitute the 'new' temple. It is forbidden in Deut. xxiii. 3 (quoted in the text) for certain persons—Ammonites, Moabites and others— to belong to the congregation of God; similarly it is forbidden for such persons to join the true Israel in the last days. Further, the rules for those who served in the temple are made conditions of membership of the Qumran community. The congregation of God applied strictly the rule that temple priests should be 'without blemish' (Ezek. xliv. 9, Lev. xxi. 17–23). The demand for purity and sanctification, as recorded in 4QFlor., thus belongs in the context of temple symbolism.[4] Another aspect of the demand for holiness in connexion with the 'new' temple was the presence of the angels, 'for his holy ones are there [for ever]'. It was formerly believed in Israel that the temple was a meeting place for God and his angels, and that the man who entered the temple came 'before the face of God'; this belief was now transferred to the holy congregation.

[1] Exod. xv. 17 is also used in later Jewish expository tradition to refer to the heavenly temple. See e.g. Strack–Billerbeck, *Kommentar*, III, 701 f.

[2] See below, p. 62, n. 1.

[3] Cf. Gärtner, 'Bakgrunden till Qumranförsamlingens krig', pp. 66 f. We might also compare Matt. xxi. 14, which tells how Jesus, after having cleansed the temple, received the blind and lame and healed them. The text may be a criticism of the emphasis placed by the Qumran community on purity in their re-establishment of the pure and holy temple (see p. 111, below). A number of Qumran texts emphasize that the lame and deformed cannot become full members of the community.

[4] See above, pp. 5 f.

Just because these holy beings dwelt in the midst of the community, it was essential to preserve its absolute purity, otherwise there was a risk that they might abandon the 'new' temple.[1]

The text of 4QFlor. continues with a further exposition of the theme of the temple and the community: '(5) He shall be seen upon it continually, and strangers shall not again make it desolate, as they desolated once (6) the sanctuary of Israel because of their sins.' The new temple is thus eternal, and is constantly able to fall back upon the promises of God, for it is holy, and cannot be corrupted by sin. This idea is entirely in accord with the community's aim of preventing, by obedience to the Law, that destruction which inevitably follows sin, and rendering themselves able to receive God's blessing by living impeccable lives. The theme of the eschatological temple, which will never be destroyed and upon which the Lord will be seen, recurs in later Jewish texts, even after the fall of the temple in A.D. 70. An example is provided by Sifre Deut. xxxiii. 12, in which it is said that a distinction must be drawn between the former temple, which was destroyed, and the latter, which is eternal. 'And in the same way you find that Abraham saw it (the temple) being built, and saw it desolated and saw it rebuilt (Gen. xxii. 14). "And Abraham called the name of that place *Yahweh-jireh* (Yahweh will see)"; behold, there it is built. "As it is said to this day: in the mount"; behold, there it was desolated. "Where the Lord will be seen"; behold, there it is rebuilt and perfect in the future.'[2] The account of 4QFlor. seems to agree with the Sifre text on this point; both appear to be based on Gen. xxii. 14. The 'Presence' of God will rest upon the temple in the last days, as is said in the story of Abraham, and it will never more be destroyed. We may compare this with the later Jewish idea that the temple was safe from destruction so long as the *Shekinah* of God rested upon it. When the temple was destroyed in A.D. 70, many had to resort to the explanation that the *Shekinah* had first left the temple.[3]

---

[1] Cf. Fitzmyer, 'A Feature of Qumrân Angelology and the Angels of I Cor. xi. 10', *N.T.S.* IV (1957–8), 55 ff., and below, pp. 94 ff.

[2] For further examples, see Strack–Billerbeck, *Kommentar*, I, 1004, and IV, 923.

[3] Cf. Ginzberg, *The Legends of the Jews*, VI, 392 f., and Ezek. xi. 23, the *Shekinah* of God leaving Jerusalem.

It seems to me that when the Qumran text speaks of the community withstanding every enemy and of God resting upon the 'new' temple, it is a similar idea which is being expressed. Despite Belial's efforts, he will be unable to lay waste this new temple; 'that means that he will give rest to them from all the sons of Belial who made them stumble to destroy them [because of their sins]...and to devise against them wicked plans, so that they will be caught by Belial through their errors' (4QFlor. i. 7ff.). A comparison may also be drawn with C.D. iii. 19f.: 'And he built for them in Israel a firmly established house, בית נאמן, the like of which has not existed from ancient times until this day. They that hold fast unto it are (destined) for life eternal....' The community, as the 'house of God', bears the seal of eternity.[1]

This eternal temple is now in process of realization in the community, in accordance with the commandment of God: '(6) And he purposed to build him a temple of (among) men, מקדש אדם, in which should be offered sacrifices (7) before him, the works of the Law.' The sacrifices offered in this temple, a temple made up of members of the community, are to be spiritual in character and are to consist of a life lived in perfect obedience to the Law. We find at this point that the symbolism of 1QS recurs in 4QFlor., in this important respect: that the sacrifice has been 'spiritualized'. It is in this part of the text that we meet with the expression מקדש אדם, which might well be translated 'a temple of men', i.e. consisting of men.[2] The simplest means of expressing the translation 'among men'

---

[1] It is likely that the expression 'a firmly established house' in C.D. iii. 19f. is taken from II Sam. vii. 16, which has the same Hebrew expression. Cf. below, pp. 73f.

[2] Yadin, 'A midrash on II Sam. vii and Ps. i–ii', p. 96, translates 'a Sanctuary amongst men', and refers to Ps. lxxviii. 60, אהל שכן באדם, 'set up a tabernacle among men', but the text in question has the preposition בְּ, 'among'. Allegro, 'Fragments', p. 352, translates 'to build for Him a man-made sanctuary', but does not say what are the implications of this translation. These would seem however to be the same as for Nötscher, 'Heiligkeit in den Qumranschriften', R.Q. ii (1959–60), 173, 'Er ist ein von Menschenhand, aber durch Gottes Gnade erbautes Heiligtum...'. This interpretation seems to agree with Rev. xxi. 3 ἰδοὺ ἡ σκηνὴ τοῦ θεοῦ μετὰ τῶν ἀνθρώπων καὶ σκηνώσει μετ' αὐτῶν (cf. Zech. ii. 14). Note however that Rev. makes no use in this context of that temple symbolism in which it is claimed that the community is the temple.

would have been by the preposition בְּ, which is however missing. To interpret the sentence as meaning that God commanded
that a temple should be built 'among men' is too vague in this
context. The theme of the text, as far as the expression מקדש
אדם, is that the eschatological temple is to be made up of
the community—a theme developed in the remainder of the
passage. It is thus consistent to speak of a 'human temple', a
temple consisting of men. This interpretation also fits in admir-
ably with the temple symbolism of 1QS.[1]

One result of the coming into being of this 'new' temple,
the community, in the last days is, according to 4QFlor., that
its members are enabled to call upon another of the promises
of God, that the sons of Belial shall have no power over them.
The Scripture quoted is II Sam. vii. 11: 'and I will give you
rest from all your enemies'. There follows an exposition of
Nathan's prophecy, based on the words '[And] Yahweh
t[ells] you, that he will build you a house, and I shall set up
your seed after you, and I shall establish the throne of his
kingdom [for] ever. I [will be] a father to him and he shall
be my son' (II Sam. vii. 11–14). This version is however
shorter than the Masoretic text; phrases have been omitted,
for example the personal words to David: 'When your days
are fulfilled and you lie down with your fathers....' The
abridgement may perhaps have been intended to fit the text
for the purposes of comparison between the promised 'house'
and the community.

Of particular interest for our purposes is that this prophecy
is interpreted as follows: '(11) He is the shoot of David, צמח
דויד, who will come forward with the Interpreter of the Law,
דורש התורה, who (12) [will arise?] in Zi[on in the la]st days,
as it is written (Amos ix. 11), "I will raise up the tabernacle
of David סוכת דויד that is fallen." That is (13) the tabernacle
of David that is fall[en and which] will arise in order to save
Israel.'[2]

[1] On the subject of the word 'house' as a description of the community,
see Aalen, '"Reign" and "house"', pp. 235ff.

[2] The formal structure of this passage is as follows: first a quotation from
II Sam. vii; then an exposition introduced by the word הואה, 'it is'; this
is then illustrated by a further scriptural quotation (from Amos) introduced
by כתוב, 'as it is written'. The same structure is dominant in the first part
of 4QFlor., see Lane, 'A New Commentary Structure', p. 345.

3-2

This text, like all Qumran expositions of this type, is highly complicated. Commentators consider that it mentions two Messiahs, the Messiah of David and the Interpreter of the Law, that is, that it is a Messianic interpretation and applies to two distinct persons.[1] This judgement is based on other Qumran texts, in which is clearly expressed an expectation of two Messiahs. But there is another possibility which is worth taking into consideration, and which may lie behind this particular text. A frequent phenomenon in the Qumran texts is that the content of the Messianic symbols oscillates between collective and individual. The founder of the community may stand as the representative of the whole community (particularly in 1QH); or he may be spoken of as the elect of God, an individual instrument for the raising up of the community. It is not always easy to tell which of the two is meant on any given occasion.[2] A similar oscillation is to be observed both in the Old Testament and in Judaism.[3] The basic themes of the 4QFlor. text we are discussing have so far been the relation between the community and the temple and the theme of the 'house' in relation to the Davidic prophecy of the temple. It may well be that at this point the author abandons this area of symbolism altogether, and proceeds instead to speak about the Messianic figures revered by the community. But this gives rise to difficulties, since after i. 14 the text reverts to the theme of the collective, the community. If we interpret this text as referring to two Messiahs, we must then ask how these two are related to the 'Messiahs of Aaron and Israel'; and that is no light task.[4]

But there is an alternative: to assume that it is the community which forms the centre; in this view there is no need to lay exclusive emphasis on the Messiahs. God is to build a 'house', a temple, we read in the text; this 'house' is linked with the

[1] See e.g. Allegro, 'Further Messianic References in Qumran Literature', *J.B.L.* LXXV (1956), 177; K. Schubert, 'Die Messiaslehre in den Texten von Chirbet Qumran', *B.Z.* I (1957), 182; Flusser, 'Two Notes on the Midrash on II Sam. vii', *I.E.J.* IX (1959), 104 ff. Cf. Lövestam, *Son and Saviour* (1961), pp. 63 ff.   [2] Cf. Gärtner, *Die rätselhaften Termini*, pp. 21 ff.

[3] See e.g. Pedersen, *Israel*, I, 13 ff., and A. R. Johnson, *The One and the Many in the Israelite Conception of God* (1942).

[4] The difficulties caused by this view are clearly seen in Liver's attempted interpretation, 'The Doctrine of the Two Messiahs', pp. 179 ff.

'seed' of David, the 'son' who is born to the father. This is the shoot of David, צמח דויד, who is to arise with the 'Interpreter of the Law' in the last days. The interpretation which suggests itself is that 'the shoot of David' is a symbol representing the community, which grows up under the leadership of the Interpreter of the Law.[1] The community, according to C.D. vi. 7, vii. 18, was founded by this Teacher; other texts regard him as being the last Teacher, 'a specially significant eschatological figure'.[2]

This interpretation appears to agree with the introduction to the Damascus Document, C.D. i, which tells the story of the founding of the community. There we read that 390 years after (?) God had given the people into the hand of Nebuchadnezzar,[3] he once more visited them and 'caused to grow up from Israel and from Aaron the root of a plantation, ...יצמח שורש מטעת, that should inherit his land and be filled by the good things of his ground', i. 7f. It is virtually certain that the 'root' mentioned here is the community, the 'holy remnant' of Israel, whose growth is evidence that the true Israel is in process of development.[4] The constitution of the community was not limited to the appearance, יצמח, of the 'root', but included the appearance of the Teacher of Righteousness as well. God calls him forth with the community (C.D. i. 11). This combination of the appearance of the community and the Teacher seems to me to be a valuable illustration of the passage in 4QFlor. which speaks of the growth of the 'shoot of David' in connexion with the appearance of the Interpreter of the Law. The same combination recurs in C.D. vi. 6ff. and vii. 16ff., the latter text making use of the same passage of Amos ix. 11 as 4QFlor.

[1] See below, pp. 132f., for the way in which the concept 'son' (the first-born son of God) is made to refer to the community.
[2] F. F. Bruce, *Biblical Exegesis in the Qumran Texts* (1959), p. 48. Note that while C.D. speaks of this as something in the past, 4QFlor. speaks of it as belonging to the future. Thus here, as in so many of the Qumran texts, past, present and future are intimately connected. It seems to me inadequate to try and explain away this fact by referring to changes in the experience of the community.
[3] There is an obvious lack of clarity in the interpretation of this text; see M. Burrows, *More Light on the Dead Sea Scrolls* (1958), pp. 191ff.
[4] On the symbolism behind the terms 'shoot' and 'plantation', see Gärtner, *Die rätselhaften Termini*, pp. 23ff.

The two expressions thus need not refer to the two Messiahs; they may well stand for the community and the Teacher.

We must now consider the meaning of the term צמח, 'root'. In late Jewish texts it is often a Messianic term describing the coming royal Messiah,[1] and is individual in its application. Although C.D. i. 4 ff. speaks of 'Israel' in collective terms as יצמח שורש, the issue is less straightforward in 4QPB,[2] the only text apart from 4QFlor. to make use of the word צמח.[3] There we find a Messianic interpretation of Gen. xlix. 10:

The sceptre shall not depart from Judah, nor the ruler's staff from between his feet, until he comes to Shiloh—There shall [not] cease a ruler from the tribe of Judah. When the rulership shall fall to the lot of Israel [there shall not] be cut off an enthroned one (belonging) to David. For 'the ruler's staff' is the covenant of the kingdom, and 'the feet' are the [thou]sands of Israel, until the Messiah of Righteousness comes, the shoot of David, for to him and to his seed has been granted the covenant of the kingdom over his people for everlasting generations which has awaited [the Interpreter] of the Law with the men of the community, for [. . .] it is the assembly of the men....[4]

When the time of Israel's supremacy comes, there will always be a king of the house of David. 'The ruler's staff' in Gen. xlix. 10 is interpreted as referring to 'the covenant of the kingdom', ברית המלכות.[5] The 'thousands', אלפי, of Israel are the 'feet'.[6] The one who 'shall come' is 'the Messiah of Righteousness',

[1] Schubert, 'Die Messiaslehre', p. 185; Strack–Billerbeck, Kommentar, I, 93 ff. Cf. Widengren, The King and the Tree of Life in Ancient Near Eastern Religion, Uppsala Univ. Årsskrift, 1951, pp. 54 ff.

[2] Allegro, 'Further Messianic References in Qumran Literature', J.B.L. LXXV (1956), 174 f.

[3] The restoration of fragmentary texts gives us other צמח-texts, e.g. 4QpIsac–d. Here, too, there is a certain ambiguity of meaning between the Messiah and/or the community, the community together with the Interpreter of the Law, see Allegro, 'Further Messianic References', pp. 180 f.

[4] Cf. Allegro, 'Further Messianic References', pp. 174 f.

[5] In C.D. vi. 7 the 'sceptre' is interpreted as referring to the Interpreter of the Law, the founder of the community. There are at this point consider-able resemblances in symbolism between C.D., 4QPB and 4QFlor., though their interpretations vary.

[6] Liver, 'The Doctrine of the Two Messiahs', p. 157, n. 27, writes: 'According to this interpretation the families of Israel, i.e. the members of the Sect and their leaders, are to be considered as legitimately having the

the shoot of David, צמח דויד, 'for to him and to his seed
have been granted the covenant of the kingdom over his
people for everlasting generations...'. The 'shoot of David'
seems here to be the expected Messiah of the house of David.[1]
Note however that the 'covenant of the kingdom' is to be given
to him and to 'his seed', זרעו,[2] an expression which, according
to 4QFlor., refers to the community. The two ideas, the shoot
of David and his 'seed', are thus intimately connected, and it
seems to me that they are symbols referring to the community
and its leader. It is conceivable that the promise of eternal rule
given to the Davidic dynasty—which no longer occupied the
throne—had been taken over by the true Israel, and that the
community as a collective unit is to be understood by the term
'the shoot of David' in these texts. It is in any case true that
the prophecy of David's eternal rule is applied to the community at the beginning of 4QFlor., in the passage which
states that the community *qua* temple shall never be laid waste
and never be overcome by the sons of Belial—a prophecy which
otherwise applied to the Davidic dynasty.[3] The exposition of
Nathan's prophecy of the future of the 'house' of David must
also be seen against the background of the double meaning of
the term: on the one hand a building and on the other a people,
a family or a community.[4]

It is difficult to surmise how the fragmentary text 4QPB
continued; we may hazard a guess that mention was made of

authority of Davidic Kingship until the coming of the anointed of righteousness, to whom and to whose descendants the covenant of kingship was given
for everlasting generations.'

[1] Cf. *Discoveries in the Judaean Desert*, I, 128f.

[2] In the O.T. the word זרע is frequently found in Messianic passages,
particularly those which promise future dominion to Israel, e.g. Gen. xii.
7, II Sam. vii. 12–15. At the same time it is connected with the idea of the
'remnant' of Israel, Isa. xliv. 3. Cf. Jer. xxxiii. 14ff., which combines the
Davidic promise with the concept of the 'remnant'. See A. Gelin, art.
'Messianisme', *Diction. de la Bible*, Suppl. v, 1170f.

[3] A text published by Baillet, 'Un recueil liturgique de Qumrân, grotte
4: "Les paroles des luminaires"', *R.B.* LXVIII (1961), 205f., col. IV, 6ff.,
has a more traditional application of the Davidic promise and the idea of
eternal kingship. The promise belongs to the future, after the victory
of Israel, but the text does not make it clear whether it is a descendant
of David or Israel as a whole who is to rule.

[4] Cf. Aalen, '"Reign" and "house"', p. 236.

'the Interpreter of the Law' who is to appear 'with the men of the community'.[1] The terminological and conceptual similarity between this and 4QFlor. is striking; it shows that the idea of the appearance of the Interpreter of the Law with the community could be connected with the prophecy of the shoot and the 'seed' of David. Although it is not possible, in the present state of the text of 4QFlor., to prove that the reference to 'the shoot of David' was intended as a collective reference to the community, it is nevertheless important to note the close relationship of the collective and the individual. This impression is strengthened by the fact that later in the same document, 4QFlor. i. 18f., there is a collective interpretation of the expression 'his anointed' in Ps. ii. 2: '[Why do] the nations [rag]e and the peoples imag[ine a vain thing? The kings of the earth set] themselves [and the rul]ers take counsel together against the Lord and against [his anointed]. The meaning of this saying [refers to the sons of Zadok, the priest]s, and th[ey are] the elect of Israel in the last days.'[2] Few words of this *pesher* exposition are preserved, but it seems feasible to assume that 'the anointed' refers to the sons of Zadok, the nucleus of the community, 'the elect of Israel in the last days'. The idea of 'the anointed one' is thus interpreted collectively on this occasion. We must however once more emphasize that it is difficult to distinguish between individual and collective in these texts; first one and then the other seems to dominate. This *caveat* is particularly significant in the context of temple symbolism, for it shows the close relation of the community's Messianism to their general forms of expression. Ecclesiology and Messianism become interwoven, not only here, but in a number of other texts as well.[3]

Returning to 4QFlor., we find a further Messianic saying linked with the concept of the temple established in the community, namely Amos ix. 11, 'I will raise up the tabernacle of David that is fallen, סוכת דויד הנופלת.' 'The shoot of David' which appears 'in Zion' is also 'the fallen tabernacle

[1] Allegro, 'Further Messianic References', p. 175, and Liver, 'The Doctrine of the Two Messiahs', pp. 156f.
[2] So Yadin, 'A Midrash on II Sam. vii and Ps. i–ii (4QFlorilegium)', *I.E.J.* IX (1959), 98: this I consider to be the best version hitherto.
[3] See below, pp. 123 ff.

of David' (13) 'which will appear in order to save Israel'.[1]
The saying of II Sam. vii about the temple and the promise
of the Davidic Messiah have here been combined with the
passage from Amos ix, which also speaks of David and his
house, or 'tabernacle', סוכה, and which points to the coming
salvation and its restoration of the kingdom and the dynasty.
This prophecy from Amos recurs in another text, C.D. vii.
14 ff., where it is made to illustrate the origin of the community,
thus providing a valuable background to the exposition of
4QFlor.[2] Here the text is based on a passage in Amos v. 26,
which it combines with certain of the community's most
important symbols (some of which are drawn from Amos v.
27): 'I shall lead into exile the Siccuth, סכות, of your king, and
the Chiyun, כיון, of your images (and the star of your God)[3]
to the tents of Damascus, אהלי.[4] The books of the Law are the
tabernacle of the king, סוכת המלך, as it is said (Amos ix. 11):
"I will raise up the tabernacle of David that is fallen." The
king is the community, קהל, and the Chiyun of the images are
the books of the prophets, whose word Israel despised. And the
star is the Interpreter of the Law who came to Damascus, as
it is written: "A star shall come forth from Jacob, a sceptre
shall arise from Israel...."' Here we find that the community
is understood by the word 'king' and the Law by 'tabernacle',
סוכה. 'The tabernacle of the king' is thus the community and
its correct interpretation of the Law.[5] Alongside the community we see references to the founder of the community: he
is the 'star', while the 'images' are the books of the prophets.

---

[1] L. H. Silbermann, 'A Note on 4QFlorilegium', *J.B.L.* LXXVIII (1959),
158 f., favours the reading 'And I will raise up the tabernacle of David that
is fallen, that is, the *branch* of David, סוכה, that is fallen', and thus links up
with 'the shoot of David' mentioned earlier. Lövestam, *Son and Saviour*,
p. 64, follows this reading, but I consider it unlikely. Nowhere in the texts
so far published does the word סוכה occur with the meaning of 'branch'.
Further, the only texts in which the word occurs outside 4QFlor. (C.D.
vii. 15 f. and xi. 8) give us no reason to vocalize it in this way.

[2] Further evidence of the close relationship between C.D. and 4QFlor.

[3] The expression is taken from Amos, and is not found in C.D., though
some editors (Hvidberg, Rabin and others) have added it.

[4] I follow Hvidberg here. Rabin, *The Zadokite Documents*, p. 28, translates 'from My tent to Damascus'.

[5] Rabin, *op. cit.* p. 29, takes 'king' to refer to the leader of the community,
and 'images' to refer to the teacher(s) of the community.

The appearance of the community and its founder are treated as a unity, as we have seen in other texts. The community is referred to by an 'individual' Messianic term, 'the king'. The difference between this text and 4QFlor. is plain, since there the expression 'the tabernacle of David that is fallen' can hardly stand for the Law; note, however, that 4QFlor. does represent the community and the Teacher as appearing together. 'The tabernacle of David that is fallen' and 'which will appear in order to save Israel' is the community,[1] appearing under its Teacher in fulfilment of the promise of a restored 'house' of David.[2] Once more we see how close is the link between ecclesiology and Messianism—a point which it will be valuable to recall when we come to examine the New Testament evidence.

C. 4QPISA^d, FRAGMENT 1, AND 1QPHAB. XII. 1 ff.

There are two other texts which cast light on the temple symbolism of the Qumran community, and which must be examined. They are perhaps not among the most central and translucent of the Qumran texts; nevertheless they help to show the importance and richness of this area of symbolism. From a fragment of a *pesher* on Isaiah, 4QpIsa^d, fr. 1, may be deduced that the community, consisting of 'priests' and 'people', makes up a house of God.[3] The image is further divided, in such a way that the foundations of the building are said to be the priests, while the members of the community, 'the elect', are the 'stones', the actual superstructure of the building. The text goes on to say that the 'priests' are 'sap-

---

[1] Cf. Acts xv. 16 where we meet a similar idea—'the tabernacle of David' is the Christian Church.

[2] An attempt to describe the relationship between the Teacher of Righteousness, the Interpreter of the Law and the 'shoot of David' has been made by Liver, 'The Doctrine of the Two Messiahs', pp. 159 ff.; he suggests that the Interpreter of the Law was the leader of the community after its founder, the Teacher of Righteousness. On the 'shoot of David', Liver sees different schools of thought in the community; some wished to suppress the idea of a Davidic Messiah, others to give it wider currency; these tendencies arose as a result of the historical development of the community.

[3] The text is published by Allegro, 'More Isaiah Commentaries from Qumran's Fourth Cave', *J.B.L.* LXXVII (1958), 220.

phires' among the 'stones', the members of the community. The whole constitutes an interpretation of Isa. liv. 11: 'Behold, I will set your stones in antimony, and lay your foundations with sapphires.'[1] The exposition need not necessarily refer to the temple-community, and may equally well form part of a more general 'house' symbolism. But the resemblance to the more specific temple symbolism of, for example, 1QS viii, with its division between Aaron and Israel, is sufficiently striking to suggest that it is here we must look for the closest comparative material.

The same is true of the name Lebanon, which belongs in the context of the same typology. 1QpHab xii. 1 ff. reads: '"For the violence done to Lebanon will overwhelm you; the destruction of the beasts] shall terrify (you), for the blood of man and violence to the land, the city and all who dwell therein" (= Hab. ii. 17). The meaning of the text concerns the wicked priest in retribution to him for the treatment that he meted out to the poor. "Lebanon" stands here for the council of the community, עצת היחד, and "beasts" for the simple-minded in Judah, who carry out the Law....' This *pesher* commentary on the text of Habakkuk thus identifies the council of the community with 'Lebanon' and the members of the community with the 'beasts'. The division of the community into two is well known from the temple symbolism, and it is interesting to note that in late Jewish texts 'Lebanon' is often used to denote the temple. Investigation of the relation between 'Lebanon' and the temple has demonstrated how well this text fits in with a distinct exegetical tradition.[2] In this tradition 'Lebanon' is taken to refer either to the Messianic king or to the kings of the future;[3] or, more frequently, to the temple and even to the temple of

[1] The text restored by Yadin, 'The Newly Published *Pesharim* of Isaiah', *I.E.J.* IX (1959), 40 ff.; his interpretation seems to fit in well with the general ideology of Qumran.

[2] G. Vermès, 'Car le Liban, c'est le conseil de la Communauté', in *Mélanges bibliques André Robert* (1957), pp. 316 ff., and 'The Symbolical Interpretation of Lebanon in the Targums', *J.T.S.* IX (1958), 1 ff.

[3] *Targum* on I Kings iv. 33, 'He (Solomon) spoke of trees, from the cedar that is in Lebanon to the hyssop that grows out of the wall', reads, 'He prophesied concerning the kings of the house of David that should rule in the world and the Messiah that should reign in the world to come'. Cf. Vermès, 'The Symbolical Interpretation', p. 2.

the Messianic age.[1] The exegetical tradition throws light on the text of 1QpHab xii. 1 ff. and its link with the symbolism of the temple; it also helps us to understand the temple–king (Messiah) complex of ideas, which we have previously encountered, and which is of such importance for the New Testament interpretation of the 'temple'.[2]

D. THE 'SPIRITUAL' SACRIFICES

In a number of the texts we have quoted, the community is represented as the new temple, with two rooms, the 'Holy place' and the 'Holy of holies'; but this is not all: the life of the community in perfect obedience to the Law is represented as the true sacrifice offered in the new temple. Thus we read in 1QS viii. 9 that the establishment of the temple (the community) has come about in order to make atonement for the land '...and a bringing forth of the sweet smell of sacrifice and a house of justice and truth in Israel...'. These are not merely images and symbols; they express a reality. Since the community has taken over the holiness and the functions of the temple it is now in point of fact the only means of maintaining the holiness of Israel and making atonement for sin. It is necessary that atonement should be made for the sins of the people; the desecration of the official temple has rendered it useless for these ends; there must be a substitute, and that substitute is the life of the community, lived in perfect obedience to all the precepts of the Law, all its commandments, purifications and prayers.[3] It is this that is implied by the words of 1QS ix. 3ff., 'When these (things) come to pass in Israel according to all these laws, it is for (*or* in order to establish)

---

[1] Vermès, 'The Symbolical Interpretation', pp. 5 and 11. On the complex of ideas surrounding the holy mountain, the temple and the holy city, see Riesenfeld, *Jésus transfiguré*, pp. 218 ff.

[2] This combination of temple and king is found e.g. in Sifre Deut. i. 7: 'And Lebanon: when you enter the country, you shall choose a king and build the elect house (the temple). How do we know that Lebanon refers to the king? Because it is written.... How do we know that Lebanon refers to the temple? Because it is written....' Cf. Vermès, 'The Symbolical Interpretation', p. 8.

[3] On the central role of the temple in making atonement, see E. Lohse, *Märtyrer und Gottesknecht*, F.R.L.A.N.T.(N.F.) XLVI (1955), 20 ff.

the foundation of the holy spirit, for eternal truth, for the atonement of the guilt of sin and misdeeds, and for the wellbeing of
the land by means of the flesh of burnt offerings and the fat of
sacrifices, (that is) the right offerings of the lips as a righteous
sweet savour and a perfect way of life as a free-will offering,
pleasing (to God)....'.[1] We encounter the same 'spiritualization'[2] of the idea of sacrifice in 4QFlor. i. 6f., 'And he purposed
to build him a sanctuary of (among) men, in which should be
offered sacrifices before him, the works of the Law'.[3] The
blood sacrifices offered in the Jerusalem temple were often
linked with some individual's confession of sin; sacrifice and
man's turning to God were closely related.[4] This was the
'atmosphere' in which the Qumran community made its severe
demands, requiring that the sacrifice offered by its members
should consist in a life lived in perfect obedience to the Law.
The works of the Law were useless without an inward turning
to God.[5]

But it is in the Rabbinic Judaism of the period following the
fall of the temple in A.D. 70 that we finally see realized the
trend toward the Law as the most vital element of the Jewish
religion, a trend which began much earlier.[6] Service in the
temple, 'abodâ, becomes replaced by the study of the Law and
the life of obedience to the Law. Other substitutes included a
rigid scheme of prayers, formerly (that is, before A.D. 70)
connected with temple worship.[7] A similar process of reorienta-

---

[1] Cf. Flusser, 'The Dead Sea Sect and Pre-pauline Christianity', *Scripta
Hierosolymitana*, IV (1958), 229 ff.; Baumgarten, 'Sacrifice and Worship',
pp. 149 ff.

[2] When we speak of the 'sacrifices' offered through the works of the Law
this is not merely a metaphor; both actual and 'spiritual' sacrifices were
regarded as being equally 'real' in the eyes of God. The problem recurs in
the N.T. A useful criticism of those who regard the Pauline sacrificial
terminology as no more than an extended metaphor is found in K. Weiss,
'Paulus—Priester der christlichen Kultgemeinde', *T.L.Z.* LXXIX (1954),
356.

[3] C.D. vi. 20 has an expression which seems to contain the same idea.
The community, constituted as the true Israel, offers the works of the Law
as they are interpreted in their own traditions; cf. Hvidberg, *Menigheden*,
p. 113.

[4] See e.g. Bonsirven, *Le Judaïsme Palestinien*, II, 119.

[5] See Gärtner, 'Bakgrunden till Qumranförsamlingens krig', pp. 59 ff.

[6] See above, pp. 17 f.   [7] Cf. Weber, *Jüdische Theologie*, pp. 38 ff.

tion is to be observed in Qumran, even before the fall of the temple. We have already discussed some of the causes,[1] but there is one further detail which we must mention here. It is striking how many of the Qumran texts hark back to passages in the Old Testament which criticize sharply any form of temple service which fails to take account of justice and righteousness according to the demands of the Law.[2] This is important for the understanding of the Qumran background, with its frequent stress laid upon truth and righteousness according to the Law as the only sacrifices of value in the eyes of God. There is a link here with a well-established tradition of criticism of the cultus, a tradition of which the prophets were the principal exponents. Thus we see how the account in 1QS ix. 3 ff. of the 'new' temple and its 'sacrifices' links up with Hosea's criticism of the cultus. The other text in 1QS which is important in this connexion, viii. 2 ff., is easily associated with Mic. vi. 6–8 and Ps. li. 19, 'The sacrifice acceptable to God is a broken spirit, רוח נשברה'. C.D. xi. 20f., which prohibits members of the community from sending sacrifices to the Jerusalem temple, the altar of which has been defiled, refers to Prov. xv. 8, 'The sacrifice of the wicked is an abomination to Yahweh, but the prayer of the upright is his delight' (C.D. amends the Masoretic text to read 'the prayer of the upright is like a pleasing sacrifice'!). Examples might be multiplied,[3] but these should serve to show how the community turned to those passages in the Old Testament which they regarded as fitting their own situation and their own critical attitude to the temple and its sacrifices. The former service in the temple they replaced by a general עבודה, a life according to the Law, a righteousness demanded of each and every member of the community.

[1] See above, pp. 17f.
[2] Cf. Maier, 'Zum Begriff יחד', pp. 161f.
[3] 1QS x. 22, 26f., and Hos. xiv. 3, Ps. li. 19; 1QS v. 3 and Isa. lvi. 1; 1QS i. 24 and Mic. vi. 6–8.

CHAPTER IV

TEMPLE SYMBOLISM IN THE
NEW TESTAMENT

WE have seen that the Qumran texts contain a consistent temple symbolism, in which the community is represented as the new temple, and in which the true sacrifice is seen as being spiritual in character, offered in the holy and pure lives, the praise and the prayer of the members of the community. No direct parallel to this temple symbolism has been traced in Judaism.[1] There are 'spiritualized' interpretations of the temple and its sacrifices in the work of such authors as Philo and Josephus,[2] but there is nothing corresponding to the Qumran community's identification of a group of men with the true temple. And although both Philo and Josephus are to some extent critical of a too realistic attitude to the presence of God in the temple and his approval of blood sacrifice,[3] their work shows no trace of the characteristic Qumran criticism, based on the Messianic self-consciousness of the community that God is in the midst of the 'true Israel' (the community) although the Jerusalem temple is defiled.

A number of these themes are of course found elsewhere. For instance, we may compare the concept of the 'remnant',

[1] An attempt to interpret some of the texts in the Book of Daniel, which mention the 'saints of the most High' over which the Son of man is to reign, as expressing the idea that these 'saints' comprise a spiritual temple is to be found in A. Feuillet, 'Le Fils de l'homme de Daniel et la tradition biblique', *R.B.* LX (1953), 197ff. This interpretation seems however to lack support in the texts. It is natural that Daniel should contain a temple criticism similar to that found in Qumran, since both represent similar Jewish circles. See e.g. Gärtner, 'Bakgrunden till Qumranförsamlingens krig', pp. 39f. Cf. below, pp. 127ff.

[2] See e.g. M. Simon, *Verus Israel* (1948), pp. 56f.; Gärtner, *The Areopagus Speech*, pp. 205ff.

[3] Schlatter, *Die Theologie des Judentums nach dem Bericht des Josefus*, Beitr. z. Förd. christl. Theol. XXVI (1932), 72f.; Daniélou, 'La symbolique du temple de Jérusalem chez Philon et Josèphe', *Serie orient. Roma* XIV (1957), 83ff., shows how the temple symbolism of these two authors is expressed mainly in cosmological categories.

which contains a number of similar ideas. The Old Testament and late Judaism speak of the 'remnant' as the company of those who are to be saved in the last days.[1] There was discussion, particularly in late Judaism, as to whether this 'remnant' was identical with the whole of Israel, or whether it was only a group within the nation. There is evidence for both views in the texts.[2] It is interesting to note that this concept was linked with the holy land, Palestine, and (more often) with Zion, Jerusalem.[3] Thus it was believed, for example, that the Lord would preserve on the holy mountain a 'remnant', a company of the saved, those with whom he was particularly pleased. This 'remnant' idea was also connected with the appearance and the saving work of the Messiah. The concept is met with, though not frequently, in the Qumran texts. The community itself is the 'remnant', that group in Israel which has turned to the will of God (C.D. i. 4) and will be saved in the distress and judgement of the last day (1QH vi. 8); for in it are fulfilled the prophecies that part of Israel would be saved: that part truly chosen by God (1QM xiii. 8, xiv. 8f.). The 'remnant' idea, when it occurs in the Old Testament and late Judaism, is connected with Zion and the appearance of the eschatological Messiah; it is thus understandable that the idea of the community as the holy, circumscribed group was readily combined with the symbolism of the temple. For in this symbolism, as we have seen, the dominant ideas were of holiness and separation, of the temple as the dwelling place of God and the focus of God's beneficence.[4] But at the same time it is characteristic of Qumran that it is the community itself that is the focus of fellowship with God, a temple well pleasing in the sight of God. This has no parallel, either in the concept of the 'remnant' or in other areas of late Judaism, at least not according to texts at present available.

A parallel to the ideology of the Qumran texts is however

[1] See e.g. Herntrich–Schrenk, art. λεῖμμα, *T.W.B.* IV, 202 ff. and E. W. Heaton, 'The Root שאר and the Doctrine of the Remnant', *J.T.S.* III (1952), 27 ff.

[2] Cf. Volz, *Die Eschatologie der jüdischen Gemeinde*, pp. 342 ff., and Jeremias, 'Der Gedanke des "heiligen Restes" im Spätjudentum und in der Verkündigung Jesu', *Z.N.T.W.* XLII (1949), 184 ff.

[3] See Herntrich–Schrenk, *op. cit.* pp. 210 ff.

[4] Cf. similar motives in Maier, 'Zum Begriff יחד', pp. 148 ff.

provided by the New Testament, where the idea of the eschatological temple is actually applied to a circumscribed group of men, in the context of a Messianic interpretation of the founder of the group, Jesus. Similarities between Qumran and the New Testament are to be noted in a number of New Testament texts, but it is not possible to examine them all in detail here.[1] We shall instead concentrate on some of the most important texts from the various traditions, endeavouring to throw light on the connexion which existed between the Christian interpretation of the temple and that found in the Qumran texts.

A. PAUL AND THE TEMPLE OF CHRIST

(1) *II Cor. vi. 14–vii. 1*

This text, which contains the clearest statement in the Pauline Epistles of the idea of the Christians as 'the temple' is at the same time the one most reminiscent in its terminology of the theology of the Qumran community. It reads:

Do not be misyoked with unbelievers. For what partnership have righteousness and iniquity, ἀνομία? Or what fellowship can light have with darkness? What accord has Christ with Belial? Or what part has a believer with an unbeliever? What agreement has the temple of God, ναὸς θεοῦ, with idols? For we are the temple of the living God; as God said, 'I shall dwell among them and move (among them), and I shall be their God, and they will be my people (Ezek. xxxvii. 27, Lev. xxvi. 11 f.). Therefore come out from them, and be separate from them, says the Lord, and touch nothing unclean (Isa. lii. 11); then I shall welcome you (Ezek. xx. 34), and I shall be a father to you, and you will be my sons and daughters (II Sam. vii. 14), says the Lord Almighty' (II Sam. vii. 8?). Since we have these promises, beloved, let us cleanse ourselves from every defilement of body and spirit, and make holiness perfect in the fear of God.

The resemblance between this text and Qumran theology is striking; the two have a large number of points in common, among them the alternatives of righteousness or iniquity (that which opposes the Law), light or darkness, Christ or Belial; the

---

[1] Cf. general works on the temple symbolism of the N.T.; e.g. M. Fraeyman, 'La spiritualisation de l'idée du temple dans les épîtres pauliniennes', *Ephem. Theol. Lov.* XXIII (1947), 378 ff.; Y. Congar, *Le mystère du temple*, Lectio Divina, XXII (1958); J. P. Pfammatter, *Die Kirche als Bau* (1961).

expression 'lot', μερίς, the idea of the community as the 'temple of God', and the exhortation to purity. All this fits in so well with the atmosphere of the Qumran texts that some have supposed the passage to be 'a Christian reworking of an Essene paragraph which has been introduced into the Pauline letter'.[1] Similar ideas are of course to be found in other late Jewish circles, but this combination of so many of them, coupled with the specifically Qumran idea of the community as the temple of God, is particularly striking. We cannot deal with all the many details, interesting *per se*, which this text and the Qumran texts have in common.[2] We concentrate instead on three ideas of particular importance for the understanding of the temple symbolism.

(1) Paul writes, 'What agreement has the temple of God with idols? For we are the temple of the living God.' This means that Christians are the true temple of God, separate from non-believers. The image of the temple appears to have been used here as it was used in Qumran, to show that the 'presence', *Shekinah*, of God had removed from the official Jerusalem temple to the 'new' people of God, the Christian Church. This particular text does not develop the idea of the new temple, but support is provided for it by certain important themes.

Why did the Apostle place these two concepts—God's temple and the idols—over against each other? 'What agreement has the temple of God with idols?' It has often been supposed that Paul, conscious of the problem of idolatry in Corinth, was thinking of idols *in concreto*.[3] But in view of the numerous correspondences between this text and the ideology

[1] Fitzmyer, 'Qumrân and the Interpolated Paragraph in II Cor. vi. 14–vii. 1', *C.B.Q.* xxiii (1961), 271 ff. Although we are not prepared to talk about 'interpolation' in this context, since that would give rise to a mass of problems of the order of 'by whom?' and 'when?', it is evident that this passage is relatively independent of the rest of the letter, causing difficulties for anyone who wishes to determine its overall disposition.

[2] See K. G. Kuhn, 'Les rouleaux de cuivre de Qumrân', *R.B.* lxi (1954), 203, n. 2; F. M. Braun, 'L'arrière-fond judaïque du Quatrième Évangile et la Communauté de l'Alliance', *R.B.* lxii (1955), 33f.; Kosmala, *Hebräer–Essener–Christen* (1959), pp. 373f; and J. Gnilka, '2 Kor. 6, 14–7, 1, im Lichte der Qumranschriften und der Zwölf-Patriarchen-Testamente', in *Festschrift J. Schmid* (1963), pp. 86–99.

[3] Michel, art. ναός, *T.W.B.* iv, 891, considers that there is a connexion here with the idols mentioned in the O.T., which brought about Israel's corruption.

of Qumran, it may be worth seeking for the background of this expression in the Qumran texts. Thus we read that true members of the Qumran community must turn their backs on hypocrites in their midst; these are to be cursed by the priests and the Levites, for they have entered into the covenant 'with the idols of the heart', בגלולי לבו (1QS ii. 11). It is clear from the context that the reference is to Deut. xxix. 18 ff., but that the actual expression is drawn from the prophet Ezekiel, who polemizes against any member of the house of Israel who takes 'his idols into his heart', xiv. 4 ff.[1] The text does not seem to have been used in Qumran to refer to the actual worship of images; instead it has been given a transferred meaning, pointing to the evil impulses which cause a man to disobey the Law and the faith of the community (1QS iv. 5, cf. ii. 17). Another text closely related to Ezek. xiv is 1QH iv. 15 ff., which describes those who have turned their backs on the covenant. Although they seek God their hearts are turned to idols (cf. C.D. xx. 9 f.). I consider that here we have the background of Paul's words. Paul's use of the concept of the 'temple' is spiritual, having nothing to do with an actual building; in the same way it is reasonable to suppose that by 'idols' he meant not the actual images, but that from which the Christian must be separated: sin and uncleanness. 'The temple of God', the company of Christians, cannot remain open to those who have fallen away from faith and purity, preferring instead the evil of their own hearts.[2]

I consider that it is this complex of ideas which provides the necessary background of Paul's antithesis between the 'temple of God' and 'idols'—confirmation being to some extent supplied by the valuable comparative material in 4QFlor. Reference is there made to Ezek. xxxvii. 23 and its warning to the people not to defile themselves with idols; in 4QFlor. i. 16 f. we read: 'And these are they of whom it is written in the book of the prophet Ezekiel: "They shall not [defile themselves any more with] their idols." They are the sons of Zadok and the

---

[1] Cf. Wernberg-Møller, *The Manual of Discipline*, p. 54, n. 29.

[2] This opposition between the temple and the idols may also be seen as an exposition of those texts which describe the placing of the idols in the temple of Israel, Fraeyman, 'La spiritualisation', p. 392. The connexion with the Qumran texts' 'idols of the heart' seems however to be more likely.

m[en] of his [coun]sel....'[1] The text of Ezekiel is here interpreted by means of a reference to the sons of Zadok and to the
community which is the true Israel of the last days. Those who
join the community thereby turn aside from the path of the
apostates. Again I do not believe that the 'idols' referred to
are in fact images; they symbolize the paths of the unfaithful
outside the bounds of the Law. As we have already pointed
out, 4QFlor. is one of the most important of the Qumran texts
from the point of view of temple symbolism and its Messianic
background.[2] Further, this exegesis of the word 'idols', combined with the principle of the community as the temple of
God, is proof of its close similarity to the Pauline text under
discussion. It is also noteworthy that Ezek. xxxvii—the passage
quoted in 4QFlor.—recurs in Paul, in the compound Old
Testament quotation which follows in explanation of the
references to 'the temple of God' and the 'idols' in II Cor. vi. 16.

(2) Paul, wishing to demonstrate the essential agreement of
his statement 'For we are the temple of the living God' with
the Old Testament, quotes freely a number of Old Testament
texts, which he combines in the manner of contemporary
Jewish exegesis. This method was at the same time typical of
the Qumran scriptures.[3] The first part of this text is taken from
Ezek. xxxvii. 27 and Lev. xxvi. 12.

II Cor. vi. 16b	Ezek. xxxvii. 27	Lev. xxvi. 11–12
ἐνοικήσω ἐν αὐτοῖς	ἔσται ἡ κατασκή-	καὶ θήσω τὴν
καὶ ἐμπεριπατήσω	νωσίς μου ἐν αὐτοῖς	διαθήκην μου ἐν
καὶ ἔσομαι αὐτῶν	καὶ ἔσομαι αὐτοῖς	ὑμῖν...
θεός	θεός	καὶ ἐνπεριπατήσω
καὶ αὐτοὶ ἔσονταί	καὶ αὐτοί μου ἔσον-	ἐν ὑμῖν
μου λαός	ται λαός	καὶ ἔσομαι ὑμῖν θεός
		καὶ ὑμεῖς ἔσεσθέ μου
		λαός

Neither of the texts quoted agrees exactly with Paul's version.
It is a striking fact that his introductory words ἐνοικήσω ἐν

---

[1] I prefer Yadin's restoration of the text to Allegro's, which does not fit
the lacuna so well, nor the interpretation. See above, pp. 31 f. Cf. Fitzmyer, 'The Use of Explicit Old Testament Quotations in Qumran Literature', *N.T.S.* VII (1960–1), 315.   [2] See above, pp. 30 ff.

[3] Cf. Fitzmyer, '"4Q Testimonia" and the New Testament', *Th.St.*
XVIII (1957), 530 ff.

αὐτοῖς are to be found nowhere in the Old Testament, and that the verb is never used in the LXX in connexion with God's 'dwelling' in the temple or among the people. But they provide an excellent paraphrase of what is said at the beginning of the Ezekiel and Leviticus texts. Ezekiel xxxvii. 27 (LXX) κατασκήνωσις corresponds to the Masoretic מֹשְׁכָּן, often used to describe the tabernacle or the temple. Leviticus xxvi. 11 (LXX) διαθήκη also corresponds to the Masoretic מֹשְׁכָּן.[1] The 'presence' or 'dwelling', Shekinah, was linked particularly to the tabernacle and the temple, and it is to this 'presence' Paul seems to be referring when he writes 'I shall dwell among them' as Scriptural proof that the Christians are now the true 'temple'. This idea, of God 'dwelling' among the Christians, is expressed elsewhere in the New Testament in different forms; for example John xiv. 23: '...and my Father will love him, and we will come to him and make our home, μονή, with him', and Rev. xxi. 3 (using Ezek. xxxvii. 27): 'Behold, the tabernacle, σκηνή, of God is with men. He will dwell, σκηνώσει, with them, and they shall be his people, and God himself will be with them....'[2] The meaning of the 'presence' of God in the Pauline text is not merely that God dwells among his faithful people: it has to do with the temple concept as well. Christians are not only the people of God; they are also the temple, ναός, of God. The use of ναός instead of ἱερόν is to be explained by the fact that ἱερόν refers to the whole temple, while ναός is normally confined to the 'Holy place' and the 'Holy of holies', the dwelling place of God.[3]

Here we may note a further resemblance to 4QFlor. A leading theme there is that the temple in which God dwells is the community.[4] This theme is illustrated by a number of Old

[1] Codex Ambrosius also reads σκηνή.

[2] Cf. John i. 14 ὁ λόγος ἐσκήνωσεν ἐν ἡμῖν and the commentary of Riesenfeld, Jésus transfiguré, pp. 184f.; F. M. Braun, 'In spiritu et veritate', Rev. Thom. LII (1952), 246f.; Congar, Le mystère du temple, pp. 161ff.

[3] Cf. Congar, op. cit. pp. 135ff.

[4] Nor was the community unfamiliar with the traditional idea that God, in fulfilment of the promises, would once more dwell in the Jerusalem temple. See Baillet, 'Un recueil liturgique de Qumrân, grotte 4: "Les paroles des luminaires"', R.B. LXVIII (1961), 205, col. IV, 1ff. But the community was the replacement for the temple during the period of judgement. See above, p. 20.

Testament texts, expounded in such a way as to fill them with new meaning. The texts in question are II Sam. vii. 10–14, Exod. xv. 17–18, Amos ix. 11, Ps. i. 1, Isa. viii. 11, Ezek. xxxvii. 23, and Ps. ii. 1. The first three of these deal with the subject of the temple of God, the dwelling of God in the midst of the people. God 'dwells' with his holy angels, in the community.[1] A related idea is the foundation of the community and its rejection of all impurity; the community is the bearer of purity, holiness and the promise of an everlasting future. Here the foundation of the community is linked with the Davidic prophecies.[2]

Of these, Paul uses in II Cor. vi. 16 the text from Ezek. xxxvii and, a little later, the passage from II Sam. vii. 14: 'and I shall be a father to you, and you will be my sons and daughters'.[3] It is not possible to say whether this compound version of the Old Testament texts in question formed part of a collection of *testimonia*, taken over by Paul from Qumran or from some other late Jewish tradition; at the same time it cannot be denied that its theme and character resemble closely such a text as 4QFlor. But the treatment and combination of the Old Testament quotations reveal certain distinct characteristics which have (so far) no parallel in the Qumran texts. For this reason it seems most likely that they originated with Paul himself, or with some other Christian interpreter. Further, the text from Lev. xxvi. 11 used by Paul is fundamental for the future hopes of Judaism in respect of the coming temple, in other traditions than that of Qumran.[4] For example, Jub. i. 17: 'And I shall build my sanctuary in their midst, and I shall dwell among them, and I shall be their God, and they will be my people in truth and righteousness.'[5] It is the concept of the community as the temple of God that brings the Qumran tradition closest to Paul.

[1] See above, pp. 30ff.

[2] II Sam. vii, Amos ix and Ezek. xxxvii belong to this category. The latter text has to do with the promise of Davidic rule, *v.* 24.

[3] The quotation is altered from 'I shall be a father to *him*' to 'to *you*'. The Pauline phrase 'you will be my sons and daughters' is a development of II Sam. vii. 14; it is probable that the common O.T. phrase 'sons and daughters' has influenced the formulation.

[4] Cerfaux, *La théologie de l'église suivant saint Paul* (1948), pp. 115 ff.

[5] Cf. Fraeyman, 'La spiritualisation', p. 391.

(3) An outstanding characteristic of the temple symbolism advanced by Paul in II Cor. vi. 14ff. is its connexion with purity. The demand for purity and holiness is most emphatic. This is to be seen in the antithetical pairs, righteousness–iniquity, ἀνομία, light–darkness, Christ–Belial, the temple–idols; it is however also to be seen in the Old Testament texts which are quoted. Thus we find a free version of Isa. lii. 11, 'Therefore come out from them, and be separate from them, says the Lord, and touch nothing unclean'.[1] A close parallel to this requirement, that the company of the sanctified must withdraw from those who will not follow the ways of the Lord, is provided by 4QFlor. i. 14ff., in which Ps. i. 1 is interpreted with reference to the community: 'A mi[dr]ash on "Happy is the man that walketh not in the counsel of the wicked" (Ps. i. 1). The meaning of this wo[rd] has to do with those [who] turned aside from the way [of the people], as it is written in the book of the prophet Isaiah concerning the last days (Isa. viii. 11): "And it was as though with a strong [hand that he turned me aside from, יסירני, following the way] of this people." '[2] The community is the sanctified group which, refusing to follow the sinful ways of the official Israel, has established its holiness in the light of the Law. There follows the saying on 'idols' which we considered above. The separation of the Christian community is expressed in similar terms, following the text 'come out from them, and be separate from them, says the Lord, and touch nothing unclean...'—a theme frequently taken up by the exclusive Qumran group.[3] It is evident that this concept is an intrinsic part of temple symbolism, particularly as expressed in 4QFlor.[4]

The theme of separation and holiness returns in the brief exhortation which concludes the passage (II Cor. vi. 14–vii. 1);

---

[1] M.T. Isa. lii. 11: 'Depart, סורו, depart, go out thence, touch no unclean thing; go out from the midst of her, purify yourselves, you who bear the vessels of the Lord.' The Pauline text is in the plural, thus fitting in better with the context of an exhortation to separate the holy community from the ungodly; it has also been abbreviated. The latter part of the text is of no significance. Cf. also Ezek. xiv. 11.

[2] The similarity with the two Isa. texts quoted extends beyond the contents of the important common term סור.

[3] See Gärtner, 'Bakgrunden till Qumranförsamlingens krig', pp. 62ff.

[4] See above, pp. 31f.

the Apostle urges the congregation to cleanse themselves from every defilement of the body and the spirit, since this is part of the holy life of the Christian in the fear of God. Here, too, there is a close relationship with the theology of the Qumran community, though the content of the exhortation has taken on distinctly Christian characteristics. It is to be explained by Paul's thesis that the true temple is the community in which Christ is light, righteousness and the living God. For proof-texts he takes Old Testament passages in which God is said to 'dwell' in the midst of his people; the consequence of which is that the people must abandon anything and everything which can pollute them and lead them astray. At this point the distance dividing Paul from the Qumran texts is minimal. Although certain of these themes recur, for example in the concept of the 'remnant', the overall resemblance to the Qumran symbolism is so striking as to prompt the question whether the temple symbolism of the early Church, a symbolism which was to become so important in the ecclesiology of the New Testament, may not have originated in the Qumran tradition.[1] We cannot of course rule out the possibility that there may have been similar traditions outside Qumran, but these, if they existed, have disappeared without trace. The possibility is in any case not large, since the typical Qumran temple symbolism, with the characteristic features we have described, depended upon the creation of a particular kind of self-consciousness in which the temple was considered to have been replaced by a living community.

(2) *I Cor. iii. 16–17*

Another Pauline text in which we find a similar view of the temple is I Cor. iii. 16–17, in which the congregation in

---

[1] It has been said that the undeniable link between Qumran and Paul on this matter of temple symbolism is not evidence that Paul was dependent in any way upon Essene sources (Congar, *Le mystère du temple*, p. 190). At all events it cannot be proved. But the idea of a temple made up of a group of people is, as far as we know, limited to Qumran and the N.T. (cf. Kuhn, 'Les rouleaux de cuivre de Qumrân', *R.B.* LXI (1954), 203 n. 1). This suggests that there must have been a link between the two groups of texts. But at the same time it is probable that this temple symbolism was reinterpreted by the early Church before the time of Paul.

Corinth is briefly described by the Apostle as a spiritual building, a temple. Earlier (in *vv.* 9–15) he described how, like a skilled master builder, he laid the foundations of this spiritual edifice, and emphasized that it was God's work which was decisive. For the foundation is Christ, and it is God who determines what will be the result of the work on the building (*vv.* 9ff.). Others will build in future, but their work will be tried in the judgement (*vv.* 12f.).[1] Paul then proceeds to give the reason for his demand for purity, in the course of which he identifies the church with the temple. Christians are God's temple, and therefore must be holy. It seems that this temple symbolism formed part of Paul's teaching in Corinth, since he begins by saying 'Do you not know that, οὐκ οἴδατε ὅτι', the implication being that he is reminding them of something they have heard before.[2] The whole text reads, 'Do you not know that you are God's temple, ναὸς θεοῦ, and that God's Spirit dwells in you? If anyone destroys God's temple, God will destroy him. For God's temple is holy, and that (temple) you are.'

There are four points of contact with II Cor. vi. 14ff., and through it with the temple symbolism of the Qumran community.

(1) Clear emphasis is placed on the typical identification of the 'temple of God' with the community. The Christian church in Corinth is the true temple; the temple is made up of the members of the church: *vide* the expressions 'you are God's temple' and 'that (temple) you are'. The Apostle paved the way for the introduction of this image a few verses previously by saying that the foundation, θεμέλιον, is Jesus Christ, and that no other foundation can ever be laid (*v.* 11); further, that the Christians are 'God's building', θεοῦ οἰκοδομή ἐστε (*v.* 9).

---

[1] H. Odeberg, *Pauli brev till korintierna* (1944), pp. 77ff., considers that when Paul speaks of the spiritual building, he is assuming that the builders themselves are part of the material out of which the new temple is constructed. Thus the Apostle is able to say that both the building and the builder are to be tested by fire.

[2] It has been pointed out that Paul may be referring to the tradition expressed in Mk. xiv. 58, that Jesus would destroy the temple and build it up again in three days, cf. Michel, art. ναός, *T.W.B.* iv, 890. It is unlikely that Paul had that particular saying in mind, but the temple symbolism he is using may well be based to some extent on that particular *logion*.

It seems to me to be perfectly justifiable to regard these more general expressions in the context of temple symbolism.[1] Note, too, that the imagery of iii. 6–17 shifts between a plantation, a building and a temple, all being related to the foundation and existence of the Church. We have earlier had occasion to point out that the background of this compound imagery is to be sought in the Old Testament and later Judaism, and that the images occur in certain of the Qumran texts, texts which express important aspects of temple symbolism and which in turn resemble Paul's symbolism at various points.[2]

(2) From this identification of the temple with the members of the Church it follows that the Spirit of God 'dwells' in the congregation, the implication being that God's *Shekinah* no longer rests on the Jerusalem temple, but has removed to the Church. It seems likely that Paul had the *Shekinah* in mind when writing 'God's Spirit dwells in you'. The Hebrew שכן means 'dwell', and is used to express the idea of God dwelling among men, among the children of Israel, in the tabernacle, or in the sanctuary.[3] We might compare II Cor. vi. 16*b*, ἐνοικήσω ἐν αὐτοῖς, which provides a parallel to I Cor. iii. 16 τὸ πνεῦμα τοῦ θεοῦ οἰκεῖ ἐν ὑμῖν. The former expression we found to be without equivalent in the LXX, being evidently intended to express God's 'dwelling' among the new people of God in the new temple. The latter corresponds directly to the former, but amplifies it somewhat by pointing out that it is the Spirit of God which dwells among the Christians, as the Spirit once dwelt among the children of Israel in the tabernacle and the temple. A further comparison may be made with relevant Qumran ideas, such as the idea that the holy angels dwell in the midst of the community.[4] And again, that the Spirit of God has a constitutive function in the texts of the Qumran community; this is part of the same complex of ideas as the holiness and purity of the 'elect' and God's 'dwelling' with his people.[5]

---

[1] Cf. Cerfaux, *La théologie*, p. 185 f.
[2] See above, pp. 28 f.
[3] See e.g. Congar, *Le mystère du temple*, pp. 27, 33 f., 117 ff.
[4] See below, pp. 95 ff.
[5] On the interest in the spirit expressed by the Qumran theology, see further Nötscher, 'Heiligkeit in den Qumranschriften', pp. 341 f.

(3) It is only natural, with this background in mind, that Paul should stress the consequences of this view, namely that 'the temple of God is holy'. In doing so, Paul is harking back to the traditional Jewish conception of the temple as the focus of holiness. An intense degree of holiness is concentrated upon the dwelling place of God; and this applies equally to the 'new' temple, the Church, the company of Christian believers. The use of the term 'holy' is thus dependent upon the image of the temple, just as 'holiness' was a dominant concept in the ideology and temple symbolism of the Qumran community.

(4) The 'dwelling' of God in the congregation and the holiness this fact implies are closely connected with the demand for purity. 'If any one destroys God's temple, God will destroy him.' The word translated 'destroy' (by the R.S.V.) is φθείρω, otherwise used only four times by Paul, apparently in connexion with heresy or immorality (II Cor. xi. 3, Eph. iv. 22).[1] It is found in the LXX on some twenty occasions, mainly as a translation of the Hebrew שחת, 'destroy', a word which often has the double meaning of 'judge' and 'destroy', and is used of man's evil work of destruction and of God's punishment.[2] Here, too, there are resemblances to the theology of Qumran. The noun שחת is found on a number of occasions in the Qumran texts, in connexion with the epithet 'men of destruction', אנשי השחת, who try to destroy the community, but fail and are themselves condemned to eternal destruction (1QS iv. 12 and ix. 16).[3] It was also a concern of the community to separate themselves from 'children of destruction' (C.D. vi. 15) as a condition of obtaining the blessing of God. If we look upon the word φθείρω in I Cor. iii. 17 against this background, we see how well it fits in with the concept of the congregation as the temple of God. Paul's exhortation not to 'destroy' the temple of God seems then to mean that they must avoid the snares of the evil one in the form of false doctrine and a life in conflict with the will of God. Earlier in the same chapter the Apostle spoke of

[1] Cf. Test. Sim. iv. 8, v. 4, Jud. xix. 4.

[2] It is occasionally eschatological in character; see A. M. Denis, 'La fonction apostolique et la liturgie nouvelle en esprit', *R.S.P.T.* xlii (1958), 420 ff.

[3] The idea of the temple and those who are seeking to destroy it is also to be found in 4QFlor., though the term used is שמם. It is not however the new temple that is to be destroyed, but its enemies.

the importance of building on the foundation of Christ, in line with his own work. Those who are trying to destroy this 'new' temple are false apostles, whose doctrines must bring them under the wrath and judgement of God since they do not agree with the message preached by the Apostle himself.

If we bring these four points together, we find that there are close resemblances between I Cor. iii. 16–17 and II Cor. vi. 14–vii. 1, but also that both resemble the temple symbolism and overall ideology of the Qumran community. The resemblance does not stop with the assertion that the community is to be identified with the temple of God; it extends to the emphasis on the 'dwelling' of God in the community, the holiness which results, the exhortation to purity and finally the warning to beware of those who threaten the life of the community. We are thus faced not only with a similar attitude to the new temple and the respective groups of believers, but with similarity in the other factors as well.

(3) *Eph. ii. 18–22*

Turning to other texts in the *Corpus Paulinum* (texts the authenticity of which is sometimes questioned, but which undoubtedly contain Pauline traditions) we see how the temple symbolism lives on. We encounter it in such texts as Eph. ii. 18–22 and I Tim. iii. 15, and although the forms of expression and the focus change, they nevertheless seem to embody a consistent tradition, similar in basic structure to the older texts from I and II Corinthians. What is particularly interesting, however, is that new characteristics and new details appear within the framework of the temple symbolism, details not to be found in I and II Corinthians, but which are paralleled in the Qumran texts.

To begin with the exposition of the 'holy temple' in Eph. ii. 21; we must note the extremely important background sketched by the Apostle in *vv.* 18–19. The theological argument which culminates in the idea of the 'holy temple' began with the result of the death of Christ on the cross: that 'Jews' and 'Gentiles' have been made into one new man in place of two (ii. 11–17). The group of people who make manifest the true people of God in the Christian Church now have privileges which were once restricted to the Jews; in short, 'access...to the Father', 'for through him (Christ) we both (Israel and the Gentiles) have access in one Spirit to the Father. So then you are no longer strangers and sojourners, but you are fellow citizens with the saints and members of the household of God...' (vv. 18–19). This text is capable of being interpreted in various ways, and it is no easy matter to find the right background to its terminology and expressions. But it seems worth while to make use once more of the comparative material from Qumran, and work on the possibility of regarding the whole passage (vv. 18–22) in the light of the temple symbolism of Qumran and the New Testament.

'Access to the Father' (v. 18), προσαγωγὴ πρὸς τὸν πατέρα, fits in well with this symbolism, since in the LXX the verb προσάγειν often denotes the presentation of a sacrifice in the temple or appearance in the temple before God.[1] The noun προσαγωγή is used on two other occasions in the New Testament, by Paul, when it means 'access' in a more general sense, connected with the Christian's privilege of appearing before God through the atonement brought about by Christ. But both the background and the actual verb seem to be cultic in character.[2] According to Eph. ii. 18 'access' to the Father is rendered possible in and through the Spirit; in other words, the term has been 'spiritualized' in meaning and application, like the temple and its sacrifices. This 'access', within the framework of temple symbolism, means that those who obtain access are of the company of the sanctified, the true people of God. It is thus entirely consistent that Paul should write to Gentile Christians that they are no longer 'strangers and sojourners, ξένοι καὶ πάροικοι'. The temple of Israel was originally the property of the chosen people; no stranger might come before the face of Yahweh. Once more we may refer back to 4QFlor., with its words about the new, pure 'house of God'. The new 'spiritual' temple might be entered only under certain conditions: 'That is the house where there shall not enter [any one

---

[1] προσαγωγή is not found in the LXX, but the verb προσάγειν is common. On the cultic implications of the word, see K. L. Schmidt, art. προσάγω–προσαγωγή, *T.W.B.* I, 131 f.

[2] See K. L. Schmidt, *op. cit.* pp. 131 ff. Schlier, *Der Brief an die Epheser*, p. 139, refers to 'eine Thronszene' (cf. I Enoch xlvii. 3 ff.).

whose flesh has a] permanent [blemish] or an Ammonite or a Moabite or a bastard or an alien or a stranger for ever,[1] for his holy ones are there [for] ever...' (i. 3 ff.). Words of particular interest here are ממזר, a foreigner who could not be incorporated into Israel, בן נכר, an alien belonging to another nation, and גר, a sojourner; all are directly related to the words ξένοι and πάροικοι in the LXX.[2] It is conceivable that the exclusion of strangers and foreigners from the temple may have influenced the strictness with which the Qumran community regarded such people. The purity and holiness of the temple demanded the exclusion of everyone who might be 'unclean' (cf. II Macc. iii. 12, 18 and Josephus, *Bell.* v, 193 f. for λίθινος δρύφακτος); similar rigorous measures were imposed by the community that claimed to be the temple of God.

Paul in Eph. ii. 19 addresses himself to former Gentiles, who have now become Christians; the link with the Jewish background seems to be that these have now become full members of the 'new' people of God, and are no longer undesirable aliens. All have 'access' to God. The text uses the same themes as 4QFlor., but fills them with new meaning, that in Christ has been created a new sphere and a new dimension of holiness, having no connexion with race or nation. This similarity with 4QFlor. is important as a statement, in the context of the new temple, of the racial qualifications for membership. (The theme of the protection of the temple against foreigners is one which recurs on a number of occasions in the Qumran texts.)[3]

But they are no longer 'strangers' and 'sojourners'; they have become 'fellow citizens with the saints and members of the household of God, συμπολῖται τῶν ἁγίων καὶ οἰκεῖοι τοῦ

---

[1] Allegro, 'Fragments', p. 351, suggests the inclusion of גר, 'a non-Israelite', in the text; this may well be so. Yadin, 'A Midrash on II Sam. vii and Ps. i–ii', p. 96, prefers to replace it with ועד, since C.D. xiv. 4 uses גר to refer to persons who were not full members of the community, but were connected with it. But the same word may have been used in different contexts with different meanings, as in the O.T. This impression is strengthened by the fact that C.D. vi. 21 has גר in the meaning 'foreigner', i.e. the non-Israelite, as in Exod. and Deut.

[2] Cf. Stählin, art. ξένος, *T.W.B.* v, 8 ff., and K. L. and M. A. Schmidt, art. πάροικος, *T.W.B.* v, 841 ff.

[3] E.g. 1QH vi. 26 f. Cf. Betz, 'Felsenmann und Felsengemeinde', p. 56. There is however another reading and interpretation in Holm-Nielsen, *Hodayot* (1960), p. 119.

θεοῦ' (v. 19). These two expressions, συμπολῖται and οἰκεῖοι, are difficult to interpret. They seem however to be parallel to each other, like the antithetical ξένοι and πάροικοι, and seem to point to a new fellowship with God. This fellowship implies that the people in question have been incorporated into the group of believers who now comprise the 'new' people of God: those who have taken over the privileges which once belonged to Israel. That the Apostle uses the word συμπολῖται might well mean that he has in mind the Greek πόλις: that Christians are citizens of a spiritual city-state. But if it is a form of 'citizenship' which Paul has in mind, then it is most likely to be citizenship of the heavenly Jerusalem. This fits in well with οἰκεῖοι τοῦ θεοῦ. The Church is the heavenly city (Gal. iv. 26, Phil. iii. 20, Heb. xii. 18 ff.), and God's heavenly house, in which the Christians are housefolk under the Father.[1]

Here again 4QFlor. provides us with a parallel. There we find emphasis laid upon the exclusion of 'aliens' and 'strangers' from the true Israel, the company of the sanctified. This the community justified by recalling their holiness, which was such as to permit the angels of God to dwell with them: 'That is the house where there shall not enter...an alien or a stranger for ever, for his holy ones are there [for] ever...' (i. 3 ff.). The angels are here called קדושו, 'his holy ones',[2] and they are able to have fellowship with the community, the 'house of God', the true temple. The community is a 'holy congregation', יחד or עדת קודש, the 'holy people' of God, עם קודשכה.[3] The Qumran community, as a holy temple, is in fellowship with God and his angels, 'Those whom God has chosen he has made into an eternal possession, and he has given them a share in the lot of the holy ones, and he has united their community with the sons of heaven into a council of the community, עצת יחד, and their community is a house of holiness[4] for an eternal

---

[1] See further K. L. Schmidt, 'Jerusalem als Urbild und Abbild', pp. 209 ff., and Schlier, Der Brief an die Epheser, pp. 140 f.

[2] Yadin's reading, 'A Midrash on II Sam. vii and Ps. i–ii', p. 96. Allegro, 'Fragments of a Qumran scroll', reads קדושי, 'my holy ones'. The context suggests that Yadin's is the correct interpretation.

[3] Cf. Gärtner, 'Bakgrunden till Qumranförsamlingens krig', pp. 64 ff.; Nötscher, 'Heiligkeit in den Qumranschriften', R.Q. II (1959–60), 323 ff.

[4] The text reads וסוד מבנית קודש. Translators disagree as to its meaning. I follow Wernberg-Møller's emendation (cf. 1QS. viii. 5).

plantation in every age to come...' (1QS xi. 7f.). The same idea of the community united with the company of the angels is to be found in other texts, e.g. 1QH iii. 21 ff.: 'And thou purifiest a perverted spirit from his manifold transgressions, that he may stand in array with the host of the holy ones and enter into fellowship with the sons of heaven. And thou hast granted unto man an eternal lot among the spirits of knowledge to praise thy name....'[1]

The link between the community and the world of the angels in heaven thus formed an intrinsic part of the temple symbolism of the Qumran texts. And it is against this background that the Apostle's words, 'fellow citizens with the saints[2] and members of the household of God', are to be seen; they express a view of the Church which has a great deal in common with Qumran teachings on fellowship with the angels and with God.[3] The account in Ephesians may of course have been influenced by other ideas derived from late Judaism but this particular combination, of the community as the temple of God and the relation of the new temple to 'strangers' and the 'household of God', suggests that the relationship between this text and the ideology of Qumran was particularly intimate.

In Eph. ii. 20-2 the Apostle goes on to develop the idea of the Christians, in fellowship with the inhabitants of the heavenly world, as a temple. He describes what is virtually a heavenly edifice, with its given foundation and its corner-stone, '...built upon the foundation of the apostles and prophets, Christ Jesus himself being the chief corner-stone, ἀκρογωνιαῖος...'.[4] I consider it impossible to draw an absolute distinction between

[1] Mansoor, *The Thanksgiving Hymns*, p. 117, points out that the expression 'to stand in array' is used in the *Hodayot* 'with reference to the Divine Presence'; this seems to fit the community's temple symbolism. The members of the community form a fellowship (earthly and heavenly) in which God is 'present'.

[2] Schlier, *Der Brief an die Epheser*, pp. 140f., takes 'the saints' to refer to the angels in the heavenly Jerusalem, with whom Christians on earth have fellowship in faith.

[3] Cf. below, p. 97.

[4] Jeremias, art. ἀκρογωνιαῖος, *T.W.B.* I, 792f., and those who have followed him (see bibl. in Schlier, *op. cit.* p. 142) interpret this by 'topstone', 'keystone'. But the older interpretation, 'corner-stone', seems to fit the Qumran texts better. See e.g. R. J. McKelvey, 'Christ the Cornerstone', *N.T.S.* VIII (1961–2), 352–9.

temple symbolism and the more general imagery of the 'building', and the 'spiritual' house in this passage.[1] The text here has a wide variety of disparate images—the people of God, the house, the temple, fellowship with the angels, etc.—and it is not easy to keep them separate. But it is of the greatest importance that the text goes on to identify the Christians expressly with the temple: '...in whom the whole structure[2] is joined together and grows into a holy temple in the Lord, εἰς ναὸν ἅγιον ἐν κυρίῳ; in whom[3] you also are built into it for a dwelling place, κατοικητήριον, of God in the Spirit'. Those who in Christ have been joined together to make one people are the true and holy temple, ναός; we are familiar with this idea from I and II Corinthians. They are also said to be the dwelling place, κατοικητήριον, of God. This expression is found in the LXX for the dwelling place of God on the holy mountain, in heaven, in the temple, in Jerusalem, and the like.[4] In ii. 22 it is thus parallel with the 'holy temple', emphasizing that it is here that God dwells. It has also been pointed out that the following phrase ἐν πνεύματι stresses that the presence of God, the Holy Spirit, has removed from the Jerusalem temple to the new temple, the Christian Church.[5] The expression ἐν πνεύματι may also be regarded as a parallel to ἐν κυρίῳ in the previous clause, the implication being that the new temple was brought into existence by the Spirit, and that the Spirit is the new reality to which the temple has removed.

We have said that the Qumran texts contain the combination, also found in the Old Testament and late Judaism, of 'temple' and 'plantation' as a description of the community. One image is of an object, the other of a living organism. The same combination occurs in I Cor. iii. 6–17, and influenced the account in such a way as to enable Paul to speak of a building, a plantation and a temple as though all were living organisms.[6] This need not imply that the 'plantation' image brought life to the other two; it is rather the case that all three were

[1] On the symbolism of the 'house', see Michel, art. οἶκος, *T.W.B.* v, 127f.
[2] On the discussion surrounding this translation, see S. Hanson, *The Unity of the Church in the New Testament* (1946), p. 132, and Schlier, *op. cit.* p. 143.   [3] See previous note.
[4] Schlier, *Der Brief an die Epheser*, p. 145.
[5] Hanson, *The Unity of the Church*, p. 134.   [6] See above, pp. 28f.

symbolically applied to a company of living persons, members of the community. Ephesians ii. 20–2 is a compound image, and the image of the object and the organism are fully complementary. Christians 'grow into a holy temple', a combination of the terminology of growth with a static object. Similarly with the imagery of Eph. iv. 12 and 16, in which the image of the growing and living organism is combined with that of the building. The same situation can arise outside the bounds of the *Corpus Paulinum*, for example in I Pet. ii. 4f., where Jesus is called the 'living stone' and the Christians 'living stones', all within the bounds of temple symbolism; these provide the materials for the construction of a spiritual temple.[1] The latter motif is also found in the Qumran texts. Here we appear to be dealing with an element of early Christian tradition which formed part of the complex of ideas surrounding the symbol of the temple.[2]

(4) *I Tim. iii. 15*

The Pastoral Epistles, which are the most recent and most discussed of the Pauline letters, also contain echoes of a temple symbolism which appears to be in line with what we have already seen of Paul's use of the image. We shall confine our attention here to one text only, a text reminiscent in certain of its forms of expression of Qumran ideology, I Tim. iii. 15: (I am writing these instructions to you so that...) 'you may know how one ought to conduct oneself in the house of God, which is the church, ἐκκλησία, of the living God, the pillar and foundation of the truth.'

Previously in the same chapter the Apostle has reviewed the conditions for the appointment of bishops and deacons. The passage concludes with a statement that there is a sacred order in the Church as a whole, just as there is in the local congregation. The phrase πῶς δεῖ ἐν οἴκῳ θεοῦ ἀναστρέφεσθαι, I consider, ought to be viewed against the Old Testament and Jewish concept, which is also of significance for the Qumran

---

[1] The verb συνοικοδομεῖν which is used in Eph. ii. 22 ('you are also built into it for a dwelling place of God in the Spirit') seems to provide a point of contact with the more elaborate image in I Pet. ii. 5, in which Christians are said to be 'stones' in the temple building.

[2] See below, pp. 75 ff.

texts.[1] The Qumran documents use the word הלך as a technical term referring to the spiritual dimension of the life of the community in conformity to the Law, as well as for the outward order which characterized the holy fellowship. The rule was to 'walk perfectly before him in accordance with all those things which have been revealed...', 1QS i. 8f.[2] The conditions laid down in I Tim. iii. 15 for life in the Church emphasize that there are rules controlling the conduct of the exclusive group of people who make up the 'house of God', οἶκος θεοῦ;[3] the reference seems to be to the new temple,[4] made up of the company of Christians. The explanation of the term 'house of God' begins: ἥτις ἐστὶν ἐκκλησία θεοῦ ζῶντος. We may note the resemblance between this and II Cor. vi. 16, ἡμεῖς γὰρ ναὸς θεοῦ ἐσμεν ζῶντος; there is little doubt that both originate in one and the same temple symbolism. It is also noteworthy that ἐκκλησία, as a term for the congregation and its members, is identified in I Tim. iii. 15 with the 'house of God', the temple.[5] Ἐκκλησία is thus connected with the 'house of God',[6] a combination of ideas found in a number of other New Testament texts, witnessing to the fact of their having belonged to a fixed early Christian conceptual scheme.[7] Thus Heb. iii. 1 ff. refers, in a *midrash*-like exposition of Num. xii. 7 (LXX) in which Moses is said to be a faithful servant in the

[1] See e.g. Nötscher, *Gotteswege und Menschenwege in der Bibel und in Qumran*, Bonner Bibl. Beitr. xv (1958), 79 ff.

[2] Cf. 1QS i. 25, iii. 9f., vi. 2, C.D. ii. 17, vii. 4f., 7f., xii. 21 ff., etc., Test. Asher vi. 3.

[3] The connexion between ἀναστρέφω and הלך is to be noted in the LXX, the meaning being to walk in accordance with the Law and the covenant, I Kings vi. 12, Prov. xx. 7. ἀναστρέφω in II Cor. i. 12 has the same meaning. Cf. ἀναστροφή in Gal. i. 13, I Pet. i. 18, etc.

[4] In the LXX the expression is used consistently to refer to the temple, see Michel, art. οἶκος, *T.W.B.* v, 123.

[5] Dahl, *Das Volk Gottes*, pp. 62 ff., shows how both ἐκκλησία and the related קהל are connected with the temple. They can refer to the people of God gathered in the temple. At the same time we see from the Qumran texts that the Heb. עדה, סוד and יחד belong in this context as well. Cf. Betz, 'Felsenmann und Felsengemeinde', pp. 57 f., and Maier, 'Zum Begriff יחד', pp. 148 ff.

[6] I Tim. iii. 5 also connects οἶκος and ἐκκλησία; although the meaning is different, the link between the two is plain. Cf. Schnackenburg, *Die Kirche im Neuen Testament* (1961), p. 87.

[7] Michel, art. οἶκος, *T.W.B.* v, 128 ff.

house of God (the people of Israel), to the fact that Christ the Son has been appointed to rule 'the house of God', that is, the congregation. The symbolic language here seems to presuppose a temple symbolism similar to that used by Paul. Further, this text identifies the members of the church with this 'house of God': 'Christ was faithful over his house as a son. And we are his (God's) house...' (iii. 6). Again, this idea of the church-temple is closely linked with important Christological statements.[1] The concept is illustrated in I Pet. ii. 3 ff.; there the 'spiritual house', οἶκος πνευματικός, is the 'pneumatic' building which has replaced the Jerusalem temple. It corresponds to the Christian Church and her local congregations, but at the same time Christology is of considerable importance for its symbolism.[2] In I Tim. iii. 15 we find the same principle as in the other texts we have been considering, that the church is the temple of God.

The connexion between I Tim. iii. 15 and Qumran is rendered even more probable by the expression used to illustrate the concept of the community, 'the pillar and foundation of the truth, στῦλος καὶ ἑδραίωμα τῆς ἀληθείας'. The expression is found nowhere else in the New Testament.[3] The best comparative material is that which we find in the Qumran texts, where the community is occasionally spoken of as a pillar and foundation. For example, 1QS v. 5 f.: '...to lay a foundation of truth for Israel, for the community of the eternal covenant, to make atonement for all those who of their own free will have dedicated themselves (to be) a sanctuary in Aaron and a house of truth in Israel...'. The founding of the community implies the building up of the true temple; it means, too, that there has been laid a 'foundation of truth', מוסד אמת, and that there has been built a 'house of truth', בית האמת.[4]

In 1QS viii. 7 ff., which is one of the most important of the 'temple symbolism' texts, we find the temple, the foundation and truth mentioned together. Here the members of the community are called 'witnesses to the truth'. They are 'the tested

<hr/>

[1] Cf. Michel, *Der Brief an die Hebräer*, pp. 97 f.; Spicq, *L'épître aux Hébreux*, II, 65 ff.   [2] See below, pp. 73 ff.

[3] Ἑδραίωμα is *hapax legomenon* in the N.T., is absent from the LXX and uncommon in secular Greek. Στῦλος is rare in the N.T., occurring only in Gal. ii. 9, Rev. iii. 12, x. 1.   [4] Cf. Schnackenburg, *Die Kirche*, p. 89.

wall, the precious corner-stone. Its foundations, יסוד, shall not be shaken and shall not be removed from their place, a most holy dwelling place for Aaron with eternal knowledge of the covenant of justice...a house of justice and truth in Israel'. Similarly with 1QS ix. 3 ff., where the founding of the community is said to be a laying of 'the foundation of the holy spirit, יסוד רוח קודש', which is 'eternal truth'. It is evident from these texts that the Qumran temple symbolism included the concepts of the 'foundation', the 'house' and 'truth' (cf. 1QH. vi. 25 ff.). The community is the temple; its foundations, which can never be disturbed, are truth—an expression denoting the revelations of God in the exposition of the Law which the community has received through its Teacher, and of which it is steward. The members of the community are those who live in truth, making up the יחד of the truth.[1]

It is important in this connexion to note that the concept of 'truth', אמת, is linked with סוד, which may be taken to mean 'the secret', i.e. the innermost core of the revelation, or the group entrusted with the truth. There is no doubt that many of the Qumran texts use the words סוד, יסד, יסוד and מסוד in a double sense; thus the reader's attention is drawn simultaneously to the foundation, the members of the community, and to the special revelation given to the community.[2] With this in mind, we might interpret the phrase 'the pillar and foundation of the truth' in I Tim. iii. 15 as an element in a temple symbolism, another of whose important terms was 'truth'. 'The ἐκκλησία of the living God' is a foundation just because it has been entrusted with the truth; in the Pastoral Epistles generally the term 'truth' stands for the revelation of Christ.[3] Hence we are led to conclude that the rare word ἑδραίωμα is to be traced back to such Hebrew concepts as סוד, מסוד, etc.[4] A further conclusion is that the symbolism of

[1] See Betz, *Offenbarung und Schriftforschung in der Qumransekte* (1960), pp. 53 ff.
[2] Cf. Mowinckel, 'Some Remarks on *Hodayot* 39. 5–20', *J.B.L.* LXXV (1956), 272 f.; Betz, 'Felsenmann und Felsengemeinde', pp. 59 f.; Mansoor, *The Thanksgiving Hymns*, pp. 102, 117, 137.
[3] I Tim. ii. 4, iv. 3, vi. 5, II Tim. ii. 15, 18, 25, etc.
[4] There does not seem to be a great difference between I Tim. iii. 15, in which the church is said to be the foundation, and I Cor. iii. 11, in which it is Christ who is the foundation, θεμέλιος. It is not remarkable, remembering the imprecision of the use of the term 'foundation' in I Cor. iii. 10–12

the house and the temple is linked with an interpretation of the person of Christ—the teacher of the revelation and the truth. It is therefore only natural that *v.* 16 should contain a hymn to Christ. The Church, the truth and Christ are indivisible.[1]

The phrase 'Great is the mystery of godliness, τὸ τῆς εὐσεβείας μυστήριον' in *v.* 16 provides us with a further point of contact with Qumran. The word εὐσέβεια, which is rare in the New Testament (occurring most often in the Pastorals), here stands for the Christian worship of God.[2] Referring back to *v.* 15, '...how one ought to conduct oneself in the house of God...', and its relation to the הלך sayings of the Qumran texts, we can interpret εὐσέβεια as an expression for the spiritual life and fellowship (including the cultus) which characterized the 'new' temple in Christ.[3] The basis and content of this εὐσέβεια is the person of Christ, who transmits a knowledge of atonement and heavenly reality: 'He was manifested in the flesh, justified in the Spirit, seen of angels....'[4]

The new temple not only has foundations; it has pillars. The image of the pillar, στῦλος, is also found in the temple symbolism of Qumran, although it is not prominent.[5]

The symbolism of I Tim. iii. 15 seems likewise to form the

and Eph. ii. 20, that I Tim. iii. 15 should read as it does, particularly since this text connects the ideas of the 'foundation' and the 'truth', the 'truth' referring to Christ and his teaching.

[1] On the connexion between verses 15 and 16, see Spicq, *Les Épîtres pastorales*, pp. 106 ff.

[2] See further Foerster, art. σέβομαι, *T.W.B.* VII, 180 ff., and Spicq, *op. cit.* pp. 125 ff.

[3] The separation of εὐσέβεια from the cultus and worship seems to be too categorical in Foerster, *op. cit.* p. 182. I consider it likely that the cultic element of this term was present in connexion with the temple symbolism of *v.* 15.

[4] When we read in *v.* 16 that in this εὐσέβεια there lies τὸ μυστήριον it suggests that the reality of Christ is a mystery, which is then described in the following hymn. Cf. Spicq, *op. cit.* pp. 107 f. and 116 ff. One might also compare the implications of the term סוד, which are easily connected with the 'secrets' and most profound revelations of the Qumran texts.

[5] Cf. Betz, 'Felsenmann und Felsengemeinde', pp. 63 ff. On this symbolism, see also Rev. iii. 12, which speaks of the faithful as 'pillars', στῦλοι, 'in the temple of my God': an expression which may be associated with the idea of the heavenly Jerusalem. The word 'pillar' is also used in Rabbinic literature to refer to 'the learned' and the 'pious', see Vielhauer, *Oikodome*, p. 20.

background of II Tim. ii. 19f.: 'But God's firm foundation stands, bearing this seal: "The Lord knows those who are his", and, "Let every one who names the name of the Lord depart from iniquity". In a great house there are not only vessels of gold and silver. . . .' In an earlier passage in the same letter certain false teachers were accused of having taught untruth. Over against these is now placed the congregation, founded on a basis of that given by God, the truth (cf. *v*. 15). 'God's firm foundation'[1] seems to me to refer to the truth revealed in Christ, guarded by the community of those who live by it. The faithful are said to bear the seal 'The Lord knows those who are his'. Once more we see how close the connexion is between the community and the 'truth'. And a little later we find an exhortation to exclude all unrighteousness from the congregation. That the background is provided by the symbolism of the temple and the house is suggested by the fact that the community is spoken of as being 'a great house', in which there are all kinds of vessels (II Tim. ii. 20f.).[2]

As far as we can judge from the concepts presented in I Tim. iii. 15–16 and II Tim. ii. 19f., we are here dealing with part of a temple symbolism found in the early Church, a symbolism which closely resembled certain areas of the ideology of Qumran. When we make comparisons with other Pauline texts we find how many-sided this symbolism was; but at the same time we find how many new and varied details appear— evidence that our information in the New Testament covers only a part of the thought of the early Church.

B. TEMPLE SYMBOLISM IN I PET. II AND HEB. XII

The temple symbolism we have encountered in the Pauline traditions, and which we have seen had a great deal in common with certain Qumran ideas, recurs in other New Testament traditions; it is thus represented in such disparate documents as the First Epistle of Peter and the Epistle to the Hebrews. A

---

[1] The expression ὁ στερεὸς θεμέλιος τοῦ θεοῦ may be connected with Isa. xxviii. 16, 'Behold, I am laying in Zion for a foundation a stone, a tested stone, a precious corner-stone, of a sure foundation...'. On the importance of this text for the temple symbolism of Qumran and the N.T. see below, pp. 76f. and 134f. [2] Cf. Schnackenburg, *Die Kirche*, p. 89.

close examination in fact shows that the temple symbolism of the New Testament is not confined to Paul, but appears to go back to an early Christian doctrinal tradition, traces of which are to be found in the various theological traditions of the young Church. It is out of the question in this context to examine in detail all the texts relating to this symbolism. Instead we shall look at a number of representative texts in which the relation between Qumran and the New Testament is illustrated. The most suitable of these are I Pet. ii and Hebrews xii, for two reasons: first, because they show how the early Christian tradition of the 'new' temple lived on in widely differing traditions outside the bounds of the *Corpus Paulinum*; and secondly, because they show how the Qumran–New Testament relationship is demonstrated by new details in the framework of temple symbolism.

(1) *I Pet. ii. 3–6*

I Pet. ii contains the most explicit statement of temple symbolism. It is not merely a matter of an exposition of the 'temple' as referring to the Christians; the text also 'spiritualizes' the concepts of the priests and of the sacrifices, and refers them to the Christians and their life.[1] The most important passage reads: 'Come to him, to that living stone, rejected by men but in God's sight chosen and precious; and like living stones be yourselves built up into a spiritual house, to be a holy priesthood, to offer spiritual sacrifices acceptable to God through Jesus Christ. For it stands in scripture: "Behold, I am laying in Zion a stone, a corner-stone chosen and precious, and he who believes in him will not be put to shame..."' (I Pet. ii. 3–6). The main characteristics which this text shares with the Qumran texts have already been described by scholars; they have said that 1QS viii. 4–10, with its numerous parallels, provides the best comparative text.[2] But there are a number of other points which deserve mention.

[1] A 'spiritualization' of these concepts is also to be found in e.g. Philo, but the object of his symbolism and allegory is unlike that of either Qumran or the N.T. Cf. Wenschkewitz, *Die Spiritualisierung*, pp. 67 ff.; Gärtner, *The Areopagus Speech*, pp. 205 f.

[2] See e.g. Flusser, 'The Dead Sea Sect and Pre-Pauline Christianity', in *Scripta Hierosolymitana*, IV, 233–6. He brings together *inter alia* 'the spiritual

(a) In I Pet. ii. 5 we read, in terms reminiscent of Eph. ii. 20–2, that the Christians are to be 'built up into a spiritual house'. This οἶκος πνευματικός, in a context in which are also mentioned priests, sacrifices and the 'corner-stone', can hardly refer to anything but the temple. It is 'spiritual', the implication being that it belongs to the new sphere created by the pouring out of the Spirit. But at the same time behind the word there seems to lie the meaning of 'true', the 'true' temple of God.[1] When we read that the believers are to be 'built up' into a temple, οἰκοδομεῖσθε οἶκος πνευματικός,[2] it may appear the obvious verb to use in connexion with the image of the temple. But it is nevertheless interesting to note

house' and 'a holy house for Israel', and 'a holy priesthood' and 'the most holy dwelling place for Aaron'. By this means he intends to show that I Pet. ii has a modified form of the symbolism of 1QS viii, in which the two rooms of the temple have become one house and one priesthood. This I consider unlikely. Flusser, also, goes too far when he sees in the 'corner-stone' passage of I Pet. ii (from Isa. xxviii. 16) so close a resemblance to 1QS viii that he is able to write of 'some literary dependence of the Greek Epistle on a Hebrew prototype which resembled the passage quoted from D.S.D. viii. 4–11'.

[1] The 'house' is said to be πνευματικός. Selwyn, *The First Epistle of St Peter* (1952), pp. 160 and 284f., considers that the word, which is not found in the LXX and which is Christian in character, describes the new state in which Christians live through the Spirit. In I Pet. ii. 5 the word tends to mean 'true' *contra* the false temple. Cf. נאמן in C.D. iii. 19, 'And he built for them in Israel a firmly established, נאמן, house', in which the emphasis is laid partly on that which is eternal and indestructible, and partly on the 'true house' *contra* the defiled temple and the apostate people in Jerusalem. Cf. C.D. xiv. 2, 1QS iv. 3, 1QpHab ii. 4, 6, 14. Rom. xii. 1 has the word λογικός ('spiritual worship') in a context similar to that of I Pet. ii. 5. It is also used in I Pet. ii. 2, λογικὸν ἄδολον γάλα, 'pure spiritual milk', where λογικός is a synonym for πνευματικός (cf. the connexion with temple symbolism in *vv.* 4f.). See Flusser, 'The Dead Sea Sect', p. 232. The fact that the 'house' in I Pet. ii. 5 is said to be 'spiritual' does not mean that it is less real than the Jerusalem temple; it stresses the new level on which the temple and its cultus have been placed through the person and work of Jesus. The Holy Spirit is the new sphere of reality to which the Church and the company of Christians belong. See also C. F. D. Moule, 'Sanctuary and Sacrifice in the Church of the New Testament', *J.T.S.* 1 (1950), 34ff.

[2] This reading seems preferable to ἐποικοδομεῖσθε, since the latter verb suggests building 'on' a foundation, as in e.g. Eph. ii. 20, where the expression reads ἐποικοδομηθέντες ἐπὶ τῷ θεμελίῳ τῶν ἀποστόλων..., cf. I Cor. iii. 12. The foundation is not mentioned in I Pet. ii. 5.

that it has a direct equivalent in the Qumran texts, which also speak of 'building up' a temple of an entirely new character. We have previously referred to one of the most important of the 'temple' texts, 4QFlor., but it is worth recalling it again here. The passage in question reads: 'And he purposed to build him a temple of (among) men, לבנות לוא מקדש אדם' (i. 6). The verb בנה, 'build', is here used to refer to the founding of the community—the temple. (The corresponding LXX term for בנה is οἰκοδομεῖν.) This verb is found on only a few occasions in the Qumran texts, and it is thus impossible to make any categorical statements as to the manner of its use. But there is a text which witnesses to its having been used as a 'foundation' term: 4QpPs xxxvii. II. 16, which reads '(God) established him (the Teacher of Righteousness) to build him the community (of elect?) [בחירו?] הכיני לבנות לו עדת ...'. Here the verb בנה is used without the object being a house, a temple or a town; instead the object is עדה, a 'community'. The Teacher of Righteousness 'built', that is founded, the community.[1] Another text says that it was God himself who 'built' the community like a house: 'And he built for them in Israel a firmly established house, ויבן להם בית נאמן' (C.D. iii. 19); this house is permanent, and those who stand by it will inherit eternal life.[2] A more common term in this connexion is כין, which can also mean 'found', 'establish'. It is in fact found in some of the most important 'temple' texts, where it describes the founding of the community (1QS viii. 5. 10, 1QH vii. 18). It seems likely that the word is to be seen against the background of the temple symbolism of Qumran, particularly since the verb is used in other New Testament texts in connexion with the setting up of the community as the new temple.[3] Associated with the image of the 'spiritual house' which is 'built up' is the common New Testament idea that the Apostles and Christians are to promote the growth of the

[1] This expression probably has to do with the O.T. concept of how God 'builds up' the house of Israel, the people. See Michel, art. οἰκοδομέω, *T.W.B.* v, 139.

[2] בנה is also found in 1QpHab x. 10, where it refers to the opponents of the community, who wish to establish an apostate town. The verb is otherwise uncommon in the texts.

[3] Cf. Michel, *op. cit.* pp. 141 ff.

Church in the Spirit; this does not however appear to be the kernel of the thought of I Pet. ii. 5.[1]

Another aspect of the image of the temple, the 'spiritual house', in I Pet. ii is the phrase 'living stones'. The 'house' is made up of individual members of the Church, and these are 'living stones'. This unusual expression has no direct equivalent in the New Testament,[2] and seems to be a special development of the concept of the 'living stone', here referring to Christ, the fulfiller of the prophecies of the 'stone that the builders rejected', the 'corner-stone' and the 'rock of stumbling' in the Old Testament. It is difficult to decide whether the term 'living' should be referred back to the Jewish conceptual background, as in the case of the expressions 'living water' and 'living bread' (John iv. 10, vi. 51).[3] So much is however clear: that the essential background is to be found in temple symbolism and the interpretation of the person of Christ: through Christ, a living person, Christians can be built up to form that 'living', 'spiritual' temple in which Christ is Lord.[4]

We have already seen that the temple imagery of the New Testament connects at a number of points with that of the Qumran texts; we can now go on to ask whether this is also true of the use of the word 'stones' to describe the members of the congregation. It is true that this detail does not occupy a prominent position in the Qumran texts,[5] but it is used, and may well bear some relation to a Messianic interpretation of the 'stone' sayings of the Old Testament used in I Pet. ii. Two of the relevant texts are unfortunately obscure, but they tell us enough to enable us to form some idea of the background of this detail in I Peter.

[1] See Michel, *op. cit.* pp. 142 ff.

[2] Eph. ii. 20 stands closest, but there the image is not developed to apply to the 'stones'. Christians grow up into a temple, but they are not called 'stones'.

[3] See Gärtner, *Die rätselhaften Termini Nazoräer und Iskariot*, p. 30; Daniélou, 'Le symbolisme de l'eau vive', *Rev. S.R.* XXXII (1958), 335 ff.

[4] Rom. xii. 1, which also contains traces of this temple symbolism, uses 'living' in the sense of 'belonging to the sphere of the Spirit', describing the 'spiritual' quality of the 'spiritualized' sacrifices. Cf. above, p. 73.

[5] I have been unable to find any direct parallel in late Jewish literature. There is the Jewish concept that God is able to bring forth children from 'stones' (cf. Matt. iii. 9), but the background in this case is different. See Jeremias, art. λίθος, *T.W.B.* IV, 274 f.

1QH vi gives an account of the community and its situation in which there are a number of images; thus in lines 25 ff. we find a brief statement to the effect that the community is a sign of the faithfulness of God, like a 'house' the foundations of which were laid by God and the walls built up: 'I was like one who comes to a fortified town and takes his refuge in a high wall, חומה נשגבה, for salvation. And I [rejoice in] thy truth, O my God, for thou dost lay a foundation upon the rock, סוד על סלע,[1] and the beams according to the measuring-line of the Law and the plumb-line [of truth?] in order to [get] tested stones, אבני בחן,[2] [for a] strong [building][3] which is not shaken, and all who enter shall not be moved. For no stranger, גר, shall enter there. . . .'

The restoration of this text is uncertain at some points, but this does not prevent our being given a good insight into the imagery of the community as a 'building'. It is not however clear what was the character of this 'building'. One possibility is a general 'house' symbolism; another might be based on the temple building.[4] The images are to some extent interchangeable. True, nothing is said which points directly to the temple, but the nature of the images used in 1QH vi. 25 ff. compared with the above-mentioned texts is such that the connexion with temple symbolism can hardly be denied. The imagery seems to a great extent to have been drawn from Isa. xxviii. 16 f., where faithfulness to God is represented as a protection against punishment and violence: 'Behold, I am laying in Zion for a foundation a stone, a tested stone, a precious corner-stone, of a sure foundation: "He who trusts in it will not be in haste." And I will make justice the line, and righteousness the

[1] Betz, 'Felsenmann und Felsengemeinde', p. 56, translates 'Denn du wirst einen Kreis (von Männern) auf einen Felsen setzen', which seems to me to place too much emphasis on the associations based on the 'foundation' and directed toward the 'council' or the 'community'. Cf. Holm-Nielsen, *Hodayot*, pp. 118 f. and his unduly harsh criticism of Betz.

[2] Mansoor, *The Thanksgiving Hymns*, p. 146, translates 'and a weighing s[tone] to [beco]me tried stones . . .'.

[3] Betz, 'Felsenmann und Felsengemeinde', p. 56, reads לב[נית] עוד. On the discussion see Holm-Nielsen, *Hodayot*, p. 119. For comparison with I Pet. ii. 5 the complement [לפנות] 'as corner-stones' is a far too good reading, Nielsen–Otzen, *Dødehavsteksterne*, p. 132.

[4] Cf. above, pp. 24 f., on the immovable walls of the future Jerusalem.

plummet....' It is this theme, permanence and certainty, which is at the heart of 1QH vi. 25 ff. It is important for the purposes of comparison with I Pet. ii to note how the word 'stone', the 'tested stone' of Isa. xxviii. 16 which late Judaism and New Testament regarded as referring to the Messiah,[1] has been transferred to the plural, 'tested stones', and made to refer to the members of the community. The 'foundation' laid by God on the rock here represents the 'truths' (revelations) on which the new covenant is based, and which are altogether decisive for the community or the 'council'.[2] The 'tested stones' are the members of the community. They are built up into a building or 'wall' which cannot be shaken. It is clear that this imagery is closely connected with the symbol of the temple if we compare 1QH vi. 25 ff. with 1QS viii. 4 ff., which speaks of the community as 'the tested wall', חומת הבחן, 'the precious corner-stone', פנת יקר,[3] and states that 'its foundations, יסוד, shall not be shaken and shall not be removed from their place, a most holy dwelling place for Aaron...'.[4] This text, too, refers back to Isa. xxviii. 16f., and describes the community as a holy building which will stand for ever. This vision of

[1] See below, pp. 133 ff.

[2] See above, pp. 68f. The context of 1QH vi. 25ff., together with the close parallel in 1QH vii. 7, shows that it is faithfulness to the revealed interpretation of the Law that creates the firm basis for the community.

[3] 1QH vi. 15ff. has the image of the 'plantation' with its usual associations, immediately before that of the 'building'; this seems to be connected with the temple symbolism of the passage (cf. above, pp. 28f.). Further, it is said in 1QH vi. 25ff. that no stranger may enter the holy building, an idea reminiscent of 4QFlor. See above, pp. 32f.

[4] The latter expression for the immovability and permanence of the 'building' may be connected with the idea of the temple rock *qua* foundation (see above, p. 27). Be that as it may, it is an important aspect of the Qumran attitude to the 'new' temple. Flusser, 'The Dead Sea Sect', p. 235, considers that when I Pet. ii. 6 quotes Isa. xxviii. 16 from the LXX ('he who trusts in him will not be put to shame, οὐ μὴ καταισχυνθῇ...') it misses the point of 1QS viii, which speaks of immovability in agreement with the Masoretic לא יחיש. But the fact that the motif of 'immovability' is lacking in N.T. temple symbolism applies to other texts as well, in which mention is made of the 'foundation' without placing any emphasis on the idea of firmness and immovability, as in Qumran. Incidentally, I Pet. ii. 6 makes better use of the LXX text, since the focus of the passage is the following words, the 'stone which will make men stumble, a rock that will make them fall', an idea found neither in 1QS viii nor 1QH vi.

permanence seems to have influenced the exchange of the 'tested stone', אבן בחן (Isa. xxviii. 16), for 'the tested wall', חומת הבחן.[1] Thus 1QS viii uses the singular form, 'wall', 'corner-stone', to describe the community, while 1QH vi uses the plural, 'stones'—further evidence of oscillation between the idea of the community and its members, between singular and plural, individual and collective. There is also an example in I Pet. ii of the term 'stone' from Isa. xxviii. 16 being interpreted first with a view to the individual, the Messiah, and being then transferred to the collective, 'living stones', referring to the members of the community.[2] The resemblance between Qumran and I Pet. ii is so striking at this point that we are compelled to assume the existence of some common tradition.

Another text illustrating the way in which the members of the Qumran community were described as 'stones' is 4QpIsa[d]. This text is, however, badly damaged and reconstruction can be little more than a hypothesis. We have earlier had occasion to mention this text, since its imagery combines the symbols of the 'house' and the temple.[3] What is particularly interesting here is that the text symbolizes the two groups, 'priests' and 'people', as 'sapphires' and 'stones'. The Isaiah text on which this *pesher* is a commentary is liv. 11 f., like xxviii. 16 f. a description of how God will protect Zion from its enemies by building a permanent structure, a new Jerusalem: 'O afflicted one, storm-tossed, and not comforted, behold, I will set your stones in antimony, and lay your foundations with sapphires. I will make your pinnacles of agate, your gates of carbuncles, and all your wall of precious stones.' That fragment of the Isaiah *pesher* so far published contains an exposition of 'I will set your stones in antimony, and lay your foundations with sapphires', which probably claims that it is the priests who form the 'foundations' of the community. The 'community of the elect' are the 'stones'; among these 'stones' the priests are 'sapphires'.[4] The distinction drawn between the two groups agrees with the general pattern of 'house' and temple symbolism in Qumran, and it is here that we must seek for the context in which 'stones' is made to apply to the members of the

---

[1] See above, p. 27. [2] Cf. below, pp. 134 ff. [3] See above, pp. 42 f.

[4] Following Yadin's attempted reconstruction, 'Some Notes on the Newly Published *Pesharim* of Isaiah', *I.E.J.* 9 (1959), 40 ff.

community.[1] This text provides further evidence that there were traditions current in Qumran according to which, starting from various Old Testament texts, it was usual to speak of the faithful as 'stones' in the holy edifice of the future. It seems likely that these traditions form at least part of the background of I Pet. ii, in which the Christians are called 'living stones'.

(b) Another element of the temple symbolism of I Pet. ii is the concept of the Christians as a 'holy priesthood', ἱεράτευμα ἅγιον (v. 5), and βασίλειον ἱεράτευμα (v. 9).[2] This statement is not otherwise found in the New Testament in connexion with the symbolism of the temple.[3] The expression is taken from Exod. xix. 6, where it is promised that the whole of Israel will become a royal and priestly people, provided that they keep the covenant, ὑμεῖς δὲ ἔσεσθέ μοι βασίλειον ἱεράτευμα καὶ ἔθνος ἅγιον. The people of Israel are thus privileged above all others. It is not possible to consider in this context all the manifold problems connected with this expression in the Old Testament, late Judaism and the New Testament. We must however take up the question of the temple symbolism under discussion, since it is this which determines its use in I Pet. ii. 5.[4]

Jewish exegetical tradition has followed a number of different lines when interpreting Exod. xix. 6 and its reference to Israel as a 'priesthood'. Alexandrian Judaism spiritualized the concept, and made of it a 'spiritual priesthood'; Jewish apocalyptic saw visions of the heavenly cultus; the Rabbis returned again and again to the thought of the kingdom which Israel had been promised.[5] But the tradition which stands

---

[1] The *pesher* text is also of interest, since it appears to speak of twelve 'priests', representing the twelve tribes of Israel.

[2] The term ἱεράτευμα, which belongs to the language of the LXX, appears to be used in a collective aspect. See Schrenk, art. ἱεράτευμα, *T.W.B.* III, 249f. Βασίλειον is probably used here as a noun; see Selwyn, *The First Epistle of St Peter*, pp. 165f.

[3] Rev. i. 6 and v. 10 speak of Christians as 'priests', ἱερεῖς, though the expression has been taken from Exod. xix. 6, apparently without reference to the temple and its sacrifices; there may of course have existed such a connexion in the traditional background.

[4] On this problem see Cerfaux's excellent account in 'Regale sacerdotium', *R.S.P.T.* XXVIII (1939), 5–39 (reprinted in *Ephem. Theol. Lov.*, *Bibliotheca* VI (1954), 283ff.).   [5] Cerfaux, *op. cit.*

closest to I Pet. ii is found in II Macc. ii. 17–18, a text which otherwise has a great deal in common with Qumran theology.[1] It forms part of the Jerusalem Jews' second letter to the Jews in Egypt, and concerns the festival of the consecration of the temple: 'But God, who has saved all his people and restored to each his heritage, together with the kingship, the priesthood and holiness, as he promised in the Law: upon him we place our trust, hoping that he will soon have mercy upon us and gather us from all the countries under heaven to the holy place.'

This text expresses the hope that the victory won by the Jews will usher in the Messianic era, in which the people will once more possess the promised land, κληρονομία, exercise kingship, βασίλειον, over it, and worship in a temple cleansed from all Gentile influence, ἁγιασμόν, with its own priesthood, ἱερά-τευμα, serving God there.[2] The exposition of Exod. xix. 6 was not confined to the idea of the priesthood, but also covered the idea of the temple and its restored holiness.[3] This tradition, with its exposition of Exod. xix. 6, has been used in I Pet. ii. 5, though more in a symbolical sense, emphasis being laid on the fact that all Christians are members of the priesthood, ἱερά-τευμα, and must offer spiritual sacrifices. In II Maccabees it was expected that the promises would be fulfilled in Jerusalem, in the temple; in I Peter this complex of ideas is given a 'spiritual-ized' interpretation, in which the temple and its priests re-present spiritual realities. The expectation we meet in the text of II Maccabees is to some extent reminiscent of Qumran, though there its constituent parts have a different function.[4]

[1] Of the Books of Maccabees, II Macc. stands closest to Qumran and Daniel, see Gärtner, 'Bakgrunden till Qumranförsamlingens krig', pp. 39f.

[2] Cerfaux, 'Regale sacerdotium', pp. 295f.

[3] Cf. Jub. xvi. 18 and xxx. 20, in which the future Israel is called (the reference is to Exod. xix. 6) a 'holy people', a 'people of inheritance', a 'priestly people' and a 'royal people'. Here too there are links with the temple and the coming restoration of its purity, as well as to the heavenly cultus of the future. Cf. Cerfaux, *op. cit.* pp. 297f.

[4] There is a resemblance here to the visions of the future described in 1QSb iii. 25ff., iv. 25ff. and elsewhere, in which the dominion and kingship which Israel (the community) will inherit are mentioned in terms reminiscent of Exod. xix. 6 and Isa. lx–lxii. All nations shall know the might of Israel. The true temple and the eternal priesthood shall be the eternal servants of

In Qumran it was believed that the community had replaced Jerusalem, its temple, its sacrifices and its priests; we are thus justified in saying that so far Qumran and I Pet. ii represent a different tradition from II Maccabees. But at the same time we must remember that the chief interest of the Qumran community was its own cultic life. The purified and restored temple was the community; the 'priesthood', the true priests, who the prophets had said would be part of the true temple worship of the future (Ezek. xliv). It is not certain whether there was any thought here of a 'priesthood' in which every member of the congregation had his place, or whether it was a limited group within the community. Sometimes one notices a tendency to apply certain demands, properly made only of the priests, to the whole company; sometimes the priests are the leaders of the community, with their traditional tasks to perform.[1] This is one of the difficulties when we try to find material with which to compare I Pet. ii on the subject of the 'holy priesthood'. The material which the Qumran texts have to offer is at this point weak.[2]

The most important of the texts which might conceivably provide us with background material is C.D. iii. 19–iv. 3, in which the founding of the community is said to have been the work of God: 'And he built for them in Israel a firmly established house the like of which has not existed from ancient times until this day. They that hold fast unto it are (destined) for life eternal, and theirs is the glory of man (the glory of Adam), even as God has sworn unto them by the hand of the prophet Ezekiel, saying: "The priests and the Levites and the sons of Zadok that kept the charge of my sanctuary when the children of Israel went astray from me, these are they that shall offer

---

God. The concept is more transcendentally expressed here than in II Macc. There is the further difficulty of reconciling the realistic Qumran view of the future victory with the heavenly visions described in the texts. Earthly and heavenly are interwoven: this applies both to the present temple worship in the community and the visions of the heavenly temple of the future. Cf. above, pp. 21f.

[1] See above, pp. 5f.

[2] We might compare Jeremias' thesis that the Pharisaic movement wished to actualize a community of 'holy priests', in 'Der Gedanke des "Heiligen Restes" im Spätjudentum und in der Verkündigung Jesu', *Z.N.T.W.* XLII (1949), 186.

unto me fat and blood".[1] By "priests" is meant the penitents of Israel, שבי ישראל, who departed from the land of Judah. [By "Levites"] is meant those that associated themselves with them. By "sons of Zadok" is meant the elect of Israel, the men called by name, who shall arise in the last days....'

The founding of the community meant that God built a 'house' that would last, בית נאמן, an expression reminiscent of the Davidic prophecy in II Sam. vii. 16.[2] 'House' is thus a metaphor for the community, and is linked, *via* the following reference to Ezek. xliv. 15, to the concept of the temple. Ezekiel's text has the expression 'the Levitical priests, the sons of Zadok', הכהנים הלוים בני צדוק; this is here made into three separate groups by the insertion of two ו: הכהנים והלוים ובני צדוק. The 'priests' are interpreted as being the first group to leave the official Israel and found the community; the 'Levites' as the name of those who joined them; and the 'sons of Zadok' as the spiritual group, the true people of God. The latter title becomes the name of the community, the establishment of which was one sign that the end was approaching. Although the first group refers to the community's priestly origin, a more general term, 'the penitents of Israel', is also used (the 'priests' of the Ezekiel text). It is an expression which recalls the idea current in Qumran that anyone who would join the community must 'repent'.[3] 'Those that associated themselves with them' may mean a larger company that joined the original nucleus, 1QS v. 6, הנלוים עליהם ליחד. 'The sons of Zadok' appears to mean the whole community.[4] Thus we may deduce from the imagery of C.D. iv. 2 f. that the terms 'priests', 'Levites' and 'sons of Zadok' were used in varying ways to denote the community and its members.

But the value of C.D. iii. 19–iv. 3 as comparative material is by no means self-evident, although we have seen that there is a combination in this text of 'house', 'priests' and 'Levites'. The 'firmly established house' refers of course to the community as the new form of fellowship with God. But the link with

[1] Rabin, *The Zadokite Documents*, p. 13, suggests that it may be possible to develop on the lines of Ezek. xliv. 15, 'they shall approach Me to minister unto Me, they shall stand before Me to offer Me fat and blood'.
[2] See above, p. 73.
[3] Cf. Gärtner, 'Bakgrunden till Qumranförsamlingens krig', pp. 58f.
[4] See above, pp. 4f.

Ezek. xliv, and its prophecies of the temple and the true priesthood, shows that there was a conscious sense that in the community had been established both the temple and the priesthood of the future; consequently the mention of 'priests' in the 'new' temple may be a reference to the descendants of priestly families in the community. Although the exposition of the terms 'priests', 'Levites' and 'the sons of Zadok' in Ezek. xliv seems to be in terms of the entire congregation, it is not impossible that behind the division into three may lie that division found in, for example, 1QS, into priests, Levites and 'the people'.[1] The account in C.D. is also unusual.[2] This is the only text so far published in which we may claim to have a background to I Pet. ii and its application of the term 'priests' to each and every member of the Church.[3] We might have expected the symbolism of the temple and its sacrifices to have been completed with a similar interpretation of the 'priests'; but instead we find a reticence—though an understandable reticence—on this point. At that time the word 'priest' was linked with a definite group in the community, whose task it was to carry out the functions of their class, and who considered that they had a right, legally and spiritually, to these functions since they were members of the priestly family and observed all the precepts of the Law. The meaning of the term was thus fixed, apparently once and for all, and could be transferred to a wider group only with the greatest difficulty. But this did not prevent the 'democratization' of certain aspects of the priestly ideal and its requirements, so that they became applicable on a broader basis; this was what took place in Pharisaism.[4] The situation was different in the primitive Church, since the temple priests had ceased to serve any practical purpose. There it was easier to make the concept of the 'priest' apply to the common man. I have the impression that C.D. iii. 19 ff.

[1] See above, p. 5.

[2] On the term 'sons of Zadok' as a priestly term, see above, pp. 4f.

[3] It is difficult to know whether 1QSb iii. 1 and 26 are referring to special priests or the community, since we know nothing of the *Sitz im Leben* of the text.

[4] See above, pp. 5f. On the position of the priest in Rabbinic Judaism and the unlikelihood of transferring priestly categories to other classes of society, see Wenschkewitz, *Die Spiritualisierung der Kultusbegriffe*, pp. 43f.

6-2

nevertheless provides us with part of the background to I Pet. ii
and its 'spiritual' priesthood, but at the same time I am conscious that the forms of expression used in C.D. are indistinct, and
that we must take account of alterations in the meaning of the
words used there. It is thus quite possible that the terms
'priests' and 'Levites' may have been applied to ordinary
members of the community.

(c) I Pet. ii. 5 calls the Christians a 'spiritual house' and a
'holy priesthood'. But we must remember that an intrinsic
part of this symbolic exposition was the task appointed for these
'priests', namely 'to offer spiritual sacrifices acceptable to God
through Jesus Christ'. The 'spiritualization' of the sacrificial
office to which this text bears witness is not the sole prerogative
of the New Testament and the Qumran community; it is an
expression of an idea common in Judaism, traceable back to
the Psalter and the prophets, and known in a number of traditions from the same period as the Qumran texts.[1] The object
of these traditions was to emphasize that the sacrificial cultus
of the temple must be supplemented by a life of ethical obedience
to the Law. Those who criticized the sacrifices had no wish to
abolish the temple cultus, only to give it its proper background.
Therefore we seldom find an account of 'spiritual' sacrifices
and a 'spiritual' temple together. This was, of course, because
a criticism of the temple and its sacrifices which advocated the
replacement of the temple and the cultus was inconceivable for
most people, at least as long as the Jerusalem temple stood.[2]
The Qumran texts however provide us with such a combination—of criticism of the temple together with criticism of the
sacrificial office and its cultus—based on their conception of
the community as the new temple, and its life of obedience to
the Law as the true sacrifice.[3] This provides us with a good
background to I Pet. ii and its mention of the 'spiritual'
temple. Here the talk of 'spiritual sacrifices' is noteworthy
only as part of a clearly enunciated temple symbolism. When
we read that sacrifices are 'spiritual', πνευματικαί, and
'acceptable to God through Jesus Christ' nothing is said except

[1] See above, pp. 45f. Cf. Wenschkewitz, *op. cit.* pp. 10ff., and Wolfson,
Philo, II (1948), 241ff.
[2] See above, pp. 16ff. Cf. Klijn, 'Stephen's Speech—Acts vii. 2–53',
N.T.S. IV (1957–8), 30f.   [3] See above, pp. 44ff.

that the sacrifices of the old covenant have been replaced by spiritual sacrifices, which are acceptable to God just because they are offered in Christ—the new sphere of life created in the new covenant, the reality of which is expressed in the Spirit.[1] Our text tells us nothing about what these 'spiritual' sacrifices are to consist of; the deficiency is however remedied in other New Testament texts.

The imagery derived from the sacrifices and the temple offices otherwise occurs on a number of occasions in the New Testament, without any evidence of direct connexion with the concept of the Christians as a temple. The idea of the 'spiritual' priesthood is however used. Thus in Rom. xii. 1 Paul speaks of the Christians' duty to live in such a way that their lives become a sacrifice acceptable to God: 'I appeal to you therefore, brethren, by the mercies of God, to present your bodies as a living sacrifice, holy and acceptable to God, which is your spiritual (temple) worship, λογικὴ λατρεία.'[2] It is probable that the concept of this spiritual sacrifice is connected with the Pauline temple symbolism we have been discussing; on the other hand Paul's language is based on the Old Testament and Jewish tradition in which the sacrifices of prayer, praise and a godly life were contrasted with the false sacrifices of blood. Since the sacrifices in question are here said to be 'your bodies' (the reference being to the common life in the Christian fellowship rather than to martyrdom), it is hard to find direct Jewish or Hellenistic parallels.[3] It is probable that we are dealing with an early Christian tradition in a special form.[4] The imagery would seem to be inspired, first, by the temple symbolism of the early Church, and secondly, by the idea of Christ as the high priest who, by the one great sacrifice of himself once

[1] See above, p. 73.

[2] In the LXX and N.T. λατρεία is mainly a cultic term, connected with sacrificial worship; see Strathmann, art. λατρεία, *T.W.B.* IV, 61 ff.

[3] It might be possible to claim as a parallel the Qumran community's life of obedience to the Law; see e.g. 1QS viii. 5 ff., ix. 3 ff.

[4] There are of course superficial linguistic resemblances between Paul (and I Pet. ii) and Hellenistic sacrificial terminology. But it is less easy to find agreement in their contents. Michel, *Der Brief an die Römer*, pp. 260 f., seems to me to have overlooked the connexion with the general temple symbolism of the N.T., the background of which is to be sought in Palestinian Judaism.

offered, brought to an end the practice of blood sacrifice.[1]
Paul also described his apostolate in sacrificial terminology
(Rom. xv. 15f., Phil. ii. 17f., etc.), there being a connexion
with Christ's own sacrifice.[2] But behind a text like Rom. xii. 1,
which deals with the duty of the Christian to present himself
as a sacrifice, we may discern the concept of a 'spiritualized'
priesthood similar to the one we found in I Pet. ii. 5. Similarly
with Rom. xv. 15–16, in which the Apostle describes his own
commission as 'a minister (priest, λειτουργός) of Christ Jesus
to the Gentiles in the priestly service of the gospel of God, so
that the offering (i.e. conversion) of the Gentiles may be
acceptable, sanctified by the Holy Spirit'.[3] Thus the terminology
of Rom. xii. 1 and xv. 15f. is such as immediately to suggest the
service of the temple priests.

Turning to the Epistle to the Hebrews xiii. 15f., we find there
a text which accords well with these traditions; its import is
that blood sacrifice has been replaced by 'spiritual' sacrifice:
'Through him then let us continually offer up a sacrifice of praise
to God, that is, the fruit of lips that acknowledge his name. Do
not neglect to do good and to share what you have, for such sacrifices are pleasing to God.' The sacrificial terminology here is
close to that of the Old Testament and Judaism.[4] The text resembles for example Ps. l. 14f., 'Offer to God a sacrifice of
thanksgiving...'. This also has the effect of bringing it close to
the temple symbolism of 1QS ix. 3ff. (cf. x. 6 and 8), a passage
which also makes use of Ps. l, and in which the 'sacrifices'
commanded consist not only of thanksgiving, but of a holy life
in accordance with the Law, 'for the atonement of the guilt of
sin and misdeeds, and for the wellbeing of the land by means of
the flesh of burnt offerings and the fat of sacrifices, (that is) the
right offerings of the lips as a righteous sweet savour and a

---

[1] Cf. Schlier, 'Vom Wesen der apostolischen Ermahnung', in *Die Zeit
der Kirche* (1956), pp. 82ff. and Wenschkewitz, *Die Spiritualisierung der
Kultusbegriffe*, pp. 125ff.

[2] On the relationship between Christ, the Apostle and the Christian,
see E. Larsson, *Christus als Vorbild* (1962), pp. 40f., 251f., 273f.

[3] See e.g. K. Weiss, 'Paulus—Priester der christlichen Kultgemeinde',
T.L.Z. LXXIX (1954), 356ff.; Michel, *Der Brief an die Römer*, pp. 327f.;
Cerfaux, *La théologie de l'église suivant saint Paul*, p. 26.

[4] See further Michel, *op. cit.* pp. 351f.; Wenschkewitz, *Die Spiritualisierung
der Kultusbegriffe*, p. 145.

perfect way of life as a free-will offering, pleasing (to God)'. The resemblance is striking, but there are important differences nevertheless. The Christian interpretation of the terminology of sacrifice in Heb. xiii. 15 f. is concentrated on the introductory words 'through him'; it is only through Christ, the true high priest (cf. *v.* 11) that the true sacrifices can be offered.[1] These do not however conflict with the 'one sacrifice', Christ himself, a subject on which the Epistle to the Hebrews has a great deal to say. The imagery of the sacrifice is pressed into service to express the ethical and moral obligations imposed by the faith of the community in Christ; hence its purpose differs radically from that in the Qumran texts, whose 'spiritual' sacrifice was no more than an element in a protracted act of atonement.[2] The sacrifices of thanksgiving and a godly life which we read about in the Qumran texts had the effect of atoning for sin: in this they replaced the blood sacrifices of the Jerusalem temple. The continuation of the sacrificial ministry was essential for the country and for the people. This is not so in the case of the 'spiritual' sacrifices of the New Testament: there the sacrifice of Christ was the only one which had an atoning effect. All subsequent 'spiritual' sacrifices were no more than expressions of the moral obligations of the new life; their fulfilment could in no way make atonement for sin. Thus when we read in I Pet. ii. 5 and other New Testament texts of 'spiritual' sacrifices, sacrifices of thanksgiving, of 'doing good and sharing what you have', the words used may well resemble the words of Judaism,[3] but the meaning is different.

We must make some final observations in connexion with I Pet. ii. The Pauline text which approximated most closely to the Qumran texts, II Cor. vi. 14 ff., had a striking combination of temple symbolism and the demand for purity and holiness. The Christian community, as the spiritual temple, must

[1] Heb. xiii. 10f. places the high priestly office of Jesus over against the office of the Jerusalem temple. A context of temple symbolism is thus found in *vv.* 15f., but its content and purpose are different from those of the texts we have been discussing.

[2] Cf. Wenschkewitz, *Die Spiritualisierung der Kultusbegriffe*, pp. 142f.; Coppens, 'Les affinités qumrâniennes de l'Épître aux Hébreux', *Nouv. Rev. Théol.* xciv (1962), 263.

[3] Ehrlich, *Die Kultsymbolik im Alten Testament und im nachbiblischen Judentum* (1959), p. 40.

maintain the standard of its holiness, vii. 1. We noted a similar combination in I Cor. iii. 16f. The passage in I Pet. ii dealing with the temple, the priesthood and sacrifices also began with an exhortation to all Christians to avoid malice, guile, insincerity, envy and slander. This purity is an element in the Church's growing up in Christ, until it becomes the 'new' temple, ii. 1–3. This combination of the demand for moral purity and the concept of the holiness of the 'new' temple was decisive for the temple symbolism of Qumran; it became no less a part of the New Testament description of the Church as the temple of God.[1]

(2) *Heb. xii. 18–24*

Another aspect of temple symbolism is worth mentioning here, since it reflects a further link between Qumran and the New Testament: that is the fellowship of the eschatological community on earth with the community of heaven. This idea is most clearly expressed in Heb. xii. 18–24. It is true that the temple is not expressly mentioned here (nor with any measure of clarity in the comparative Qumran material), but the ideas expressed here are relevant to our subject, and cast light upon an aspect of temple symbolism which is easily overlooked.[2]

---

[1] There are other details, quite apart from temple symbolism, which point to a link between I Pet. ii and Qumran, e.g. the expression γένος ἐκλεκτόν, which seems to hark back to Isa. xliii. 20 עַמִּי בְחִירִי, and which is found nowhere else in the N.T. The O.T. background is clear (see art. λέγω, in *T.W.B.* iv, 152ff.) but the use of בָחִיר and בָחַר is typical as an expression of the self-consciousness of the Qumran community as the elect. The phrase בְחִירֵי עַם קוֹדֶשׁ, 'the elect of the holy people', is found in 1QM xii. 1 and 5 (see Carmignac, *La Règle de la Guerre*, pp. 172 and 176f.). 'Elect' and 'holy' belong together. I Pet. ii. 9 has γένος ἐκλεκτόν and ἔθνος ἅγιον (see also Nötscher, 'Heiligkeit in den Qumranschriften', *R.Q.* ii (1959–60), pp. 328ff.). A similar expression occurs in I Enoch, see Dahl, *Das Volk Gottes*, pp. 85ff.

[2] There are other texts in Heb. connected with the temple, the priestly office and the sacrifices, but we cannot analyse them all here; see e.g. Spicq, 'L'Épître aux Hébreux, Apollos, Jean-Baptiste, les Hellénistes et Qumrân', *R.Q.* i (1958–9), 382. Most of the temple texts fall outside the bounds of the type of temple symbolism we have been discussing. Most of the texts in Heb. speak of the sacrifice offered by Jesus in the heavenly temple, the temple not made with hands, and of the relation (as conceived in Jewish thought) between the heavenly and earthly temples. Of interest here is the fact that Heb. xii. 18–24 speaks of a connexion between the

In xii. 18–24 the writer to the Hebrews contrasts two blocks of ideas. On the one hand, the old covenant, its relationship to God, and its cultic approach to the place of God's revelation, described with images drawn from Sinai (Exod. xix–xx, Deut. iv. 11 f., v. 23, etc.); and on the other the fellowship with God himself and his Son enjoyed through the new covenant, and the new cultic fellowship with the heavenly world: 'For you have not come to what (i.e. a mountain[1] which) may be touched, a blazing fire, and darkness, and gloom, and a tempest, and the sound of a trumpet, and a voice whose words made the hearers entreat that no further messages be spoken to them. For they could not endure the order that was given, "If even a beast touches the mountain, it shall be stoned". Indeed, so terrifying was the sight that Moses said, "I tremble with fear".'

This describes the situation of the old covenant, in which God revealed his presence in a variety of ways, through the 'mountain', 'fire', 'gloom', 'tempest' and 'the sound of a trumpet'.[2] At the same time emphasis is laid on the terrible aspect of these revelations, and the immense distance which divides the worshipper from God.[3] The mountain mentioned in *v.* 18 is not given a name, but it is obviously Sinai that is meant; in late Jewish traditions Sinai was often interpreted in Messianic and eschatological terms, as the pattern of the mountain of the coming salvation.[4] (Other mountains were mentioned in this connexion as well.) This 'mountain of the future' was also the

earthly and heavenly communities. This passage determines the temple symbolism of Heb. In one verse the Christians are said to be a temple (iii. 6, discussed above, pp. 67 f.), but otherwise there is little resemblance between this view and the temple symbolism we have examined.

[1] Probably we should understand 'mountain', ὄρος, remembering the contents of the text and the parallel to the following Σιὼν ὄρος, *v.* 22. See Michel, *Der Brief an die Hebräer* (1949), p. 314, and Spicq, *L'Épître aux Hébreux*, I, 430, and II, 403 f.   [2] Riesenfeld, *Jésus transfiguré*, pp. 217 ff.

[3] See Michel, *Der Brief an die Hebräer*, p. 314.

[4] The theme of Sinai recurs in the introduction to I Enoch. There Sinai is the place of God's future revelation, from whence judgement is passed on the non-elect and peace and light granted to the elect. There are undoubted resemblances between Heb. xii and I En. i, but the themes have been made to fulfil different functions. I En. is also close to the Qumran texts we have quoted, particularly 1QM xii. 1 ff., where the ideas of judgement and victory form part of the concept of the community's fellowship with the angels.

foundation of the 'new' temple and the 'new' Jerusalem. In Hebrews the Sinai experience symbolizes the old order, replaced in the new community by a 'mountain of the future', called Mount Zion. Zion is manifested in the Christian Church, the ultimate goal of which is to be incorporated into the heavenly reality.[1] 'But you have come to Mount Zion and to the city of the living God, the heavenly Jerusalem, and to innumerable angels in festal gathering, and to the assembly of the first-born who are enrolled in heaven, and to a judge who is God of all, and to the spirits of just men made perfect, and to Jesus, the mediator of a new covenant, and to the sprinkled blood that speaks more graciously than the blood of Abel.' Here the proximity of the new covenant to the heavenly world is described. Members of the community are able to experience, here and now, fellowship with the great and glorious ones of the heavenly world.

The mountain that symbolizes this new dimension of fellowship with God is Zion, just as Sinai stands for the old order. 'Mount Zion, ὄρος Σιών', refers to the rock on which stood Jerusalem, the holy city, the dwelling place of God.[2] In some Old Testament traditions and in late Judaism (for example I Maccabees) 'Zion' is used to denote the rock of the temple, or the temple itself, in which God dwelt.[3] Hebrews xii mentions 'Mount Zion', 'the city of the living God' and 'the heavenly Jerusalem' consecutively, all three denoting that place in which God is said to 'dwell', and in which he reveals himself. There was also a direct connexion in Jewish tradition between the actual temple and city and the future temple and Jerusalem, the mark of which was eternity. The earthly mountain corresponded to the heavenly mountain, with its holy city and its temple.[4] It is this link between 'mountain'

---

[1] Sinai and Zion are contrasted in Gal. iv. 24 ff., where they stand for the old and new covenants respectively. Sinai is not mentioned by name in Heb. xii—evidence of the way in which the old has been set aside. See Spicq, *L'Épître aux Hébreux*, II, 403.

[2] Riesenfeld, *Jésus transfiguré*, pp. 217 ff. On the view of the heavenly city expressed in Heb., related to other N.T. texts, see Michel, *op. cit.* p. 349.

[3] Spicq, *L'Épître aux Hébreux*, II, p. 405, and Fohrer, art. Σιών, *T.W.B.* VII, 307 ff.

[4] Jeremias, *Golgotha*, p. 186; H. Bietenhard, *Die himmlische Welt im Urchristentum und Spätjudentum*, Wiss. Unters. z. N.T. II (1951), 123 ff.

and temple which provides a reason for taking up this passage here.

Hebrews xii begins with an exhortation to Christians to exert themselves in the fight against sin and everything standing in the way of the maintenance of 'holiness'. They simply must not allow the community to become 'defiled' by deliberate sins (*vv.* 14–16). This the letter motivates by pointing to the Christians' fellowship with God, the saints in heaven and the holy city and holy temple of the age to come. Thus the point of the exhortation to holiness is that the community on earth has fellowship with the 'community' in heaven.

It was just this attitude to the community—as the realization of the holy eschatological company, characterized by purity and by fellowship with the dwellers in the heavenly world—which formed such a powerful basis for the self-consciousness of the Qumran sect. There is an important resemblance at this point between Hebrews xii and Qumran. The connexion between earth and heaven is however not expressed in Qumran through images of the order of 'Zion', 'the city' and 'Jerusalem' (as far as we know from the texts so far published):[1] here the Qumran texts differ from Hebrews xii. 'Zion' is used in a more general sense, to refer to the true Israel (4QFlor. i. 12, 1QM xii. 13),[2] or, more traditionally, to the holy city and temple of the future, in which God dwells: 'They (the Gentiles)

[1] It is possible that certain fragments are remains of a description of the 'new' Jerusalem, *Discoveries in the Judaean Desert*, I, 134f., and Baillet, 'Fragments araméens de Qumrân 2. Description de la Jérusalem nouvelle', *R.B.* LXII (1955), 222 ff. (the character of these texts is doubted by Rengstorf, *Ḥirbet Qumran*, pp. 68f.). Cf. also 4QpPs xxxvii. II. 11, which tells how Israel is to 'occupy the mountain of the heights of Israel', probably recalling Ezekiel's prophecy of the future dominion of Israel, Ezek. xvii. 23, xx. 40 and xxxiv. 14. On the idea of the community as the spiritual centre, the Jerusalem, of Israel, see above, pp. 23f.

[2] The latter text, 1QM xii. 13f. (with parallel in xix. 5) combines Ps. xcvii. 8 and Zech. ix. 9, and reads: 'Rejoice greatly Zion. Shine forth in rejoicing Jerusalem. Rejoice all towns of Judah. Keep open your doors for ever, that the treasures of the nations may be brought to you.' As in Heb. xii. 22, Zion and Jerusalem are linked as the centre of the coming salvation. A psalm discovered in 1956 speaks exclusively about Zion, the reference being to the community as the true Israel, 'I remember thee for blessing, O Zion. With all my might I loved thee. May thy memory be blessed forever. Great is thy hope, O Zion...' (published in *Chicago Tribune*, 8.iii.1962).

come with their gifts, silver, gold and precious stones, with all the treasures from their countries to glorify thy people and Zion, thy holy city and thy marvellous house....'[1] The theme of the fellowship of the earthly and heavenly communities, on the other hand, is common in the texts; this applies, too, to the area of thought covered by the temple symbolism. It was normal for the Jew to regard the temple as the dwelling place of both God and his holy angels. The phrase 'before the face of God' in the temple meant 'in the presence of God and his hosts'. The throne of God was surrounded by heavenly beings.[2]

The Qumran community was concerned to stress that God and his angels dwelt in their midst, since they had become the temple of the new relationship with God.[3] One of the most important of the texts on this subject is found in 1QM xii. 1 ff. The text is damaged, but its import is clear nevertheless.

'(1) For a multitude of holy ones are [with th]ee in heaven and hosts of angels in thy holy dwelling place, זבול, to glo[rify] thy [name]. And the elect of the holy people (2) hast thou placed for thyself in [thy house and the book?][4] with the names of all their hosts is with thee in thy holy dwelling place, במעון קודשכה,[5] and the num[ber of the ho]ly ones are in the dwelling place of thy glory, זבול. (3) The gracious works of thy [good][6] blessing and the covenant of thy peace hast thou inscribed for them with the pen of life in order to rule [...] in all the ages of eternity (4) and to order the ho[sts] of thy cho[sen][6] by their thousands and tens of thousands together with thy holy ones [and with] thy angels, that they might overcome (5) in the war, [and thou dost make them the aven]gers of the earth[6] at the multitude of thy judgements, and they shall

---

[1] Baillet, 'Un recueil liturgique de Qumrân, grotte 4: "Les paroles des luminaires"', *R.B.* LXVIII (1961), 207, col. IV. 10 ff. Cf. 1QM xii. 12 ff.

[2] See e.g. Bietenhard, *Die himmlische Welt*, pp. 101 ff.; Michl, art. 'Engel', *R.A.C.* V, 63, 70, 78, etc.

[3] Maier, 'Zum Begriff יחד', *Z.A.T.W.* LXXII (1960), 164.

[4] I follow here Carmignac, *La Règle de la Guerre*, p. 173.

[5] E. Hochmuth, *Die Gebete der Kriegsrolle*, Inaug.-Diss., Karl-Marx-Univ., Leipzig (1959), p. 27, translates 'Auserwählte des heiligen Volkes hast du dir auf E[rden] gesetzt. [Das B]uch der Namen aller ihrer Heerscharen befindet sich bei dir...', which emphasizes the link between the community and the angels of the heavenly world.

[6] Van der Ploeg, *Le Rouleau de la Guerre*, pp. 144 f., gives an account of the various alternatives which have been tried.

[conquer] with the chosen ones of heaven (6) [...] (7) And thou, O God, ter[rible] in the glory of thy kingdom and (in) the community of the holy ones, art in the midst of us as an eter[nal] help...(8) the king of glory is with us, a company of saints. Heroes among a host of angels[1] are mustered amongst us. (9) The power (courage?) of war is in our community and a host of his spirits are with our infantry and our cavalry....'[2]

The object of this description of the fellowship between the Qumran community and God and his angels is to demonstrate that the decisive eschatological war, which was declared when the community was founded, must end in victory for the 'children of light', since they are not fighting alone: they have the support of the army of the angels of heaven. But it witnesses at the same time to the fundamental position of the community as a line of communication between the true people of God on earth and the hosts of God in heaven, between the 'temple' (community) on earth and the dwelling place of God in heaven. As in Hebrews xii, the eschatological and eternal fellowship with God and his angels has been initiated in the founding of the community.

We cannot take up all the resemblances between these two texts here, but we can point to certain likenesses in matters of detail, likenesses which cast further light on our subject of temple symbolism. Hebrews xii. 22 speaks of Mount Zion and the heavenly Jerusalem as entities in which the community already has a share. The author writes: 'For you have not come to (a mountain), οὐ προσεληλύθατε...' (v. 18)—'But you have come, προσεληλύθατε, to Mount Zion...' (v. 22). It has been supposed that the verb is of cultic significance, referring to those who approach God in the cultus or in worship; this I consider to be justified, and it places the passage in its correct context.[3] Christians are enabled to approach the lofty figures of the heavenly world without perishing; this 'approach' is made in the context of the whole community.

---

[1] We might also read: 'the king of glory is with us, with the holy heroes, and a host of angels...', Ploeg, *op. cit.* pp. 47 and 146.

[2] Carmignac, *La Règle de la Guerre*, pp. 179 f.

[3] Michel, *Der Brief an die Hebräer*, pp. 313 f.; Schneider, art. ἔρχομαι, *T.W.B.* II, 681 f. Compare the ingress to the 'temple' text discussed above, I Pet. ii. 4 πρὸς ὃν προσερχόμενοι....

1QM xii. 1 ff. mentions fellowship with the heavenly world in connexion with its description of the 'holy war'. The passage has the character of a hymn or a prayer; hence its oscillation between the third and the first person. The community can be called 'the elect', 'they'; it can also be called 'us', 'God dwells in the midst of us', 'we, a company of holy ones'. This terminology shows how the community considered itself to be a dwelling place for heavenly beings, and how they believed themselves, through the cultus, to be living a life of fellowship with heaven. The saints of heaven were on high, but they were also present in their midst. It is extremely difficult to offer any detailed exegesis of such a fragmentary text, particularly on the subject of the different expressions for God's 'dwelling place' and the links with heaven. The heavenly dwelling place of God and his angels is mentioned four times, 'in heaven', 'in thy holy dwelling place, זבול', 'in thy holy dwelling place, מעון', and 'in the dwelling place of thy glory, זבול', v. 1–2.[1] Both זבול and מעון are used in the Old Testament to denote the dwelling place of God in heaven and in the temple.[2] This applies to מעון[3] in the Qumran texts 1QS viii. 8 (the community as the temple) and x. 3 (heaven). When we read in 1QM xii. 1 ff. of the dwelling place of God, the home of God and all his angels and 'saints', this appears to be an expression for heaven as a temple, an idea found in the Old Testament, in late Judaism and in the New Testament.[4] And when we read, later in the same text, that God himself and his angels are in the midst of the community, we may interpret this as evidence of a direct link between heaven and earth, between the heavenly temple and the earthly; and further, that the earthly congregation is to some extent a reflection of the heavenly world.[5] Thus we find that in Qumran, too, there was talk of a relationship between the community and the Jerusalem temple, and between the earthly community and the dwelling place of God in heaven.

[1] Our translation above, pp. 92f., has 'thy house', but we cannot use it here, since the reconstruction is uncertain in the extreme.

[2] I Kings viii. 13, Isa. lxiii. 15, II Chron. xxxvi. 15, Deut. xxvi. 15, etc.

[3] זבול seems only to refer to the heavenly dwelling place.

[4] See e.g. S. A. Cook, 'Notes on the Relevance of the Science of Religion', in *Festschrift A. Bertholet* (1950), pp. 122ff.; Ahlström, *Psalm 89* (1959), p. 60; Riesenfeld, *Jésus transfiguré*, p. 185.

[5] On the idea of this connexion, see Spicq, *L'Épître aux Hébreux*, II, 234ff.

These ideas on the subject of a link between heaven and earth are found elsewhere in the Qumran texts, for example in 4QFlor. i. 4f., 1QS xi. 7f., 1QH iv. 21 ff.[1] They are also connected with the complex of ideas surrounding the temple. Of particular value is a group of fragments from Cave 4, which give us an insight into the Qumran attitude to angels, heavenly worship and the heavenly temple.[2] The cult of the heavenly temple had been regarded in Judaism as a model for that of the earthly temple.[3] The intense preoccupation with the heavenly temple and its worship which we find in the fragment from Cave 4 may have to do with the community's severe criticism of the Jerusalem temple and the 'transfer' of the 'dwelling place' of God from this temple to the community.[4] Nor is this liturgical fragment merely a description of the worship practised by the angels; it is related to the worship of the community, in which the angels took part.[5] When other texts speak of angels in the community, the reference is undoubtedly to the idea of the temple and worship in heaven (1QSa ii. 8, 1QH vi. 13). This connexion characterizes the whole of that document known as 1QSb. Unfortunately its present state of preservation is such as to make it difficult to estimate its contents, a problem complicated still further by our lack of knowledge of its place in the liturgy and teaching of the community. We can however distinguish the way in which the priestly leader (?) and the 'priests' are described by means of images drawn from the heavenly temple service. A basic theme is the blessing of God bestowed on the 'faithful', which proceeds from the holy dwelling. The priestly leader, whoever he may be, is said to be 'like an angel of the Presence in the holy dwelling,

---

[1] See above, p. 62.

[2] Strugnell, 'The Angelic Liturgy at Qumrân—4Q serek šîrôt 'ôlat haššabāt', *V.T., Suppl.* VII (1960), 318 ff.

[3] Cf. Strack–Billerbeck, *Kommentar*, III, 700 ff.; Volz, *Die Eschatologie der jüdischen Gemeinde*, p. 375.

[4] Strugnell, 'The Angelic Liturgy', p. 335, 'The Essenes, however, whose critique of the Jerusalem Temple doubtless led them away earlier from any confusion between God's dwelling in heaven and His dwelling in the Temple, are already here showing interest in the heavenly sacrificial cult, the priestly quality of the angels and the structure of the heavenly Temple —a further aspect where their beliefs are in some relation to those presupposed in Hebrews'.   [5] Strugnell, *op. cit.* p. 320.

מעון, [to serve] the glory of the God of hosts [for ever. And thou] shalt be a faithful servant in the temple of the kingdom, היכל מלכות, sharing the lot of the angels of the Presence, and in the council of the community [with the holy ones] for ever and for all eternity, for [all] thy commandments are [sure]...'
(iv. 25 ff.).[1]

This text has been interpreted as referring to that time in the future when victory shall have been won over all the powers of darkness, and the final link shall have been established between heaven and earth. But this seems to be an unnecessary limitation. It is likely that this text also reflects the attitude of the present community to their cultic contacts with the heavenly world, it being a general and natural characteristic of the cultus to combine and interweave present and future in this way.

Another passage combines the idea of the community as God's temple with the idea of fellowship with the angels: 'Those whom God has chosen he has made into an eternal possession, and he has given them a share in the lot of the holy ones and he has united their community with the sons of heaven into a council of the community, and their community is a house of holiness...' (1QS xi. 7f.).[2] The community believed that one of the necessary conditions of their existence was this link with the heavenly world, the only assurance of success in the final conflict. The angels, 'the sons of heaven', together with the members of the Qumran sect, make up a holy council of eternal significance.[3] This permanent congregation forms the nucleus of the coming glorious company. Thus the community already has a share in eternal life. It is this which is meant in 1QH iii. 20 ff.: 'And I know that there is a hope for him whom thou hast created out of the dust to (belong to) an eternal foundation (council? סוד). And thou purifiest a perverted spirit from his manifold transgressions, that he may stand in array with[4] the host of the holy ones and enter into fellow-

[1] *Discoveries in the Judaean Desert*, i, 126. On the temple of the 'new' Jerusalem in late Jewish texts, see *ibid*. p. 127.
[2] Cf. above, pp. 63f.   [3] Cf. Nielsen–Otzen, *Dødehavsteksterne*, p. 95.
[4] Mansoor, *The Thanksgiving Hymns*, p. 117, is led to think of the angels and the ranks of the righteous around the Lord, I En. lx. 2. Cf. 1QS ii. 23 on the place of each member of the community in the hierarchy.

ship with the sons of heaven. And thou hast granted unto man an eternal lot among the spirits of knowledge to praise thy name. . . .'

When we compare these texts with the idea of the temple in Eph. ii. 19, 'you are fellow citizens with the saints and members of the household of God', we see how closely it fits into the context of Heb. xii. 22 if we interpret it as referring to fellowship with the citizens of heaven.[1] There seems to have been a common tradition in which the Christian community *qua* God's new temple was regarded as being in contact with heaven. Christians are 'holy', and as such live in fellowship with the 'holy ones', the saints in heaven.

The text of Hebrews xii calls the citizens of the heavenly Jerusalem by three different names: 'innumerable angels', a 'festal gathering' and 'the assembly of the first-born who are enrolled in heaven'.[2] Opinions differ as to the interpretation of these three groups. The 'innumerable angels' and the 'festal gathering', πανήγυρις, are normally regarded by commentators as referring to the angels. But 'the assembly of the first-born' and 'enrolled in heaven' are usually taken to refer to the members of the earthly community, since these two phrases are often used in the New Testament to refer to believers on earth.[3] It is of course possible that all three refer to the angels, though in that case we are faced with uncommon usages in certain cases. But at the same time it is entirely in accord with the basic attitude to the link between the congregations in heaven and on earth, if some of these expressions should refer to the company of believers on earth. We must beware of making a categorical statement that it is *either* the angels *or* believers on

---

[1] See above, pp. 62f. Cf. I Tim. v. 21, which expresses the relation of the community to the angels; Spicq, *Les Épîtres pastorales*, p. 178.

[2] Many read the first two expressions together: see Michel, *Der Brief an die Hebräer*, pp. 316f. But groups of three dominate the text: three terms for the heavenly world, 'Mount Zion', 'the city of the living God' and 'the heavenly Jerusalem'; three terms for the dwellers in heaven; three terms for the act of salvation, 'God, the judge', 'Jesus, the mediator' and 'the sprinkled blood'. The only expression which does not fit into this pattern is 'the spirits of just men made perfect', which seems to belong to the image of 'God, the judge'.

[3] For different expositions, see Michel, *op. cit.* pp. 316f., and Spicq, *L'Épître aux Hébreux*, II, 406ff.

earth who are meant; it is rather a case of both–and.[1] The
'first-born' mentioned in the text may be the Christians[2] whose
name is written in the book of life.[3]

We encounter the same ambiguity in the passage we quoted
from 1QM xii. 1 ff., where the 'holy ones' seem now to be the
company of angels, and now the sanctified members of the
community; this is likewise typical for the other texts we
quoted.[4] Similarly with such expressions as 'Mount Zion',
'the city of the living God' and 'the heavenly Jerusalem' in
Hebrews xii, which indicate that the community on earth and
the community in heaven are united. The fact that typical
correspondences with the Qumran texts are to be found in
other details of Heb. xii. 22 ff.[5] is further evidence of the undeniable proximity of the New Testament and Qumran in this
matter of temple symbolism. The Qumran literature thus provides us with a most illuminating background to the concept

[1] Similarly with the following καὶ πνεύμασι δικαίων τετελειωμένων.
Commentators refer sometimes to members of an earthly community, sometimes to the spirits of dead Christians, or to the righteous dead from the
O.T. What is important is that earthly and heavenly are combined. See
e.g. Michel, *op. cit.* pp. 318f., and Spicq, *op. cit.* II, 408f.

[2] The N.T. consistently refers to Christ as the 'first-born' (Col. i. 15,
Heb. i. 6, etc.). But the word 'first-born' can be used of the Christians. So
probably here. Cf. Michaelis, art. πρωτότοκος, *T.W.B.* VI, 882. It is also
conceivable that the word may be used of the angels, since 'first-born' does
not mean 'born first in time', but 'the object of God's especial love'.

[3] Luke x. 20, Phil. iv. 3, Rev. iii. 5. Cf. 1QM xii. 2!

[4] See e.g. Carmignac, *La Règle de la Guerre*, pp. 171 ff. and on the three
'groups', p. 18, and Spicq, *L'Épître aux Hébreux*, II, 378.

[5] Among these details may be mentioned: the word πανήγυρις, *hapax
legomenon* in the N.T., rare in the LXX, may correspond to the Heb. מועד
(Hos. ii. 11, ix. 5, Ezek. xlvi. 11), which some Qumran texts use to refer to
the community in its sacred gatherings, 1QSa ii. 2, 11, 13, 1QM iii. 4. At
the same time the object of attention is the coming 'festal community'.
The 'first-born' in Heb. xii. 23 are said to be 'enrolled in heaven'. The idea
that the members of the community have their names written in the 'book
of life' is not unknown in Qumran, and it may be that when a man was
'enrolled' in the community he was regarded as having been enrolled in
heaven at the same time. On this theme, see Nötscher, 'Himmlische Bücher
und Schicksalsglaube in Qumran', *R.Q.* 1 (1958–9), 405 ff. The concept of
the list of saints, written in the books of heaven, is probably hinted at in
1QM xii. 1 ff. (the best parallel to Heb. xii.). See above, pp. 92 f. 1QM xii. 4
also speaks of 'myriads' of angels, לאלפיהם ולכבואותם, cf. Heb. xii. 22
μυριάσιν ἀγγέλων.

of the union of the heavenly and earthly communities. It is of course possible that these ideas may have developed along different lines elsewhere. Similar ideas on the subject of the heavenly Jerusalem, its liturgy and its links with its earthly equivalent are for example to be found within late Judaism.[1] But nowhere, it seems to me, is there textual material which is of such comparative value as that from Qumran. The bond which binds together Qumran and the New Testament is undoubtedly the intense self-consciousness of the two communities represented; both considered themselves to have been set up in opposition to the temple of the old covenant and its cultus; both believed themselves to have replaced the old temple, for in both the community was the temple. This applies quite apart from the general resemblance between the Epistle to the Hebrews and Qumran.[2]

C. THE GOSPELS AND THE TEMPLE OF CHRIST

(1) *Faith in Jesus as the Basis of the Temple Symbolism of the New Testament*

We have seen how that form of temple symbolism which appears in the *Corpus Paulinum*, in I Peter and in Hebrews, contains a number of striking resemblances to corresponding phenomena in the Qumran texts. The two groups share the basic idea that the Jerusalem temple and its sacrificial cultus have been replaced by a community of the faithful, an idea which seems to have no equivalent in contemporary Judaism. The Qumran community wanted to replace the temple because they considered it to have been defiled, and therefore unable to fulfil the precepts of the Law. Most texts seem to indicate that its replacement was temporary. When the final victory had been won the temple would once more resume its position at the heart of national affairs. But so long as its defilement lasted,

---

[1] See e.g. Volz, *Die Eschatologie der jüdischen Gemeinde*, pp. 372 ff.; Cerfaux, *La théologie de l'église suivant saint Paul*, pp. 270 ff.; Riesenfeld, *Jésus transfiguré*, pp. 218 ff.

[2] See Yadin. 'The Dead Sea Scrolls and the Epistle to the Hebrews', *Scripta Hierosolymitana*, IV, 36–55; Spicq, 'L'Épître aux Hébreux, Apollos, Jean-Baptiste, les Hellénistes et Qumrân', *R.Q.* 1 (1958–9), 365–90; Coppens, 'Les affinités qumrâniennes de l'Épître aux Hébreux', *Nouv. Rev. Théol.* XCIV (1962), 128–41, 257–82.

THE TEMPLE AND THE COMMUNITY

other things—life in accordance with the Law, the cultus—had to fulfil the functions of the temple in making atonement for the sins of the people and winning the acceptance of God. And this could be accepted in perfect confidence, since the community believed itself to be the holy people of God, marking the start of the last days and claiming the promises and the dominion.

The early Church's point of departure was somewhat different. The Church believed that the temple and its sacrifices had ceased to have any significance in the new Messianic age, and that it had been replaced, once and for all, by Jesus and the fellowship around the Risen Lord. There was no further need of its sacrifices as a means of making atonement, since Jesus had made the final atonement for all men. The 'temple' was now the fellowship of Christ; its 'sacrifices' the Christian life, no longer a means of making atonement for sins but an intrinsic part of the Messianic way of life. When reading Acts i–v, however, we observe that the primitive Church was unable to dissociate itself entirely from the temple as the centre of the religious life. The first Christians continued to attend temple worship, though not the blood sacrifices (Acts ii. 46, iii. 1), the inference being that the idea of the Christian community as the true temple of God had not as yet assumed the dimensions we have noted in Paul, I Peter and Hebrews. Stephen's criticism of the temple, Acts vii, may have been one element in the growth of temple symbolism in the early Church.

The temple symbolism of Qumran and the New Testament was thus based on three factors: criticism of the Jerusalem temple and its sacrifices; a belief that the last days had begun; and belief on the part of both groups that God had come to dwell with them. As he had once 'dwelt' in the temple, so he now lived in the midst of the community. Consequently the community had to take care to preserve its purity, lest the presence of God should be withdrawn. The blood sacrifices once offered in the temple had been replaced by 'spiritual' sacrifices: a blameless life, the sacrifice of the lips and deeds of mercy. And those who offered these 'spiritual' sacrifices were the ordinary members of the community. Further, alongside the belief in the presence of God there was the belief that the community lived in fellowship with the life and worship of the hosts of heaven. The resemblance between Qumran and the

New Testament on this point of temple symbolism is sufficiently detailed to suggest that there must have existed some form of common tradition. Some of these resemblances are to be found in other Jewish texts, but there are so many which are to be found only in Qumran and the New Testament that one is tempted to conclude that certain elements in the Qumran tradition were taken over by the early Church.

But although the degree of resemblance is sufficiently striking to point to a common tradition, we must not forget that there are also striking differences between the two. It is only natural that these should be found in various details of the form taken by the temple symbolism of the two communities, since the communities grew up in different religious milieus, and may have been influenced separately by similar concepts from other Jewish circles. Most important for the purposes of this study is the essential difference between the basis of temple symbolism in the two communities. We have already mentioned a difference in historical background. This we might express as follows. The thought-world in which the temple symbolism of the New Testament was placed had one unique feature: that Jesus, the founder of the Church, was believed to be the Messiah, and that this Messiah had died and risen again from the dead as the Son of God. And since Jesus was believed to be the Son of God, who now lived with the Father and whose Spirit constituted the Church, all things were centred upon him. True, the Qumran community had its Teacher of Righteousness, the founder of the community and the revealer of the deepest meaning of the Scriptures, but the basis of the community was identical in principle with that of the official Israel—the Law as life and the guarantee of God's blessing in the last days. If it be allowed, then, that Qumran and the New Testament shared the same basic temple symbolism, it must nevertheless be admitted that its 'function' and contents differed as between the two groups. Between the temple symbolism of Qumran and that of the New Testament there stands the fact of faith in Jesus as the Messiah and the Son of God. Therefore the distinguishing feature of the temple symbolism of the New Testament is that it depends entirely upon this faith in Jesus. Jewish ideas about the 'new' temple were given a new substance in the person of Christ.

All the New Testament texts we have been discussing are directly connected with this faith in Christ. The one which is least affected by this element of faith is II Cor. vi. 14–vii. 1; this is also the text which, both in language and content, stands closest to Qumran.[1] The clearest evidence of the 'christianizing' of the tradition is in the antithesis 'What accord has Christ with Belial?' in *v.* 15.[2] This gives the passage a different character from that created by the more general terms 'light' and 'darkness', 'righteousness' and 'iniquity'. The setting up of Christ against Belial marks the decisive role played by Christ in the battle of God and evil. The Teacher of Righteousness in the Qumran texts is never set up against Belial; the battle against Belial and his followers is won by God and his host.[3] In the New Testament view it is Christ who represents God in the final conflict against Belial, the evil one, a conflict which he has in a sense already won. This was vital to the Christian Church, particularly in the interpretation of the phrase 'we are the temple of the living God', which meant the creation of an entirely new fellowship with God on an entirely new basis.

The same is true of I Cor. iii. 16–17. Although Christ is not mentioned, and although if removed from its context it loses most of its Christian character,[4] Paul is here paving the way for his statement of the nature of the Christian Church as the 'new' temple by saying that Christ is the foundation of the 'spiritual' edifice which is the company of believers (*v.* 11). The statement in *v.* 16 that 'you are God's temple' suggests that Paul's teaching contained an exposition of the Church as a temple, closely linked with his doctrine of the person and work of Christ.

A more comprehensive treatment of the theme of the temple

---

[1] See above, pp. 49 ff.

[2] We might mention the terms πιστός and ἄπιστος, *vv.* 14 and 15, which are related to the faith of the N.T., and not to the 'faithfulness' of Qumran to the community's interpretation of the Law and the eschatological message of the Teacher of Righteousness.

[3] 1QH suggests that the Teacher of Righteousness may be in a state of war with Belial; but the 'I' of the hymns represents the whole community, and the Teacher therefore fought on God's behalf against Belial as a member of the community. It is impossible to parallel the Teacher and Christ on this point.   [4] See above, pp. 56 ff.

and the person of Christ is found in Eph. ii. 18ff.[1] Several times emphasis is placed upon the fact that it is only in and through Christ that the 'new' temple is constituted and can function. Christ is the corner-stone of the building, the temple, of which the Christians are the materials. The temple grows in the Spirit, and 'the whole structure is joined together' in the Lord. It is the atoning work of Christ which provides the conditions for the creation of this 'new' temple (*v.* 18). It exists in the Spirit (*v.* 18). Thus Christ is both the corner-stone and the one through whom the building came into existence (*vv.* 20f.). Here the text is combining two separate ideas. First, that the company of Christians makes up the temple, and secondly, that the whole is encompassed by the Spirit of Christ. In the latter case the idea expressed is virtually identical with that of the Church as the body of Christ (*vv.* 22 ff.). The temple building is said to be a living being, capable of growth. Note however that it is nowhere said in the texts we have examined that the company of Christians comprises the temple of Christ: it is always the temple, house or dwelling of *God*.[2] Further, Christ is never said to be the temple; only the foundation, corner-stone and basis of the new temple. The image is thus linked to current expressions: the temple of God or the house of God.

I Tim. iii. 15, which speaks of the household of God as 'the church of the living God' gives evidence of further points of contact with the thought of the Qumran community.[3] But here again the terms used have been given a new content derived from faith in Christ. The expression 'the pillar and foundation of the truth', expressing the nature of the Church, is directly connected with the theme of revelation in Christ, as is clear from the verse which follows, which is a hymn to the mystery of Christ: 'He was manifested in the flesh, justified in the Spirit, seen of angels...' (*v.* 16).

The text which most clearly connects temple symbolism with the interpretation of the person of Christ is perhaps I Pet. ii. 4ff. We have already said that there is in this text an intimate

[1] See above, pp. 60ff.
[2] The only dubious passage is Heb. iii. 6, where the text may mean that we are the house of Christ. But it is most likely that this passage, too, refers to the house of God. See above, p. 68.   [3] See above, pp. 66ff.

relationship between the concept of the 'living stone', Christ, and the 'living stones', the members of the Christian community and elements of the spiritual building.[1] The basis of this relationship is faith in Jesus as the 'living stone'. This Christological statement, which is grounded in Jesus' interpretation of his own Messiahship as recorded in the Gospels, suggests that the source of the New Testament interpretation of the 'new' temple is to be sought in the self-consciousness of Jesus—his desire to be the Messiah and break through the Jewish religion and its cultus. It may be possible, following this line, to show how Jesus himself and faith in Jesus were together responsible for giving the temple symbolism of Qumran a new content and a new outline.

Hebrews xii. 18–24, with its clear links with concepts important in the Qumran texts, also has certain aspects which may be understood as resulting from 'christianization' of the temple symbolism.[2] The foundation of the boldly drawn account of the connexion between the earthly and heavenly communities here (over and above that found in the Qumran writings) is the mediatorial function of Christ. The new covenant represented by the Christian Church is based on the atoning death of Christ, 'the mediator of a new covenant' (v. 24). Through him the terrible aspect of contact with God, as it was in the old covenant, has been exchanged for close fellowship with the Lord and the hosts of the heavenly world.

The decisive difference we have seen to exist between the temple symbolism of Qumran and that of the New Testament is thus based on the New Testament's attitude to the person and work of Jesus. The Teacher of Righteousness played an important role in the theology of the Qumran community, but he was no more than a revealer of secrets. He was not the Messiah, and his person and work cannot be compared in their significance with those of Jesus for the Church. The Qumran community was therefore able to 'spiritualize' the temple and its sacrifices, and allow them to fulfil the same functions they held in Judaism. But the temple symbolism of the New Testament is built on the work of Christ; this it was believed had replaced the temple and its sacrifices once and for all. In

<hr>

[1] See above, pp. 72 ff.   [2] See above, pp. 88 ff.

short, the boundary between Qumran and the New Testament, in this matter of the content and function of temple symbolism, goes through the person of Christ.

(2) *Jesus and the Temple in the Gospel Tradition*

If this be so, then we must go on to ask whether the reinterpretation of those traditions we have noted as appearing in the temple symbolism of Qumran took place in the early Church, with its new faith in Christ, or whether its principal features are to be traced back to Jesus himself. This means going back to the gospel traditions, to see whether we can trace an attitude to the temple similar to that we noted in the Epistles. It must of course be remembered that the gospel texts do not give us a wholly authentic account of the Jesus traditions, since they lived and were formed in the early Church, but they are sufficiently comprehensive to indicate what was Jesus' attitude to the temple, as conveyed in his teaching; this will at the same time cast light upon the origins of the temple symbolism of the New Testament.

A great deal might be said on the subject of Jesus and the temple. But not all the texts in the Synoptic Gospels which have to do with this theme are relevant for our purposes. We shall therefore concentrate on those texts which may possibly give an indication of the origins of the temple symbolism of the Epistles. Nor do we need to give an account of the whole of Jesus' attitude to the temple, since the task has already been carried out elsewhere.[1] We shall be most concerned with texts in which Jesus is represented as criticizing the temple, and which illustrate his attitude to fellowship with God, in the temple and in his own person; and further, such eschatological sayings as may cast light upon his attitude to the hopes the Jews pinned to the 'new' temple.

The late Jewish attitude to the future sometimes included an element of hope in a 'new' and better temple alongside their expectation of the coming Messiah. One aspect of the work of the Messiah in the last days was believed to be the renewal of the temple. In such cases, quite irrespective of whether these hopes were interpreted in immanent or transcendent terms, the coming Messiah was coupled with hopes of a new temple and

[1] See Congar, *Le mystère du temple*, pp. 139 ff.

a new Jerusalem.[1] It is probable that an attitude of this kind
to the temple and the Messiah forms the background to the
pericope of Jesus' cleansing of the temple, in Mk. xi. 15–19
with par. The context of these passages in the Synoptics is
similar, and illustrates Jesus' Messiahship in various ways. So
for example the entry into Jerusalem is clearly Messianic in
character, as is the symbolic cursing of the fig-tree,[2] in which
episode the tree represents the people of Israel when con-
fronted by Jesus the Messiah. The 'authority' pericope also
has to do with the self-consciousness of Jesus, and his claim to
ἐξουσία. The parable of the wicked husbandmen, too, must be
reckoned with this group, since it leads to a reference to Ps.
cxviii. 22, the stone which the builders rejected which became
head of the corner; this text is linked with temple symbolism
in other traditions as well. The fact that these pericopae were
collected into one account based on the question of the temple
and the Messiah seems to witness to a conscious theological
attitude in the first gospel tradition, before it became fixed by
the Evangelists.[3] The unanimous witness of the Synoptics seems
also to be evidence that Jesus himself connected the Messiahship with those hopes centring on the temple. Such a combination was by no means out of the question in the Jewish milieu
in which Jesus lived. We may also note that although the
Fourth Gospel places the account of Jesus' cleansing of the
temple at the beginning of the Gospel narrative, it still connects it clearly with the question of the Messiahship. This we
observe by the Jews' questioning of Jesus' authority, which is
placed immediately after the account of the actual cleansing

[1] Cf. M. Simon, 'Retour du Christ et reconstruction du Temple dans la
pensée chrétienne primitive', in *Mélanges M. Goguel* (1950), pp. 247 ff.;
Jeremias, *Jesus als Weltvollender*, pp. 25 ff.; J. Schmid, *Das Evangelium
nach Markus* (1958), pp. 212 f., treats the idea of the Messiah's renewal of
the temple and the cultus with a good deal of scepticism.

[2] Luke does not have the pericope of the fig-tree, but otherwise includes
the same material as Mk. and Matt. (It is possible that the parable of the fig-
tree in Luke xiii. 6–9 is a replacement for the pericope.) See e.g. Riesenfeld,
in *Sv. Exeg. Årsbok* xx (1955), 50. Cf. C. W. F. Smith, 'No Time for Figs',
J.B.L. lxxix (1960), 324.

[3] The problem of composition is discussed by e.g. Doeve, 'Purification
du Temple et desséchement du figuier', *N.T.S.* 1 (1954–5), 297–308;
Congar, *Le mystère du temple*, pp. 148 ff.; E. F. Scott, *The Crisis in the Life
of Jesus* (1952), pp. 17 ff.

(John ii. 18 ff.). There then follows a statement of principle, that the temple and the body of Jesus are related.[1]

Further, the actual events described in the pericope of the cleansing of the temple are an expression of the Messianic consciousness of Jesus.[2] They express the idea that Jesus *qua* Messiah now had the authority to demonstrate, in word and deed, that the time had come for the establishment of the 'new' temple and a new and better basis of fellowship with God.[3] Many attempts have been made to explain why Jesus acted as he did on the occasion of the cleansing of the temple; reverence for the temple, a desire to show up the priests' cupidity, a consciousness of his calling as a prophet—all have been advanced as motives for his actions.[4] But I find it difficult to avoid interpreting the pericope as an expression of Jesus' Messianic attitude to the temple. The only one who can behave in this way is the Lord of the temple.[5] And if we compare the words of Jesus, recorded by the Synoptics in connexion with Isa. lvi. 7 and Jer. vii. 11, it becomes even clearer that the cleansing of the temple was to Jesus a way of showing what the 'house of God' was to be in the last days: a house of prayer, a house in which the true fellowship with God could be found.

A great many problems follow upon the different placing of the various pericopae and material peculiar to the individual Gospels in this passage. But there is a further common motif here, in the context of the Messiah and his relationship to the people and temple of Israel, that is, the important theme of judgement. The traditions make it clear that to the entry of Jesus into Jerusalem belonged not only the cleansing of the

---

[1] The relationship between the Synoptics and the Johannine versions is a problem too profound to permit of treatment here. See however S. Mendner, 'Die Tempelreinigung', *Z.N.T.W.* XLVII (1956), 93 ff.; I. Buse, 'The Cleansing of the Temple in the Synoptics and in John', *E.T.* LXX (1958–9), 22–4; E. Haenchen, 'Johanneische Probleme', *Z.Th.K.* LVI (1959), 34 ff.

[2] The essential historicity of this pericope may be accepted; it is supported unanimously by the traditions.

[3] Cf. Jeremias, *Jesus alt Weltvollender*, pp. 42 ff.

[4] Cf. Scott, *The Crisis in the Life of Jesus*, pp. 62 ff.; Léon-Dufour, 'Le signe du Temple selon saint Jean', *Rech. S.R.* XXXIX (1951–2), 161 ff.

[5] Lohmeyer–Schmauch, *Das Evangelium des Matthäus* (1956), p. 299; Burkill, 'Strain on the Secret: An Examination of Mark 11, 1–13, 37', *Z.N.T.W.* LI (1960), 37 f.

temple but also the cursing of the fig-tree (in Matthew and Mark; a symbolic action representing the judgement of Israel consequent upon their refusal to accept the Messiah) and the prophecy of the destruction of Jerusalem (in Luke). Jesus' cleansing of the temple thus becomes simultaneously a judgement and an expression of hope in a better fellowship than that based on the temple as it then was. This impression is strengthened by the fact that all three Synoptics motivate the cleansing with no more than a reference to Isa. lvi. 7, 'my house shall be called a house of prayer', and Jer. vii. 11 in which the temple is called 'a den of robbers'.

The context of these two Old Testament quotations is important for our understanding of the cleansing of the temple. Thus Isaiah describes, in contrast to the decline and decay of the temple of his time, the future in which the new Zion shall be established and 'foreigners' be given their rightful place in Israel. The necessary condition is that the Law be observed and the covenant be kept. When this takes place, then the way to the dwelling place of God stands open: 'these I will bring to my holy mountain, and make them joyful in my house of prayer; their burnt offerings and their sacrifices will be accepted on my altar; for my house shall be called a house of prayer for all peoples' (lvi. 7).[1] What is required to ensure the functioning of this new temple of Zion is a life in accordance with the precepts of the Law, and the observance of the conditions of the covenant. This demand for righteousness and worship in the same context is fully in accordance with the prophetic tradition of criticism of the cultus.[2] The 'den of robbers' passage in Jeremiah vii is also connected with a sharp criticism of those who fail to observe the Law, notwithstanding their faithful attendance at worship in the temple. The blessing of

[1] Note that C.D. xi. 20ff. justifies the practice of the community in refusing to sacrifice in the temple by quoting Prov. xv. 8, which says that prayer is the sacrifice of the righteous; see above, p. 46. Prayer, the temple and sacrifice are thus brought together, both in the text of C.D. and in Isa. lvi. 7, quoted by Jesus (though the latter text says nothing about the replacement of sacrifice by prayer). John iv. 21 ff. also deals with the subject of the temple and prayer; Jesus says that, in the future, prayer shall be offered neither in Jerusalem nor Samaria, but 'in spirit and truth'. This may be a trace of a common tradition around this theme.

[2] See above, pp. 45 f.

God cannot be secured, save as a reward for complete obedience to the Law. We thus see that both texts stress the principle on which the Qumran community laid its strongest emphasis: only when there was perfect obedience to the Law could there be blessing in the house of God. And the community had broken away from the temple just because the Law was *not* observed. Now although the historical basis of the criticism levelled at the temple by the Qumran community and by Jesus differed, it is interesting to see how both hark back to the prophetic tradition pointing at the lack of correspondence between temple worship and observance of the Law. This principle is also to be found in Matt. xii. 7, the reference being to Hos. vi. 6.

It is obvious that behind Jesus' actions in the temple lay the thought that the temple and its worship had been defiled; hence he directed his attention to one of the symbols of this pollution, the selling of sacrificial apparatus in the temple court. But Jesus did not merely come to terms with a too extensive and vulgar business enterprise, though it might appear so from the account in the Gospels. There are other matters which underline his criticism of the temple, and which we may glimpse in the narrative. For example, we find preserved in Mark an observation connected with the cleansing: 'and he would not allow any one to carry anything (tools, vessels, etc.) through the temple' (xi. 16). In this way Jesus opposed the bringing into the temple of anything which was not duly consecrated.[1] His action in driving the merchants and money-changers out of the temple hit the priests, and those whose responsibility it was to see that the temple functioned properly. They had broken the Law of God under the terms of the covenant, by failing to keep the temple and its worship holy, the very things emphasized by Isa. lvi and Jer. vii. We may observe here how similar were the grounds of Qumran's criticism of the temple; the priests had been guilty of profaning the temple, and hence it could no longer function as the true cultic link with God.[2] The altar has become defiled; the temple and its worship must be replaced. But the solutions of this problem reached in Qumran and in the teaching of Jesus differed

[1] Cf. Strack–Billerbeck, *Kommentar*, II, 27.
[2] See above, pp. 19 f.

radically: in Qumran they seem to have broken with the temple; Jesus retained the links and criticized on eschatological grounds.[1]

The temple had been profaned; but what was the positive meaning of Jesus' action? It is not usual to interpret the pericope of the cleansing of the temple as a direct attack by Jesus on the temple and its worship. But I consider it unlikely that Jesus wanted to purify the worship of the temple as it was organized at that time; his desire was to demonstrate a temple criticism in the context of the better worship of the eschatological temple (cf. Isa. lvi and Jer. vii). It has been said that Jesus shared the belief of the Jews, that the 'Presence' of God rested upon the temple; attention has been called to his words in Matt. xxiii. 16–22.[2] This seems feasible. But at the same time he was able to speak of the time in the very near future when the temple would be laid in ruins, Mark xiii. 1 ff. with par. (cf. Matt. xxiii. 38), a 'future' intimately connected with Jesus' own person. Those apocalyptic *logia* of Jesus which have survived, and which speak of the coming fall of the temple, have sometimes been reckoned as later traditions, connected with the destruction of Jerusalem in A.D. 70. But remembering the atmosphere which surrounded certain groups at the appearance of Jesus, we no longer have any reason to suppose that Jesus did not, as a result of the reception he received at the hands of the Jewish leaders, speak of a judgement which would very soon fall upon the people, the holy city and its temple.[3] Thus it seems to me that the cleansing of the temple belongs in the context of those actions and words through which the leaders of the people were informed that something new was coming. The temple building was soon to go and to be replaced by better fellowship with God.

There are two details which seem to point in this direction and show how the early Church understood the cleansing as an element in Jesus' teaching about a new and better temple: (*a*) Mark quotes a further phrase from Isaiah, 'for all peoples'

[1] Cf. H. H. Rowley, 'The Qumran Sect and Christian Origins', pp. 132f.

[2] Congar, *Le mystère du temple*, pp. 142 ff.

[3] See e.g. Cullmann, 'L'opposition contre le temple de Jérusalem', *N.T.S.* v (1958–9), 167.

('my house shall be called a house of prayer for all peoples'). This seems to be a later addition, expressive of the universalist idea that the new temple would be for all people, and not for Israel only;[1] (*b*) Matthew is alone in saying that Jesus cured the blind and the lame in the temple (xxi. 14). Remembering what we know of the Qumran community and its strict conditions of membership in the 'new' temple, this verse may well have been incorporated into the narrative at this point by way of polemic against those whose concept of holiness was to restrict entry to the Christian fellowship in any way. Both these appendices seem to express the same principle, and to hint at the positive side of Jesus' teaching on the subject of the temple.

Jesus' attitude to the temple is also reflected in one of the accusations levelled at him during his trial. He is reported as having said, 'I am able to destroy the temple of God, and to build it in three days' (Matt. xxvi. 61; cf. 'I will destroy this temple that is made with hands, χειροποίητος, and in three days I will build another, not made with hands, ἀχειροποίητος', Mk. xiv. 58). It is impossible to prove that Jesus expressed himself in just these terms, but when taken in the context of Jesus' teaching as a whole they seem to express the essence of what he taught on his relationship to the temple.[2] The false witnesses evidently misunderstood the point of his teaching, and took it literally; similarly with John's version of the Jews' reaction: 'It has taken forty-six years to build this temple, and will you raise it up in three days?' (ii. 20). It is probable that Jesus, conscious of his Messiahship, harked back to that criticism of the temple which was already to be found in certain circles and at the same time spoke of a new temple; this was not to be a new building, however, but a new fellowship with God established by Jesus himself.[3] The 'made with hands...

---

[1] J. Schmid, *Das Evangelium nach Markus*, pp. 212f., and others consider the Marcan version to be the original, and suggest that Matt. and Luke have dropped the expression 'for all peoples'; the reason given—not a very good reason—is that they wrote after the fall of Jerusalem in A.D. 70.

[2] See e.g. M. Goguel, *Vie de Jésus* (1932), pp. 491 ff.

[3] On the subject of Jewish hopes of a new temple, see M. Simon, 'Retour du Christ et reconstruction du Temple dans la pensée chrétienne primitive', in *Mélanges Goguel* (1950), pp. 250 ff.; and above, pp. 16f. We cannot here discuss the whole of the complex of problems surrounding this saying of

not made with hands' of the Marcan version also emphasizes the distinction between the present concrete temple and the heavenly and spiritual fellowship with God which is to characterize the coming temple. This distinction recurs in Stephen's speech in Acts vii, and it has been supposed that it belonged to the catechetical tradition of the early Church, which was based on Jesus' criticism of the temple and on the expectation of a new and better temple. Resemblances have also been noted between Stephen's speech and the Qumran texts, further evidence that we are here dealing with a related tradition.[1]

But although the accusations levelled against Jesus tell us a certain amount about his Messianic teaching on the subject of the temple, they give us little information on what he meant by the 'new' temple that would come to replace the old one. A hint is however provided by the antithetical use of material and spiritual terms in the Marcan version. The subject was a new 'spiritual' cultus. It may be that his expression 'in three days' ('and in three days I will build another...') gives us a clue to his intentions. The expression is in fact found elsewhere, in Matt. xii. 40 in connexion with an exposition of the sign of Jonah: 'For as Jonah was three days and three nights in the belly of the whale, so will the son of man be three days and three nights in the heart of the earth.' It is probable that these two passages should be considered together. Although the form of the saying of Jesus in Matt. xii. 40 bears the marks of a later origin, there is behind it some teaching of Jesus about his return from death. It has commonly been supposed that the introduction of the sign of Jonah here took place after the establishment of faith in the resurrection, and that the sign of Jonah originally applied only to his person and message (Mark and Luke). But we have cause to regard the Matthaean version as quite in accordance with the teaching of Jesus, and to see it in line with the relatively unanimous traditions preserved in Matthew, Mark and John that Jesus taught that he

Jesus; discussions will be found in C. F. D. Moule, 'Sanctuary and Sacrifice in the Church of the New Testament', *J.T.S.* I (1950), pp. 29 ff.; A. Cole, *The New Temple* (1950), pp. 23 ff.; Gärtner, *The Areopagus Speech*, pp. 206 ff. Cf. Bultmann, *Die Geschichte der synoptischen Tradition* (1958), pp. 126 f. (and *Ergänzungsheft*, 1958, pp. 17 f.).

[1] See A. F. J. Klijn, 'Stephen's Speech—Acts vii. 2–53', *N.T.S.* IV (1957–8), 28 ff.

would establish a new temple in three days. The Jewish material available for comparison on the subject of the sign of Jonah shows that the example of Jonah was used as a sign of the power of God to save from death and danger, '...die Legitimierung des Gottgesandten durch die Errettung aus dem Tode'.[1] But there are also parallels to the expression 'three days'; thus the third day is the day of salvation[2]—a common Jewish idea which may have been realized in a special way by faith in the resurrection. The hint we find in the alleged saying of Jesus—'and in three days I will build another'[3]—is thus that the 'better' temple is related to the return of Jesus from Sheol, and connected with the person and the return of Jesus.[4]

We have seen that Jesus set himself up in opposition to the Jerusalem temple and criticized its priests because they had polluted it and made it into a 'den of robbers'. This criticism went as far as to foretell the fall of the temple. There was however nothing new in this, if we compare tendencies in contemporary Judaism. Such criticism was by no means unique; we can of course refer to the Qumran texts, but there is a great deal of other material as well.[5] Though there are concepts in the Synoptic material we have been discussing which resemble Qumran, it is not possible to demonstrate any exact parallelism between Jesus and Qumran. It is conceivable that Jesus may have been influenced in his criticism by Essene passion for a pure and holy temple. But not until we come to the question of what it was that Jesus meant would replace the temple do we find comparative Qumran material. The Qumran texts criticized the temple without wanting to do away with the

[1] Jeremias, art. 'Ιωνᾶς, *T.W.B.* III, 413, regards this as the original meaning of the *logion*, Luke xi. 30. The 'three days' he regards as 'sekundäre Ausdeutung'.

[2] On this question as a whole, see P. Seidelin, 'Das Jonaszeichen', *Stud. Theol.* V: 2 (1952), 119 ff. Cf. Cole, *The New Temple*, pp. 16 ff.

[3] The tradition of the 'three days' is found in Mk. xiv. 58, xv. 29, Matt. xxvi. 61, xxvii. 40, John ii. 19, (Acts vi. 14)—evidence of the importance and reliability of the tradition.

[4] Jeremias, *Jesus als Weltvollender*, p. 40, considers that Jesus was referring to the building up of the heavenly temple, 'die verklärte Gemeinde'. Cf. also p. 81.

[5] See above, pp. 19 f., and Flusser, 'Two Notes on the Midrash on II Sam. vii', *I.E.J.* IX (1959), 99 ff.

temple and its cultus; they wanted to replace it because, although it was incapable of functioning properly, it was still a necessity. This replacement took place by the transfer of the true 'spirituality', the presence and approbation of God, to the community. It is this which is unique in the Qumran texts. (It is difficult to say from the texts whether this replacement was believed to be permanent or only temporary.)[1]

Turning now to the Synoptics, we find in their account of Jesus' teaching on the subject of the temple no suggestion that Jesus was in favour of immediately abolishing the temple and all it stood for. He criticized its cultus, but did not urge its abolition. Here he is in line with the Qumran tradition. He did not follow apocalyptic Judaism in describing the glories of the coming temple. Instead he did as had been done in Qumran: he transferred the activities of the temple from Jerusalem to another entity. This entity was Jesus himself and the group around him as Messiah. This transference and replacement had to do with his death and its creative significance for the people. A new fellowship with God would be set up through his death and resurrection; in effect, he himself would become the replacement for the temple. The 'presence' of God would no longer be linked with the temple, but with him and those whom he had gathered to himself. Jesus' saying, 'For where two or three are gathered in my name, there am I in the midst of them' (Matt. xviii. 20), expresses substantially the same idea as the Jewish belief that the *Shekinah* of God was in the midst of the people of God when they were met together to observe the cultus or to study the Law. It is this idea of the *Shekinah* which I consider is referred to in the positive element of Jesus' accusation, 'and in three days I will build another'.[2] But this was not just another temple of the same kind as that which was to be destroyed: it was to be essentially different. It is this transference of the 'presence' of God in the temple and its cultus which Qumran and the New Testament have in common. In comparison with the world around both appear to be *sui*

---

[1] See above, p. 21.

[2] Note the greater precision of the Marcan version, when compared with Matt.: 'I will destroy *this* temple,...and in three days I will build *another*....'

generis in their claim that a man and a fellowship constitute a spiritual temple. And even though this principle is expressed in two entirely different ways, due to their widely divergent ideas about the nature of salvation and the work of the Messiah, it nevertheless provides a common basis. It is this resemblance which also provides the foundation for the agreements which we have seen to exist in Paul, in I Peter and in Hebrews.

This transference of the cultic centre from the Jerusalem temple is said in Jesus' teaching to belong to the future, and to be connected with his death. But at the same time there are hints that the transference has already begun. It seems to be this which is meant by the statement in Matt. xii. 6, 'I tell you, something greater than the temple is here', which seems to be a genuine saying of Jesus, though one which is difficult to localize in its original context. This *logion* is only found in Matthew, and has been placed in a pericope of sayings concerning Jesus and the sabbath. With it are associated two other *logia* with significance for the 'temple' theme, so that the text reads: 'Or have you not read in the law how on the sabbath the priests in the temple profane the sabbath, and are guiltless? I tell you, something greater than the temple is here. And if you had known what this means, "I desire mercy, and not sacrifice", you would not have condemned the guiltless' (*vv.* 5–7). The placing of these sayings in the context of the plucking of ears of grain on the sabbath seems to serve the following purpose. When serving in the temple the priests had the right according to the Law to transgress the sabbath in the carrying out of necessary cultic duties. Jesus refers his disciples to this principle. In Jesus there is that which is superior to the sabbath. It seems reasonable to recall the *Shekinah* idea, and interpret the verse to mean that God 'dwells' in him more than in the temple. The disciples, as servants of one whose authority is greater than the temple, need not observe these laws. The 'mercy' of God manifested in the person and work of Jesus is a more acceptable sacrifice than anything that can be brought about by the Jerusalem cultus.[1] Jesus is thus able to justify the transgression of the sabbath commandment by claiming to represent the 'presence' of God among the people more fully

[1] See e.g. Cole, *The New Temple*, pp. 8 ff.; Doeve, *Jewish Hermeneutics*, pp. 163 ff.; Jeremias, *Golgotha*, p. 78.

than the temple. The *Shekinah* of God belonged to the temple, and was revealed there in the cultus.[1] And Jewish visionaries could speak of the holy Israel in whose midst God would once more dwell in his temple, the inference being that the 'presence' of God was specially linked with the temple.[2] Part of the background of the saying of Jesus in Matt. xii. 6 is provided by the principle that even in his earthly life Jesus, and not the temple, provided a 'dwelling place' for God. Jesus, who is superior to both David and the temple, becomes Lord over the sabbath and the temple[3] because he possesses the 'Spirit' of God.[4] Here we have a plain statement that the Jerusalem temple is being replaced by something better, and this 'something' is connected with the person of Jesus and what he stands for.[5]

Another concept which must be dealt with in this connexion, a concept of great importance for Jesus' Messianic self-consciousness, is that he possessed the Spirit of God; this is stressed

[1] See Strack–Billerbeck, *Kommentar*, I, 1003; Riesenfeld, *Jésus transfiguré*, pp. 98 ff. and 184 ff.

[2] Bonsirven, *Le Judaïsme Palestinien*, I, 432 and 453. Since it was inconceivable that the *Shekinah* of God could have left the people, the 'dwelling place' of God was transferred, after the fall of the temple, to the synagogue, the Torah, etc. See *ibid.* II, 108. Cf. Wenschkewitz, *Die Spiritualisierung der Kultusbegriffe*, pp. 37 ff.

[3] Jeremias interprets the saying of Jesus in Matt. xii. 6 as evidence that Jesus is 'das himmlische Urbild der Gotteswohnung'—'Wir haben also wahrscheinlich in Mt 12:6 eine Selbstaussage Jesu, in der er sich mit dem himmlischen Heiligtum vergleicht', *Golgotha*, p. 78.

[4] On the role of the Spirit in connexion with Matt. xii. 6, see Cole, *The New Temple*, pp. 13 ff.

[5] Matt. xii. 7 quotes Hos. vi. 6, 'I desire mercy, and not sacrifice', a verse which was also used in Qumran in connexion with their view of the community as the temple. This may be a criticism of sacrificial worship detached from a life lived according to the Law. The quotation from Hosea may be an expression of Jesus' mercy towards sinners and the lost children of Israel—a more excellent way than all the sacrifices offered in the temple (Matt. ix. 13). This quotation is also found in Qumran in connexion with the idea of a life lived in accordance with the Law, which is felt to be more important than blood sacrifices offered in the temple at Jerusalem. But in Qumran 'mercy' and 'justice' are taken to refer to the keeping of the Law and the covenant, and not, as in the N.T., to the love of God, breaking through the Law in the person of the Messiah, and revealing something new. See above, p. 46, and on Matt. xii. 7 cf. Wenschkewitz, *Die Spiritualisierung der Kultusbegriffe*, pp. 94 f.

in Matt. xii. 18, 28, 32.[1] The account of the baptism of Jesus in the River Jordan, with its description of the descent of the Spirit, has to do with the idea of the initiation of Jesus into his Messianic office, the ushering in of the Messianic age, and is also linked with Old Testament and Jewish prophecies of the Messiah-King.[2] But it is possible that the 'anointing' scene described in the baptism narrative may be linked in some way with the temple. For instance, we might refer to the Messianic hymn in Test. Levi xviii, which has been connected with the narrative of the baptism of Jesus.[3] The hymn describes the 'new priest' who shall appear in the last days, and who shall be anointed with the Holy Spirit. Here, too, comes the theme of the heavens opening and pouring out 'holiness', ἁγίασμα, over him. This is combined with the idea that the holiness of the 'new priest', by which seems to be meant his high-priestly office, comes to him from the 'temple of glory' in heaven. 'And the angels of the glory of the presence of the Lord shall be glad in him. The heavens shall be opened. And from the temple of glory, ἐκ τοῦ ναοῦ τῆς δόξης, shall come upon him sanctification with the Father's voice as from Abraham to Isaac. And the glory of understanding and sanctification shall rest upon him...' (xviii. 5–7).[4] Here the 'new priest' is placed in relation to the temple in heaven; thence he receives his anointing.[5] The motifs of the opened heavens, the voice from heaven and the Spirit descending upon Jesus may well have been

---

[1] Mention of the Spirit in this context is made only by Matt., the only Evangelist to have preserved the saying of Jesus about the one who is 'greater than the temple'. See Cole, *op. cit.* pp. 13 ff.

[2] See e.g. Barrett, *The Holy Spirit and the Gospel Tradition* (1947), pp. 35–45; G. Friedrich, 'Beobachtungen zur messianischen Hohepriestererwartung in den Synoptikern', *Z.Th.K.* LIII (1956), 281 ff.; Feuillet, 'Le baptême de Jésus d'après l'Évangile selon saint Marc', *C.B.Q.* XXI (1959), 468–90.

[3] The relation of the text to the baptismal narrative is emphasized by Barrett, *op. cit.* pp. 43 f.

[4] Translation from Charles, *The Testament of the Twelve Patriarchs* (1908), pp. 63 f.

[5] The expression 'with the Father's voice as from Abraham to Isaac' may be connected with Gen. xxii. 8, and the account of the sacrificial lamb, and may refer to 'the idea of the Priestly Messiah as sacrificial victim'. See further Black, 'The Messiah in the Testament of Levi xviii', *E.T.* LX (1948–9), 321 f.

interpreted by the early Church as evidence that the glory, δόξα, of God rested upon Jesus. And this in turn may have been combined with the belief that the Spirit of God dwelt in him more than in the temple.

This idea, that Jesus possessed the Holy Spirit of God, could thus be taken in the early Church to mean that the *Shekinah* of God rested upon Jesus the Messiah. It is quite possible that it is this which lies behind John i. 51, 'Truly, truly, I say to you, you will see heaven opened, and the angels of heaven ascending and descending upon the Son of man'. This text has been interpreted as a Johannine exposition of Jesus' baptism, the implication being that the Spirit now rests upon Jesus instead of the temple, and it is through Jesus that the fellowship with the angels 'functions'.[1] The allusion to Jacob's experience in the holy place with the ladder, the angels and the stone (Gen. xviii. 11–19) may also be taken as an expression of the idea that Jesus is a high priest in a new temple.[2] The resemblance to Test. Levi xviii supports this. In the Johannine tradition Jesus, as Son of man, is the only true connexion between earth and heaven; only through him is it possible to gain access to spiritual and heavenly reality.[3]

It is tempting at this point to associate the idea of Jesus as high priest and the sacrifice he offers—his own body. We find traces in the Synoptics of the idea that Jesus constituted the basis of the new temple fellowship, and likewise that he occupied a position superior to that of the earthly high priest.[4] Jesus' sayings on the subject of his own sacrificial passion and death may also be interpreted to mean that the practice of blood sacrifice in the temple was to cease from the moment when Jesus died. We cannot here go into the question of the true high priest and his sacrifice, concepts clearly developed in Hebrews, but we must keep them in mind, since they witness to the fact that the temple and sacrificial symbolism of the New Testament was firmly grounded in Jesus' Messianic self-consciousness.

[1] Cullmann, 'L'opposition contre le temple de Jérusalem', *N.T.S.* v (1958–9), 170.

[2] Cf. Jeremias, *Golgotha*, p. 53.

[3] Odeberg, *The Fourth Gospel* (1929), pp. 38f. Cf. Jeremias, *Jesus als Weltvollender*, pp. 50f.

[4] See Friedrich, 'Beobachtungen', pp. 287ff.; Cullmann, *Die Christologie des Neuen Testaments*, pp. 86ff.

Further, it seems to be correct to say that the Gospel of John lays theological emphasis on Jesus' polemic against the Jerusalem temple and its cultus, and attempts to give clear expression to the idea that Jesus himself is the 'new' temple of the Messianic age.[1] The first mention of the incarnation of Jesus (John i. 14) contains a hint to the effect that the *Shekinah* of God came and took up his abode with Jesus. We read there that the Word, λόγος, 'dwelt among us, ἐσκήνωσεν ἐν ἡμῖν', in such a way that the 'presence' of God among men became realized through God's 'representative', the Word. God 'dwells' in Jesus, who is the Word, as it were in a temple in the midst of men. Hence God's *kabod* can be seen to rest upon him.[2] The question of the temple and the cultus is also brought to the fore in Jesus' conversation with the Samaritan woman (John iv). They talk of the true cult centre and the true worship. The woman believes that Samaria's Mount Gerizim and Israel's Mount Zion, with the Jerusalem temple, are set up in opposition to each other. But Jesus says that neither is the true centre of worship; the coming of the Messiah and the creation of a new fellowship around him makes it possible to worship in 'spirit and truth'.[3] Worship is connected with the Spirit, which proceeds from Christ (iv. 14), and with the truth which is revealed through Christ. Thus Christ is shown to be the replacement for the old cultus and cult centre.[4]

The Johannine version of Jesus' teaching on the subject of the destruction and rebuilding of the temple is important

[1] See further Cullmann, 'L'opposition', pp. 169 ff.

[2] On the question of the *Shekinah* of God and the person of Jesus, see e.g. Riesenfeld, *Jésus transfiguré*, pp. 183 ff., 257; F. M. Braun, 'In spiritu et veritate', *Rev. Thom.* LII (1952), 245 ff.; Congar, *Le mystère du temple*, pp. 161 ff.; Cullmann, *op. cit.* pp. 169 f. (Cf. *Idem* 'The Significance of the Qumran Texts for Research into the Beginnings of Christianity' in Stendahl, *The Scrolls and the New Testament*, pp. 28 f.)

[3] Braun, *op. cit.* pp. 266 ff.; Cullmann, 'L'opposition', p. 169.

[4] Note that behind the 'identity' sayings (e.g. 'I and the Father are one', John x. 30) there may be the idea that God and his *Shekinah* (which rested upon the temple) are here united. There was in Jewish thought an idea that the sin of man was capable of separating God from his *Shekinah*. The two were thus reunited, and the union manifested, in the relationship of Jesus and the Father. It is this which Odeberg expresses in *The Fourth Gospel*, p. 332: 'In me the Šᵉkinā is present, and now (in me) the Father and the Šᵉkinā are united, and Salvation is brought about.'

evidence of the way in which the early Church was able to connect the 'new' temple with the body of Jesus. After the description of Jesus' cleansing of the temple (ii. 13–17) there follows the Jews' questioning of his right to act in this way. The answer is a saying of Jesus which echoes the accusation levelled against Jesus according to the Synoptic accounts: 'Destroy this temple, and in three days I will raise it up' (v. 19).[1] The criticism implied in this saying, and in the action which preceded it, is that the old temple has reached the limit of its usefulness and must be replaced. This replacement takes place in the person of Jesus, who is 'destroyed' and 'raised up' in three days. The Evangelist comments, 'But he spoke of the temple of his body, περὶ τοῦ ναοῦ τοῦ σώματος αὐτοῦ' (v. 21). The body of Jesus, the person of Jesus, replaces the old temple. The Evangelist, wanting to stress this still further, goes on to refer to the resurrection: 'When therefore he was raised from the dead, his disciples remembered that he had said this '(v. 22). The new fellowship in replacement of the temple and its cultus is created through that Jesus whose body has passed through the gates of death and resurrection. Thus when the Jews demanded a 'sign' to prove his authority to cleanse the temple, they were referred to his own person; Jesus is the 'sign' by virtue of his death and resurrection.[2] This concept is also expressed in the Book of Revelation, in its vision of the world to come, where God and Jesus replace the temple.[3] Furthermore, the idea of Jesus as high priest and final sacrifice has its distinct place in the Fourth Gospel.[4]

It is not easy to decide how much of this Synoptic and Johannine material expresses Jesus' own attitude and how much the faith of the early Church in his death and resurrection. But it seems to me that we have behind the texts at our

[1] On the Johannine version, see Léon-Dufour, 'Le signe du Temple selon saint Jean', *Rech. S.R.* xxxix (1951–2), 164 ff.

[2] Léon-Dufour, *op. cit.* p. 166; Cullmann, 'L'opposition', pp. 168 ff.

[3] Rev. xxi. 22 reads: 'And I saw no temple in the city, for its temple is the Lord God the Almighty and the Lamb.' Elsewhere in Rev. there is a double attitude to the heavenly temple: it is said to exist, and its worship to be connected with that of the Church on earth; it is also said to have been replaced by God and Jesus. See Braun, 'In spiritu et veritate', pp. 492 ff. Cf. Feuillet, 'La demeure céleste et la destinée des chrétiens', *Rech. S.R.* xliv (1956), 361 ff.   [4] See Braun, *op. cit.* pp. 255 ff. and 491 ff.

disposal a historical nucleus in which Jesus, criticizing the temple and teaching its replacement, referred to his own person. He represented the new dimension of fellowship with God which was to outdistance the old cultus. In its negative aspect this meant a sharp criticism of the actual temple and its worship; in its positive aspect, it meant a new fellowship with God, centred on himself and replacing the temple. The Synoptics and John are agreed on this point. This replacement is conceived as an eschatological fact. The texts which speak of the Spirit coming over Jesus provide the conditions on which this replacement can be realized, once Jesus' commission—suffering and death—has been carried out.

When we compare these texts with the Qumran material we find in effect two different forms of expression for one and the same principle. Criticism of the temple leads to the notion of the transfer of the role of the old temple in maintaining fellowship with God to a new temple. In Qumran it was believed that the presence and the glory of God had already been transferred to the community; the Gospels as a rule place Jesus the Messiah over against the temple only after his death. But the Spirit of God was upon him during his earthly ministry. It is this principle of replacement of the old by the new, whether the new be conceived as a person or a community, individual or collective, which is so distinctive for Qumran and the New Testament. This doctrine is to be found in the Epistles of the New Testament, where it in fact stands closer to the Qumran texts than in the Gospels. The Epistles never say that Jesus is the 'new' temple; it is always the community, the Church, which has this position. It is true that this 'new' temple is brought into being through Christ or the Spirit, but the actual temple is the collective, the community, as in Qumran. The resemblance to Qumran also extends to details in the Epistles, details which have no equivalent in the Gospels; here the Epistles are much nearer Qumran than the Gospels.

This is capable of a number of different interpretations. It may mean that Jesus was not acquainted with Qumran's example of a closed community to which the temple and the cultus were transferred, but that this idea was introduced into the early Church at a later date, and christianized. Hence the resemblances between the temple symbolism of Qumran and the New Testament Epistles. But in that case the infiltration of Qumran traditions must have taken place at a very early date, or it would not be represented in such divergent traditions as Paul, I Peter and Hebrews. It is more likely, however, that Jesus knew of Qumran's sharp criticism of the Jerusalem temple and its cultus, and knew also that they claimed to be the true temple of God. It is similarly possible that he may have adopted the principles followed in Qumran: criticism and replacement. In his case, the replacement took place in his own person and the new dimension of fellowship with God which he represented. This depended in the last resort upon his consciousness of being the Messiah, which determined the whole of his dealings with Israel and his own personal attitude to his task. Whereas the Qumran texts represent the 'new' temple as a collective, namely the community, the Gospels lay the stress on the replacement of the temple by an individual, Jesus the Messiah. Paul and the other writers of the Epistles return to the collective view, in that they represent the Church as the 'new' temple. But this collective is founded by, and owes its existence to Jesus. This need not imply a conflict between Gospels and Epistles on this point. The fact that Jesus' positive teaching on the 'new' temple was concentrated around the person of the Messiah need not imply total subordination of the collective aspect; we have every reason to regard Jesus in the light of the common Jewish principle that the individual can represent the collective, the people.

The knowledge at our disposal is as yet too sparse to say whether this hypothesis is fully acceptable. But we may perhaps come a step closer to the final solution by comparing the relative positions occupied by the concepts of individual and collective in the Qumran texts and the Gospels. This is a matter of the self-estimation of the Qumran community and Jesus respectively in the situation created by the coming of the last days, and its implications for the subject of temple symbolism. We have already seen in the texts we have quoted that Messianic self-consciousness and temple symbolism were organically connected, both in Qumran and the New Testament; Christology and temple symbolism condition each other.[1]

---

[1] See above, pp. 99 ff.

CHAPTER V

TEMPLE SYMBOLISM AND CHRISTOLOGY, COLLECTIVE AND INDIVIDUAL

THERE are a number of expressions in the Synoptic Gospels which are of the utmost importance for the expression of Jesus' Messianic consciousness. Prominent among these are the expressions Son of man, Son of God and Son of David. We might also reckon *Ebed Yahweh* in this group, for although the actual term is relatively unimportant in the Gospels, the Old Testament figure it represents provides a background to a number of sayings of Jesus.[1] These terms express various aspects of the person and calling of Jesus the Messiah. They are consistently used in the synoptic traditions to refer to Jesus and to illustrate his work; they thus apply to an individual. But at the same time these Messianic terms are applied in late Judaism not only to an individual Messianic figure but also to the people of Israel, in which case they refer to a collective. This oscillation and combination of individual and collective is of course typical of the Old Testament and late Judaism. What is interesting in this context is that the Qumran texts make use of parts of the different idea complexes to which these terms belong in order to describe the tasks of the collective community in the last days; they do not use these terms to refer to an individual Messiah.

If we begin with the term *Ebed Yahweh* and the texts from Deutero-Isaiah, it seems that the ideas they represent were in a number of cases applied to the Qumran community. The *Ebed* was able to make atonement for sins by his suffering: the Qumran community believed itself, and its individual members, to be called to make atonement for sins. The verb כפר is frequently used in this context, a verb which in the Old Testament refers to the 'atoning' activities of the priests.[2] Thus we

---

[1] See e.g. Jeremias, art. παῖς θεοῦ, *T.W.B.* v, 698 ff.

[2] This must be considered in the context of other priestly characteristics in the ideology of the community. See above, pp. 4 ff.

can read in 1QS iii. 6 ff. that the man who lives in accordance with the Law, and with the community's interpretation of the Law, thereby makes atonement for all sins, becomes clean from them and can sprinkle himself with the water of purification and attain sanctification. When such a man accepts the rule of the community, and follows its precepts and purifications, he obtains a share in the spirit which the community possesses, and wins atonement (cf. C.D. ii. 5, iii. 18). But this atonement is not merely a matter for the individual; it concerns the whole of the community and the people, and affects what will happen in connexion with the final assault of evil. When the community functions as 'the new temple', atonement is made for sins, since the following of the precepts of the Law implies that there is laid 'a foundation of truth for Israel, for the community of the eternal covenant, to make atonement for all those who of their own free will have dedicated themselves to (be) a sanctuary in Aaron and a house of truth in Israel...' (1QS v. 5 ff.). The atonement which takes place in and through the community is related to the temple cultus, since faithful observance of the rule of the community is regarded as being a sacrifice pleasing in the sight of God, the effect of which is to make atonement for sins.[1] We encounter the same idea in another of the 'temple' texts (1QS viii. 3 ff.), in which the community is called the 'new temple'; sacrifices are offered in this temple, with the result that 'atonement is made for the land and judgement over the evil one' (cf. 1QS ix. 4, which is also a 'temple' text). As in 1QSa i. 3 'the land' refers to the land and people of Israel; it is this for which atonement is made through the work of the community. But at the same time judgement is proclaimed on all those who refuse to accept the fact of the community, its task and its election; this judgement means the ultimate end of all its enemies.

But these texts do not merely contain general impressions on the subject of 'atonement': we find expressions which are undoubtedly connected with the 'Servant' passages in Deutero-Isaiah.[2] It seems likely, therefore, that the community regarded

---

[1] In other Jewish circles the works of the Law could be regarded as having atoning significance; see E. Lohse, *Märtyrer und Gottesknecht*, F.R.L.A.N.T.(N.F.), XLVI (1955), 24 ff.

[2] See W. H. Brownlee, 'The Servant of the Lord in the Qumran Scrolls, I', *B.A.S.O.R.* CXXXII (1953), 8 ff., and II, *B.A.S.O.R.* CXXXV (1954), 33 ff.;

itself as that Servant of the Lord who was to carry out the works of the Lord for the salvation of the 'land'. The life of the community in perfect obedience to the precepts of the Law and the terms of the new covenant meant atonement for the people of God. But at the same time there are other themes from the 'Servant' passages which may have been used. 1QH thus contains passages which may refer to the *Ebed Yahweh* as the one who possesses the Spirit of the Lord and has knowledge (cf. Isa. xlii. 1), which in the case of the community meant that it possessed the Spirit of God and the secret of wisdom.[1] Although the *Hodayot* texts are often in the first person singular, and may have been the work of the Teacher of Righteousness, the collective aspect is dominant,[2] in the sense that emphasis is placed not on the personal experience of the Teacher but on that which is typical of the situation of the community. All that happens to him happens to the community: the Teacher is the type of the community. Another aspect of the *Ebed* complex is the figure of the despised Servant of the Lord. This is the description of the community in for example 1QH vii. 26f. The community is stricken and smitten (cf. Isa. liii. 4).[3] The work of the Servant as a witness to truth and justice (Isa. xlii. 3f., 6; xliii. 10, 12) is likewise applied to the community.[4]

Thus the themes of the 'Servant' texts of Deutero-Isaiah have been used by the community in the description of its own function; the *Ebed* has been interpreted collectively, in line

Bruce, *Biblical Exegesis in the Qumran Texts*, pp. 50ff.; Black, *The Scrolls and Christian Origins*, pp. 128f.; Betz, 'Felsenmann und Felsengemeinde', pp. 50f., etc.   [1] Cf. Bruce, *op. cit.* p. 54.

[2] This is not to say that there is no individual subject. But the 'I' of the *Hodayot* is one who considers himself to represent the collective, the community. Taken in this way, there is no conflict between individual and collective. See e.g. Holm-Nielsen, *Hodayot*, pp. 329ff.

[3] See Bruce, *Biblical Exegesis in the Qumran Texts*, pp. 54f. 1QH iv. 8f. says that 'I' have been despised and rejected, despite the mighty deeds done by God through 'me'. 'For they banish me from my land as a bird from its nest and all my companions and kinsmen were banished from me and have esteemed me as a useless tool.' This suggests the saying of Jesus: 'Foxes have holes, and birds of the air have nests; but the Son of man has nowhere to lay his head' (Matt. viii. 20, Luke ix. 58). The indirect reference here to the sufferings of Jesus has been pointed out e.g. by Fuller, *The Mission and Achievement of Jesus* (1954), p. 104. This is confirmed by the 1QH iv text.   [4] Cf. Black, *The Scrolls and Christian Origins*, pp. 128f.

with the collective aspect of certain of the Deutero-Isaiah texts (for example Isa. xlix. 3). It is also worth noticing that the functions of atonement, judgement and the stewardship of truth and justice have been combined with temple symbolism (this is particularly true of 1QS). We may take the best example, the term 'to make atonement'. It would seem that the prominence of this concept had to do with the main implications of atonement, connected as they were with life in accordance with the Law and the cultic purifications which replaced the sacrifices and consequent atonement of the Jerusalem temple. Little is said, on the other hand, about death, suffering and persecution having atoning effect. That side of the work of the *Ebed Yahweh* is not prominent. It is just possible that it can be traced behind such texts as 1QpHab v. 4 f., and an occasional text in 1QH.[1] But it seems unlikely that the suffering which the community and its leader had to undergo was regarded as atoning.[2] The main interest seems to have been concentrated on that atonement which was connected with the concept of sacrifice: atonement is therefore centred on the idea of the cult of the new temple.[3] Nor had the vicarious aspect of the suffering of the Servant a prominent place in late Judaism. When martyrs and prophets had to suffer, their suffering, though it might have had some atoning aspect, had not

[1] Cf. Bruce, *op. cit.* pp. 55f.

[2] Carmignac, 'Les citations de l'Ancien Testament, et spécialement des Poèmes du Serviteur, dans les Hymnes de Qumrân', *R.Q.* II (1959–60), 384 ff., is a useful corrective to the hasty conclusion that there must be a link between the *Hodayot* and the *Ebed Yahweh*. Carmignac's view, that the sufferings of the Teacher of Righteousness were never given atoning significance, I consider preferable to that of Bruce.

[3] We observe that the interpretation of the *Ebed* which is given in Targum Jonathan liii is also combined with the idea of a 'new temple'. At the close of ch. lii it says that the *Shekinah* of God has left Zion because of the sin of the people, but that it will return when the 'holy remnant' appears and purifies itself (8 ff.). The same idea recurs in liii. 3 ff. 'The righteous one' shall 'build up the sanctuary that was polluted because of our transgressions and given up because of our iniquities...'. The people of Israel shall be forgiven for the sake of the 'anointed one'. At the same time there are striking resemblances in the theme of Targ. liii. 2, which deals with the growth of the 'righteous one' as a tree, stretching out its roots to the fountains of life, and in 1QH viii. 6 ff., which takes up the same subject from the point of view of the community. Cf. Gärtner, *Die rätselhaften Termini*, pp. 21 ff.

the same significance as the voluntary vicarious suffering of the *Ebed*.[1]

In the Gospels, on the other hand, it is an individual—Jesus —who appears as the *Ebed* of the Lord. The atonement which he claimed to make was not so much a result of his life of obedience to the Law as of his suffering and death. It is his death on the cross which brings about atonement.[2] So although the Qumran texts and the Gospels interpret the *Ebed* in different ways, both make it clear that the community and Jesus respectively have been given the task of fulfilling the function of the *Ebed* among men—whether it is a matter of a collective or an individual who does so.

The figure of the Son of man (Dan. vii) was undoubtedly of great importance for Jesus' Messianic consciousness, and it seems to me that he himself was responsible for choosing the term to express certain vital aspects of his work. The application of the concept of the Son of man to Jesus the individual is entirely in line with the complex surrounding the figure of the *Ebed*. But there is another fact to be taken into account: that the Son of man in Daniel vii was interpreted collectively by many of Jesus' contemporaries. In Daniel he is the representative of the holy people, and must be seen in connexion with the most prominent figures in the account, 'the saints of the most High'.[3] According to Daniel vii the Messianic task of the Son of man was to judge and to exercise universal dominion.[4] But at the same time 'the saints' are said to have a similar function, and they must suffer and be refined until the time of their

---

[1] Cf. Cullmann, *Die Christologie des Neuen Testaments*, pp. 56f.

[2] See further Jeremias, art. παῖς θεοῦ, *T.W.B.* v, 698ff.

[3] On the interchange of individual and collective in the term 'Son of man', see Cullmann, *Die Christologie des Neuen Testaments*, pp. 141 ff.; Bruce, *Biblical Exegesis in the Qumran Texts*, pp. 56f.; and Coppens, 'Le Fils de l'homme daniélique et les relectures de Dan., VII. 13, dans les apocryphes et les écrits du Nouveau Testament', *Ephem. Theol. Lov.* xxxvii (1962), 7f. Coppens expresses doubts as to the identification of the Son of man with the 'saints of the most High', but I consider that his grounds for doing so are inadequate (pp. 11ff.). See rather T. W. Manson, 'The Son of Man in Daniel, Enoch and the Gospels' (publ. in *Studies in the Gospels and Epistles*, 1962, pp. 126ff.).

[4] This is a theme which has points of contact with the Wisdom literature. See Feuillet, 'Le Fils de l'homme de Daniel et la tradition biblique', p. 336, and Larsson, *Christus als Vorbild*, pp. 128ff.

dominion comes. The terms in which their suffering is expressed
in the texts leads our thought naturally to the *Ebed Yahweh*
texts and it has already been pointed out, and rightly so, that
in Daniel we have an interpretation of the *Ebed* figure in terms
of the suffering of the 'saints'.[1] The collective 'the saints' must
suffer and be purified as an *Ebed* of the Lord. References to
the Qumran texts have been made in connexion with this
combination of themes from the 'Servant' texts and the Son
of man.[2] Here too there have been noted slight but undeniable
resemblances between the terminology used in the Son of man
passages and 'the saints of the most High'. Although as far as
we are aware the former term does not occur in the Qumran
texts,[3] it seems that the community regarded itself as a collective, with the Messianic task of judging and administering
universal dominion. It seems on the other hand possible to
interpret 'the saints of the most High' in C.D. xx. 7 f. as referring
to the community: 'Let no man agree with him in property and
work, for all the saints of the most High, קדושי עליון, have cursed
him.' The term is used here as an expression of the character
of the community as the saints of God,[4] who are unable to
tolerate the presence of an unrighteous person in their midst.[5]
But the suffering of 'the saints of the most High' does not
play a particularly prominent role in the Qumran texts which

[1] H. L. Ginsberg, 'The Oldest Interpretation of the Suffering Servant',
V.T. III (1953), 400 ff., starts with the fact that 'the saints' who in Dan. are
said to suffer, are called *maskilim*, and that the *Ebed* is called *maskil*, Isa. lii.
13. He also compares Dan. xii. 3, which speaks of the *maskilim* which
justify 'many', with Isa. liii. 11, which says that the *Ebed* will 'make many
to be accounted righteous'. The same theme is discussed by Brownlee,
'The Servant of the Lord in the Qumran Scrolls, 1', 12 ff., and Feuillet, 'Le
Fils de l'homme de Daniel et la tradition biblique', *R.B.* LX (1953), 336 f.

[2] Black, 'Servant of the Lord and Son of Man', *S.J.Th.* VI (1953), 8 f.
The terms *Ebed Yahweh* and 'Son of man' (and 'Son of God') are combined
in other contexts; see W. Manson, *Jesus the Messiah*⁶ (1952), pp. 99 ff.

[3] We have no certain evidence of the term 'Son of man' in Daniel's
sense.

[4] Hvidberg, *Menigheden*, p. 193, interprets the term as referring to the
angels, but this seems unnecessary, since the members of the community
are often called 'saints' and are accorded the function of judgement.

[5] Van der Ploeg, *Le Rouleau de la Guerre*, p. 143, couples the expression 'the
elect of the holy people' (1QM xii. 1) with Dan. xii. 7 and vii. 27—a likely
connexion between the 'saints' of Dan. and the elect and holy Qumran
community.

have been quoted in this context. The functions of judgement and witnessing to the truth, on the other hand, have their definite place. The combination of *Ebed* and 'Son of man' themes (the latter representing 'the saints') which has been sought in the Qumran texts in connexion with the functions of atonement, witnessing and judgement thus has support in the material—provided that no attempt be made to read into the concept of atonement the specifically vicarious element from the *Ebed* passages of Deutero-Isaiah.[1] We have reason to believe that the Qumran community made use of Daniel's motif of 'the saints of the most High', applying its details to their own situation. The motifs from Daniel which Jesus is represented in the Gospels as applying to himself thus correspond to a collective interpretation on the part of the Qumran community.

The most suitable Qumran text from which to illustrate this subject of the *Ebed* theme and Daniel is perhaps 1QS viii, which is also an important text for the study of temple symbolism. Here, too, we find clear associations with the concept of the 'new temple' and the new fellowship with God. As in Targum Jonathan liii, where an exposition of the *Ebed* theme is combined with the idea of the return of God's *Shekinah* to the temple, so we find in Daniel a combination of 'the saints of the most High' and the idea of the 'new temple' which is to be established in the last days. On the subject of the evil to come it is said that one of the 'horns' of the 'he-goat' shall attack 'the Prince of the host', take away the daily sacrifice and defile the temple (viii. 11 ff.). But the good to come also stands related to the temple; atonement shall be made for the evils of the people and eternal righteousness shall be established, 'to seal both vision and prophet, and to anoint a most holy place' (ix. 24). This vision of the future has sometimes been interpreted in spiritual categories, the implication being that

---

[1] Bruce, *Biblical Exegesis in the Qumran Texts*, p. 55, writes 'When we consider how the statement of Isa. liii. 10, that the Servant will "make many to be accounted righteous", is echoed in Dan. xii. 3, where "those who are wise" (the presented *maskilim*) are described as men "who turn many to righteousness", we may find further significance in the fact that the members of the community called themselves *maskilim*, claiming no doubt to be in the succession of Daniel's *maskilim* (a claim which in all likelihood was historically justified)'.

'the saints' make up a new temple, a spiritual temple. It is the kingdom of 'the saints' which is called an anointed sanctuary upon which rests the presence of God (vii. 13–14).[1] Although it is not easy to support this 'spiritual' interpretation on a basis of the diffuse material we are given in Daniel, it is important to note that the concept of the 'anointed sanctuary' is connected with the ideas of the Son of man and the 'saints of the most High'.[2] This combination is particularly significant in view of the close relationship between Daniel and the Qumran texts.[3]

Another of the Christological terms rich in associations which are used in the Gospels is 'son', 'the Son of God'. Jesus is called 'the Son', that is the one who is specifically chosen.[4] The concept is interpreted in the Old Testament and in late Judaism both collectively and individually. It may thus be used to denote the people of Israel. Israel is God's 'first-born son, בני בכרי' (Exod. iv. 22). But it can also be used in an individual sense to refer to the angels, or to the king.[5] A collective interpretation of the term 'son' can also be found in late Jewish texts (for example Ps. Sol. xviii. 4, ὡς υἱὸν πρωτότοκον μονογενῆ). Again Israel is like the first-born and only son of God. Scholars differ as to whether the term could be used in late Judaism as an appellation of the Messiah.[6] But since it

[1] Feuillet, 'Le Fils de l'homme de Daniel', pp. 197 f., also has references to older literature.

[2] The expression is unusual, and may indicate that the temple was regarded as being a collective of persons. So Feuillet, op. cit. p. 197. Brownlee, 'The Servant of the Lord, 1', pp. 13 f., considers this to be an interpretation of the Ebed as the 'saints', and writes that 'the collective interpretation of the Servant of the Lord would seem to embrace Jerusalem and its temple as well as the "prince" and his people...'.

[3] The difference between Dan. and the Qumran texts is particularly clear in this respect: for the latter, the temple was to be replaced on account of its profanation, not by Antiochus, but by the priests of the people. Nor is the emphasis in Qumran laid on a future temple; their temple is already in existence.

[4] On this problem see e.g. Cullmann, Die Christologie des Neuen Testaments, pp. 281 f.; van Iersel, 'Der Sohn' in den synoptischen Jesusworten (1961).

[5] See Cullmann, op. cit. pp. 279 ff.; Bieneck, Sohn Gottes, Abh. Theol. A.u.N.T. xxi (1951), 13 ff.; de Kruijf, Der Sohn des lebendigen Gottes, Anal. Bibl. xvi (1962), 3 ff.

[6] See e.g. Lövestam, Son and Saviour, pp. 15 ff., though he does not draw a clear distinction between 'son', the 'anointed one' and παῖς. Cf. de Kruijf, op. cit. pp. 20 ff.

has been seen that the concepts of the Son of man and the 'saints' (as in Daniel) were made to illustrate the task of the Qumran community in the last days, it is no longer surprising that the term 'son' could be used in the same way. One of the texts from Cave 4 speaks in traditional Old Testament terms of Israel as God's 'first-born son'.[1] The text reads: '...and thou hast created us for thy glory and thou hast called us thy sons before all peoples. For thou hast called Israel "my first-born son". And thou hast chastened us as a man chastens his son....' We can interpret 'Israel' in this passage as meaning the people of God, but there are phrases in the text which suggest that it is the Qumran community—the true Israel—which is meant. The community is God's first-born son, chosen and loved by God; and he shall lead them to their reward.

A much-discussed text which seems to me to belong in this same context is 1QH iii. 7 ff. Some have attempted to discern references to the Messiah, born in the period of distress which belongs to the Messianic age, and destined to bring salvation to his people.[2] But this individual interpretation is probably wrong;[3] lines 8 and 11, for example, have verbs in the plural. It is more likely that this text refers to the 'birth' of the community and to 'the Messianic birth-pangs' which attended it; in other words, the persecution and difficulties which accompanied the founding of the community. The passage seems to emphasize that the community is the first-born son. Further, it is possible that the one who 'gives birth' is the Teacher of Righteousness, the founder of the community. But the main point of the narrative is that it is by the power of God that the community has been brought to birth (cf. C.D. i. 5 ff., which states that the community was created by God).

The text, in 1QH iii. 7 ff., reads: '[And] I was in distress as a woman in travail, bringing forth her first-born, for [her] birth-pangs came suddenly, and agonizing pain to her pangs,

[1] Baillet, 'Un recueil liturgique de Qumrân, grotte 4: "Les paroles des luminaires"', *R.B.* LXVIII (1961), 203, col. III, 4 ff.

[2] For this view see Betz, 'Das Volk seiner Kraft. Zur Auslegung der Qumran-Hodaja iii. 1–18,' *N.T.S.* V (1958–9), 67.

[3] See e.g. Betz, *op. cit.*, and 'Die Geburt der Gemeinde durch den Lehrer', *N.T.S.* III (1956–7), 314 ff.; Black, *The Scrolls and Christian Origins*, p. 150; Mansoor, *The Thanksgiving Hymns*, pp. 91 f.

to cause writhing in the womb of the pregnant one, for children have come to the pains of death. And she who conceived a male-child was distressed by her pains, for with the waves of death she shall be delivered of a man-child. And with pains of Sheol there shall break forth from the womb of the pregnant one a wondrous counsellor in his might. And there shall come forth safely a male-child from the throes of birth by the woman who was pregnant with him....'[1] Here, too, we seem to have a collective interpretation of a concept which the Gospels interpret as referring to an individual. The community is the people of God, the true and first-born son of God,[2] having a Messianic commission in the distress of the last days to bring in the day of salvation.[3] At the same time we see how even the Messianic prophecy of Isa. ix. 5 ('a wondrous counsellor in his might...') is applied to the community. The community is this 'son', and hence it has fellowship with the 'sons of heaven', the angels in heaven and the spirits of the knowledge of God (iii. 22f.).

We might also refer in this connexion to 4QFlor. i. 10ff., an exposition of the prophecy of Nathan which reads: 'I [will be] a father to him, and he shall be my son' (II Sam. vii. 14). The context of this prophecy in 4QFlor. makes it not unlikely that by 'son' may be meant the collective unit, the community.[4] Again, the most convincing reconstruction of the text of 4QFlor. i. 19 gives the expression 'the anointed one' a collective interpretation.[5] The expression in Ps. ii. 2, 'his anointed', against whom the kings of the earth rise up, seems to be applied to the leaders of the community or to the community as such: 'The elect of Israel in the last days.' It may be that in another Messianic term we have echoes of the same principle. Behind the word ναζωραῖος in Matt. ii. 23 there may be an interpretation according to which Jesus is the Messianic 'root', a word

[1] For the translation, see Mansoor, *op. cit.* pp. 112ff., and Black, *op. cit.* p. 149.

[2] The text reads בכור, 'first-born'.

[3] Black, *The Scrolls and Christian Origins*, p. 150.

[4] See above, pp. 35 and 40.

[5] Yadin, 'A Midrash on II Sam. vii and Ps. i–ii (4QFlorilegium)', *I.E.J.* IX (1959), 98, interprets the text as follows: 'The hidden interpretation of this refers [to the Sons of Sadok the pri]ests and th[ey are] the elect of Israel in the End of Days.'

which the Qumran texts normally use with reference to the community, and which the early Church also interpreted collectively (Acts xxiv. 5).[1] The expression 'son of David' is also interpreted in the Qumran texts in such a way as to suggest that it is the community which fulfils the Davidic prophecies.[2]

Another of the Christological terms in the Gospels which is important for the understanding of the subject of temple symbolism is the 'stone', λίθος. According to Mk. xii. 10 with par. and Luke xx. 18 Jesus regarded himself, both in respect of his person and his commission, as the 'stone' chosen by God, that is the one on whom the new fellowship with God should rest, the 'corner-stone' of the new temple.[3] But there is another aspect which Jesus may have used, namely that summed up in the expression 'the rejected stone'. This phrase is found in late Jewish texts in connexion with the figure of the *Ebed*,[4] but it is not impossible that this combination may have existed in Jesus' day. In addition there are late Jewish traditions in which the 'stone' represented the Messiah, the King.[5] The text quoted in the Gospels is that of Ps. cxviii. 22: 'The stone which the builders rejected has become the chief corner-stone.' The same term, with Christological implications, recurs in traditions of more recent date, for example I Pet. ii. 4ff., where Jesus is said to be the 'living stone'. He is a precious stone to the believer, but a stone of offence and a rock of stumbling to the unbeliever. In this account reference is made to three Old Testament texts, Ps. cxviii. 22, Isa. xxviii. 16 ('Behold, I am laying in Zion for a foundation a stone, a tested stone, a precious corner-stone, of a sure foundation')[6] and Isa. viii. 14 ('a stone of offence, and a rock of stumbling').

[1] See Gärtner, *Die rätselhaften Termini*, pp. 21 ff.
[2] See above, pp. 36 ff.   [3] See Jeremias, art. λίθος, *T.W.B.* IV, 277 ff.
[4] Gärtner, 'טליא als Messiasbezeichnung', *Sv. Exeget. Årsbok* XVIII–XIX (1953–4), 98 ff.   [5] Cf. Jeremias, *op. cit.* pp. 276 f.
[6] I Pet. ii. 6 follows the LXX text closely. An important disagreement between this text and Isa. xxviii. 16 is that the 'foundation' is never mentioned, though both the Masoretic and LXX have it twice in this passage. The 'foundation' is a key-word in the Qumran texts, and it is surprising that it should be missing from I Pet. ii, particularly in view of the considerable resemblances there are between I Pet. ii and Qumran. It may be due to a polemical attitude to the claims of the Qumran community; or to a complete shift in focus, from the firmly based community to faith in Christ.

In our exposition of I Pet. ii. 4 ff. we showed the importance in certain Qumran texts of the idea of the 'stone' in the context of the community as the 'new temple'. For example 1QS viii. 4 states, with reference to the community, that it comprises 'the Holy place' and 'the Holy of holies' in the temple, and that its sacrifices helped make atonement for the 'land'. But the 'temple' also has 'the tested wall, חומת הבחן', and 'the precious corner-stone, פנת יקר'. The community, the temple, is 'the tested wall and the precious corner-stone. Its foundations shall not be shaken and shall not be moved from their place, a most holy dwelling place for Aaron....' There can be no doubt that these words are based on Isa. xxviii. 16, though the word 'stone' has been exchanged for 'wall' (perhaps because the theology of the community laid such stress on the idea of the immovable foundation).[1] Once more it is a case of a concept which in certain late Jewish traditions was Messianic in character being applied to the collective unit, the community. It is not the Messiah, or any other spiritual leader, who is the 'stone': it is the community which fulfils the prophecies of 'the precious corner-stone'. As the Gospels and I Pet. ii called Jesus 'the stone' who is either an offence or a blessing for men, so it is with the Qumran community. It is either a glory and a fulfilment or a judgement and a vengeance. But there is no parallel in the Qumran texts to the theme of the 'rejected stone', as we find it in the teaching of Jesus. The Qumran picture is dominated by 'immovability'.

Another of the Qumran texts which we have already seen to contain important comparative material, 1QH vi. 25 ff., has this interpretation of Isa. xxviii. 16 f.: 'for thou dost lay a foundation upon the rock, and the beams according to the measuring-line of the Law and the plumb-line [of truth?] in order to [get] tested stones, אבני בחן, [for a] strong [building] which is not shaken, and all who enter shall not be moved...'.[2] The subject of this psalm is how 'I' came to be in a desperate situation, like a ship in a storm. The pit called 'me' but God helped 'me' through his mighty works, the 'foundation', the 'rock', 'a strong building' and 'tested stones'—all of which express the might of God, and his immovability in the face of

[1] See above, pp. 27 and 76f.
[2] On the restoration of the text, see above, p. 76.

even Belial's attacks. It seems to me that this text gives a clear account of how 'I' (speaking on behalf of the community) am saved from the wrath of unrighteousness, placed on the firm foundation of the Law of God, and made into a firmly established 'house', a 'strong building'. It is of little consequence in this text whether the one speaking is the Teacher of Righteousness or some other, since the theme of the hymn is the community as a collective unit. God has laid the 'foundations' (this has to do with the concept of revelation), and the community has to hold fast to the 'truth' which is revealed. The community thus becomes the unshakable building; its members the 'tested stones', which cannot be stirred from their place. The interpretation of Isa. xxviii. 16 seems to be based on the idea of the collective, and one result is that the singular 'a tested stone' is changed to the plural, though we cannot say whether this is due to the image of the 'building' or the actual collective interpretation. What is essential in this context is that there was in Qumran a collective interpretation of the 'stone' motif which was linked with a symbolism based on the image of a 'building', whether a house or a temple.

A similar theme is found in one other passage in the *Hodayot*. This is 1QH vii. 8f., which is similar in many ways to the previous text: '...thou hast made me as a strong tower, into a high wall, חומה. And thou hast placed my building on a rock and the eternal bases (are) my foundation. And my walls are a tested wall, חומת בחן, which cannot be moved....'[1] Once more we can trace an interpretation of Isa. xxviii. 16 behind these words. This passage uses the same familiar expressions as those we met with in the other texts: the strong tower, the tested wall, the building, the rock, immovability, etc. Again it seems that all these expressions refer to the community. It is the collective, the community, which is created by God and which can withstand all the onslaughts of the evil one in the last days, because it is based on the truths of the Law. But at the same time the text says that God has made 'me' into a strong tower and a high wall, and speaks of 'my' walls. This need not mean that we are compelled to assume an individual interpretation; the meaning seems to be that the 'I'

[1] Once more 'wall', חומה, replaces 'stone'; this seems to be a distinct Qumran exegetical tradition.

stands for the fixed and immovable element in the community as the work of God in the last days. What the 'I' says applies both to him and to the community as a whole. Once more, as in the Old Testament, collective and individual are interwoven so closely as to be inseparable. A comparison with 1QH vi. 25 ff., however, makes it clear that it is the community which is particularly referred to here—a principle which applies to other of the texts we have discussed above.

Thus we see that certain Qumran texts reveal the existence of a special exegetical tradition of the 'stone' motif of Isa. xxviii. 16, a tradition in which the typical element is that the whole is based on the collective concept of the community, which is the precious stone and the tested wall of which the Scripture speaks. This interpretation is linked, in the texts we have been considering, with a temple symbolism. If we compare this tradition with that of the Gospels we find that there too is a tradition in which Jesus is called the 'stone'. As Messiah he is the precious corner-stone. This interpretation is based for the most part on Ps. cxviii. 22, but also on Isa. xxviii. 16, a text closely related to Ps. cxviii.[1] Further, it seems possible to connect this 'stone' tradition with the idea of the new temple and the new fellowship with God.[2] This tradition recurs in I Pet. ii. 4 ff., once more in connexion with an exposition of the theme of the temple. Of particular interest here is the fact that the individual interpretation of the 'stone' as Jesus is combined with a collective interpretation, in which all Christians are said to be 'living stones' in the temple. It may be thought that the plural ('living stones') here has simply developed out of the idea of Jesus as the 'stone' and the Christians as the temple, and that it is unnecessary to look for a background in the Qumran texts or elsewhere. But we have seen the important comparisons which can be made between these texts and I Peter, and I am inclined to think that the basis of this usage should be sought in the oscillation between collective and individual we have tried to describe. Further, I Pet. ii provides evidence that both these interpretations were known and used. We conclude that the plural form 'stones' belongs in the context of the tradition of the community as the temple.

[1] Cf. Jeremias, *Golgotha*, pp. 77 f.
[2] This is the view energetically advocated by Jeremias in a number of books.

In our examination of these Christological and Messianic terms—*Ebed Yahweh*, Son of man, Son, 'stone'—we have seen how the Qumran texts for the most part interpret them collectively. Part of the self-consciousness of the community was made up of the idea that they were the group who were called to fulfil the Old Testament prophecies connected with these terms. The Gospels represent Jesus as having made use of these same terms, though he gave them a new content and a new meaning by applying them to himself. He had to fulfil these prophecies as an individual. There is of course a great deal that is uncertain in this interpretation of the situation, but it seems to extend to the question of temple symbolism as well. In the Qumran texts it is the community that is the temple; in the Gospels, as far as we can see, the interest is centred on Jesus himself. He is the temple; it is through him that a new fellowship with God is established. There is no suggestion that his disciples or his followers constitute a 'new temple'. In Qumran the temple was replaced by the community; in the New Testament by Jesus himself.

But when we observe the way in which these Old Testament terms are applied to Jesus the Messiah (or to the community) we should remember that the collective and individual aspects are not mutually exclusive; nor do they stand in opposition to each other. Behind Jesus' self-consciousness as Messiah there is also a clearly defined sense of representation. He represents the true Israel in his own person; he represents the people of God, to whom the promises are made.[1] The main focus of interest is nevertheless his own person. When we say that the individual in the Qumran *Hodayot* represents the community, there is no doubt that it is the fate, situation and commission of the community which lies uppermost. The individual, whether the Teacher of Righteousness or some other, in no way occupies the same dominant position as the Jesus of the Gospels. And although individual and collective are interwoven, the focus of interest can shift; thus in the Qumran texts it is often the collective aspect which is most prominent, while in the Gospels it is the individual.

[1] On the relationship between individual and collective, see T. W. Manson, 'The Son of Man', pp. 140 ff.; Cullmann, *Die Christologie des Neuen Testaments*, pp. 53 f., 290.

We have noted in the Epistles of the New Testament that Jesus is never said to be the 'temple', the term being reserved for the Christian community. This being so, we appear to be faced with a number of possibilities. One is that Jesus or the early Church arrived at a view of the temple and its symbolism *via* an independent study of the Old Testament and late Jewish tradition. This seems however to be the least likely alternative. Another possibility is that the Qumran temple symbolism entered the Church through the conversion of important individuals to the Christian faith. Jesus, on the other hand, would on this hypothesis have known nothing of the Qumran temple criticism or symbolism. But it is not really feasible to draw such a hard and fast distinction between Jesus and Qumran, or between Jesus and the early Church. The explanation must be sought elsewhere, and since our knowledge of the factual situation is strictly limited, we must present our findings in the form of a hypothesis.

It is possible that the various interpretations of temple symbolism that we have described have their background in a development which we might describe as follows. The centre of gravity for the Qumran texts was the actual community, as the only certain factor in the last days—certain because based on the Law; hence their comparatively minor interest in a saviour, a Messiah. The Teacher of Righteousness, though he seems to have founded the community, made no claim to be the expected Messiah; nor were the common Messianic texts, found elsewhere in late Judaism, expounded with reference to him. Nor had the expected Messiahs of Aaron and Israel any particular soteriological character. One is a high priest, a spiritual leader in the time of victory; the other a warrior, the general of the final conflict. These provide us with little or no material which we can compare with the Jesus of the Gospels, and with the central terms Son of man, Son of God and *Ebed Yahweh*. The texts so far published show that interest was instead concentrated on the community, its life, its rule and its expectations. And this being so, it is easy to understand how it was that the collective unit became the bearer of so many Messianic characteristics, and how the community came to be regarded as the chief source of fulfilment of the prophecies of Scripture.

I consider it not unlikely, from the Gospel material, that Jesus was aware of the principal Qumran tenet, that the community had replaced the desecrated Jerusalem temple. But since the teaching of Jesus was concentrated on the person of the Messiah and an individual interpretation of the Messianic terms, it is not surprising that the replacement for the temple which he offered was his own person, and the fellowship he established. His body, which was to be 'destroyed' in death, was also the new temple which was to be built.

The simplest explanation of the detailed form taken by this temple symbolism in the New Testament Epistles seems to be that the early Church was able to carry on from this point, that Jesus and the fellowship around him had replaced the temple. The doctrines of the Risen Christ and the coming of the Holy Spirit to the community were later able to create the conditions in which these Qumran temple traditions could be adopted and developed. It may be that the traditions in question were brought into the Church by former members of the Qumran sect or other Essene groups; be that as it may, they received new meaning from the faith and the teachings based on Christ.[1] That is why the idea of the community as the spiritual temple appears in forms reminiscent, both in outline and detail, of the Qumran texts. And since the Qumran temple symbolism was linked, as we have seen, with certain Messianic concepts, it is not impossible that a similar association of temple symbolism and Messianic terminology took place in the New Testament. Hence the bond between temple symbolism and Christology. It is typical of the temple symbolism of the New Testament that Jesus should be called the 'foundation' of the entire structure, the entire temple. He is the revealer of 'truth'; through his death and resurrection there have been brought about the divine works which provide the conditions for the emergence of this new temple symbolism. The new order is determined 'through Christ' and 'in Christ'; the collective temple image of Qumran has become renewed, through faith in Christ, and united with the positive teaching which the Gospels represent Jesus as giving on the subject of the 'new

[1] Some consider that Qumran traditions were introduced into the early Church during the Apostolic age. See bibliography in Rowley, 'The Qumran Sect and Christian Origins', pp. 149f.

temple'. It would hardly have been possible for these texts to have called both Christ and his followers the 'temple' at one and the same time, and as a result one aspect—the collective —gradually became more prominent. This enabled the symbolism of the temple to be expounded in terms relevant to the individual Christian, as we see in, for example, I Pet. ii. Of course the Qumran texts provided a consistent symbolism to fall back upon. A reminiscence of these two ideas, that both Jesus and the community are the 'new temple', is to be seen in Eph. ii. 20–2, where we read that Christians, as the temple, are built upon the foundation of the apostles and prophets, stewards of the mysteries of God, but that the decisive factor is Christ himself, the chief corner-stone. In him 'the whole structure is joined together and grows into a holy temple in the Lord; in whom you also are built into it for a dwelling place of God in the Spirit'. The Christian Church is the temple in which the Spirit of God dwells. But the whole of this reality is based on Jesus and his work of salvation. Christ is not the temple in his own person only; but he is the one without whom the temple could not exist.

Another element in the development of this doctrine in the early Church is the connexion between the two images 'temple' and 'body'. It has been correctly pointed out that these come into contact in Eph. ii. 20–2. The image of permanency is here linked with the image of growth.[1] The relationship is even clearer in Eph. iv. 12 and 16, though that does not mean that it is to be found nowhere but in Ephesians. We read in the Fourth Gospel, for example, in a comment on Jesus' saying about the destruction and rebuilding of the temple, 'But he spoke of the temple of his body, περὶ τοῦ ναοῦ τοῦ σώματος αὐτοῦ' (ii. 21). This is a straightforward statement of the direct relationship between the body of Christ, which passed through death and resurrection, and the 'new temple' of fellowship with God.

The association of the idea of the body of Christ, broken in death, and that of the 'new temple' is found in the Synoptics (Matt. xxvi. 61 with par.),[2] but the theological implications of this association are most clearly expressed in the Johannine

---

[1] See above, pp. 65 f.   [2] See above, pp. 111 f.

comment. But neither the Synoptics nor John say a word about the relation between those who believe in Christ and this temple. John, too, agrees with the other Gospel traditions in interpreting the temple image individually, as referring only to Jesus. It is evident that the concepts of the temple and the body were united at a very early stage in the traditions; thus we find them connected in I Cor. vi. 15–19, in a way which may give us some hint as to the process by which the image of the body of Christ emerged as a collective term. Paul, correcting members of the church of Corinth who had been guilty of immorality, states why such immorality is incompatible with the profession of Christianity. He begins with the body of Christ. Christians are to regard their bodies as members of the 'mystical' body of Christ; to have relations with a prostitute is thus to desecrate the body of Christ (vv. 15ff.).[1] He goes on to say that immorality is also a serious sin, because the body of the individual Christian is the temple of God. 'Do you not know that your body is a temple of the Holy Spirit within you, which you have from God?' (v. 19). Here the dominant thought is that of the holiness of the temple—a prominent feature of the temple symbolism of Qumran and the New Testament alike. Again we see how close was the relationship between the images of the temple and the body, and how indistinct is the line dividing individual from collective.[2] This

[1] Cf. J. Reuss, 'Die Kirche als "Leib Christi" und die Herkunft dieser Vorstellung bei dem Apostel Paulus', *B.Z.* II (1958), 105f.

[2] It is not easy to say how the individual Christian can be called a temple in which God dwells with his Spirit. Many scholars have isolated this text from the idea of the community as a temple, relating it instead to the Hellenistic background. See most recently Fitzmyer, 'Qumrân and the Interpolated Paragraph in II Cor. vi. 14–vii. 1', *C.B.Q.* XXIII (1961), 277, who refers to K. G. Kuhn and others. But this is unnecessary. The combination of the images of the body of Christ and the temple is evidence that we are in the same current of tradition as that of New Testament temple symbolism as a whole. We see, too, that the idea of the individual believer's body as the temple is not altogether dominant; the Apostle also has in mind the collective, the community. He writes, by way of explanation, that 'your body is a temple of the Holy Spirit *within you*, ἐν ὑμῖν'. The Holy Spirit is in the midst of the congregation, as was the 'Presence' of God in the temple. This may perhaps be a typical case of ambiguity in matters concerning collective and individual. Paul begins in *v.* 15 by talking about the body of the individual Christian; he goes on to talk about the collective, the body of Christ; finally he returns to the theme of the individual.

may perhaps be a link in the obscure development which separates the idea of the human body of Christ from that of the 'mystical' body, expressing the collective aspect of the Church. The Christological background of the complex of ideas surrounding the 'temple' shows how short was the step from the idea of the temple as a community to the idea of the body of Christ as a community. Jesus represents in his own person the new people of God. What happens to his body is of vital significance for every member of his Church. It is through Jesus that the temple in Jerusalem is replaced by a new fellowship with God, and it is through the body of Jesus that salvation is won and the way to the Father opened. Everyone who has faith in him is given access through him to the new fellowship, and becomes the new temple; through him the company of believers becomes his 'body'. The close connexion of the temple image with the image of the body in the teaching of Jesus makes it easier for us to understand the relationship of the two in later Christian thought. We cannot of course go so far as to say that the Pauline doctrine of the body of Christ is based on this temple symbolism; but there is certainly a close relationship between the two. It is highly likely that other concepts have had their share in influencing the idea of the Church as the body of Christ, but at the same time we cannot entirely overlook the fundamental association between this idea and that of the temple. I am led to conclude that the basis of both the temple symbolism and the doctrine of the body of Christ in the theology of Paul is to be sought in the Palestinian rather than the Hellenistic background.[1]

[1] See the review given by Reuss, 'Die Kirche als "Leib Christi"', pp. 113ff.; E. Schweizer, 'Die Kirche als Leib Christi in den paulinischen Homologumena', *T.L.Z.* LXXXVI (1961), 161ff.

BIBLIOGRAPHY

Aalen, S. '"Reign" and "House" in the Kingdom of God in the Gospels', *N.T.S.* VIII (1961–2), 215–40.

Ahlström, G. W. *Psalm 89. Eine Liturgie aus dem Ritual des leidenden Königs* (Uppsala–Lund, 1959).

Allegro, J. M. 'Fragments of a Qumran Scroll of Eschatological *Midrāšim*', *J.B.L.* LXXVII (1958), 350–4.

—— 'Further Messianic References in Qumran Literature', *J.B.L.* LXXV (1956), 174–87.

—— 'More Isaiah Commentaries from Qumran's Fourth Cave', *J.B.L.* LXXVII (1958), 215–21.

Baillet, M. 'Fragments araméens de Qumrân 2. Description de la Jérusalem nouvelle', *R.B.* LXII (1955), 222–45.

—— 'Un recueil liturgique de Qumrân, grotte 4: "Les paroles des luminaires"', *R.B.* LXVIII (1961), 195–250.

Bardtke, H. *Die Handschriftenfunde am Toten Meer*, I–II (Berlin, 1953–8).

Barrett, C. K. *The Holy Spirit and the Gospel Tradition* (London, 1947).

Barthélemy, D. and Milik, J. T. (ed.). *Discoveries in the Judaean Desert* (Oxford, 1955).

Baumgarten, J. 'Sacrifice and Worship among the Jewish Sectarians of the Dead Sea (Qumrân) Scrolls', *H.T.R.* XLVI (1953), 141–59.

Benoit, P. 'Qumrân et le Nouveau Testament', *N.T.S.* VII (1960–1), 276–96.

Betz, O. 'Das Volk seiner Kraft. Zur Auslegung der Qumran-Hodaja iii. 1–18', *N.T.S.* V (1958–9), 67–75.

—— 'Die Geburt der Gemeinde durch den Lehrer', *N.T.S.* III (1956–7), 314–26.

—— 'Felsenmann und Felsengemeinde. (Eine Parallele zu Mt 16. 17–19 in den Qumranpsalmen)', *Z.N.T.W.* XLVIII (1957), 49–77.

—— 'Le ministère cultuel dans la secte de Qumrân et dans le christianisme primitif', in *La secte de Qumrán et les origines du christianisme* (Bruges, 1959), pp. 163–202.

—— *Offenbarung und Schriftforschung in der Qumransekte* (Wiss. Unters. z. N.T., 6; Tübingen, 1960).

Bieneck, J. *Sohn Gottes als Christusbezeichnung der Synoptiker*. (Abhandl. theol. A. u. N.T., 21; Zürich, 1951).

Bietenhard, H. *Die himmlische Welt im Urchristentum und Spätjudentum* (Wiss. Unters. z. N.T., 2; Tübingen, 1951).

Black, M. 'Servant of the Lord and Son of Man', *S.J.Th.* VI (1953), 1-11.

—— 'The Messiah in the Testament of Levi xviii', *E.T.* LX (1948-9), 321-2.

—— *The Scrolls and Christian Origins. Studies in the Jewish Background of the New Testament* (Edinburgh, 1961).

Bonsirven, J. *Le Judaïsme Palestinien au temps de Jésus-Christ*, I-II (Paris, 1934-5).

Borgen, P. '"At the Age of Twenty" in 1QSa', *R.Q.* III (1960-1), 267-77.

Braun, F. M. 'In spiritu et veritate', *Rev. Thom.* LII (1952), 245-74, 485-507.

—— 'L'arrière-fond judaïque du Quatrième Évangile et la Communauté de l'Alliance', *R.B.* LXII (1955), 5-44.

Brownlee, W. H. 'The Servant of the Lord in the Qumran Scrolls, I', *B.A.S.O.R.* CXXXII (1953), 8-15.

—— 'The Servant of the Lord in the Qumran Scrolls, II', *B.A.S.O.R.* CXXXV (1954), 33-8.

Bruce, F. F. *Biblical Exegesis in the Qumran Texts* (The Hague, 1959).

Büchler, A. *Die Priester und der Cultus im letzten Jahrzehnt des Jerusalemischen Tempels* (Vienna, 1895).

Bultmann, R. *Die Geschichte der synoptischen Tradition*[4] (Göttingen, 1958).

—— *Theologie des Neuen Testaments* (Tübingen, 1948-53).

Burkill, T. A. 'Strain on the Secret: An Examination of Mark 11, 1-13, 37', *Z.N.T.W.* LI (1960), 31-46.

Burrows, M. *More Light on the Dead Sea Scrolls. New Scrolls and New Interpretations with Translations of important Recent Discoveries* (New York, 1958).

Buse, I. 'The Cleansing of the Temple in the Synoptics and in John', *E.T.* LXX (1958-9), 22-4.

Carmignac, J. *La Règle de la Guerre des Fils de Lumière contre les Fils de Ténèbres* (Paris, 1958).

—— 'Les citations de l'Ancien Testament, et spécialement des Poèmes du Serviteur, dans les Hymnes de Qumrân', *R.Q.* II (1959-60), 357-94.

—— 'L'utilité ou l'inutilité des sacrifices sanglants dans la "Règle de la Communauté" de Qumrân', *R.B.* LXIII (1956), 524-32.

Cerfaux, L. *La Théologie de l'Église suivant saint Paul*[2] (Paris, 1948).

—— 'Regale sacerdotium', *R.S.P.T.* XXVIII (1939), 5-39 (reprinted in *Ephem. Theol. Lov., Bibliotheca* 6 (1954), 283-315).

Charles, R. H. *The Testament of the Twelve Patriarchs.* Translated from the Editor's Greek Text and edited with Introduction, Notes and Indices (London, 1908).

Cody, A. *Heavenly Sanctuary and Liturgy in the Epistle to the Hebrews* (St Meinrad, Indiana, 1960).

Cole, A. *The New Temple. A Study in the Origins of the Catechetical 'Form' of the Church in the New Testament* (London, 1950).

Congar, Y. *Le mystère du temple* (Lectio Divina, 22; Paris, 1958).

Cook, S. A. 'Notes on the Relevance of the Science of Religion', in *Festschrift A. Bertholet* (Tübingen, 1950), 114–33.

Coppens, J. 'Le Fils de l'homme daniélique et les relectures de Dan., VII. 13, dans les apocryphes et les écrits du Nouveau Testament', *Ephem. Theol. Lov.* xxxvii (1962), 5–51.

—— 'Les affinités qumrâniennes de l'Épître aux Hébreux', *Nouv. Rev. Théol.* xciv (1962), 128–41, 257–82.

Cross, Fr. M. *The Ancient Library of Qumrân and Modern Biblical Studies* (London, 1958).

Cullmann, O. *Die Christologie des Neuen Testaments* (Tübingen, 1957).

—— 'L'opposition contre le temple de Jérusalem, motif commun de la théologie johannique et du monde ambiant', *N.T.S.* v (1958–9), 157–73.

Dahl, N. A. *Das Volk Gottes. Eine Untersuchung zum Kirchenbewußtsein des Urchristentums* (Oslo, 1941).

Daniélou, J. 'La symbolique du temple de Jérusalem chez Philon et Josèphe', *Serie orient. Roma*, 14 (1957).

—— 'Le symbolisme de l'eau vive', *Rev. S.R.* xxxii (1958), 335–46.

De Kruijf, Th. *Der Sohn des lebendigen Gottes* (Anal. Bibl. 16; Rome, 1962).

Denis, A. M. 'La fonction apostolique et la liturgie nouvelle en esprit. Étude thématique des métaphores pauliniennes du culte nouveau', *R.S.P.T.* xlii (1958), 401–36, 617–56.

Doeve, J. W. *Jewish Hermeneutics in the Synoptic Gospels and Acts* (Leiden, 1954).

—— 'Purification du Temple et desséchement du figuier. Sur la structure du 21ème chapitre de Matthieu et parallèles', *N.T.S.* i (1954–5), 297–308.

Ehrlich, E. L. *Die Kultsymbolik im Alten Testament und im nachbiblischen Judentum* (Stuttgart, 1959).

Feuillet, A. 'La Demeure céleste et la destinée des chrétiens. Exégèse de II Cor., V, 1–10 et contribution à l'étude des fondements de l'eschatologie paulinienne', *Rech. S.R.* xliv (1956), 161–92, 360–402.

—— 'Le baptême de Jésus d'après l'Évangile selon saint Marc (1, 9–11)', *C.B.Q.* xxi (1959), 468–90.

Feuillet, A. 'Le Fils de l'homme de Daniel et la tradition biblique', *R.B.* LX (1953), 170–202, 321–46.

Fitzmyer, J. A. 'A Feature of Qumrân Angelology and the Angels of 1 Cor. xi. 10', *N.T.S.* IV (1957–8), 48–58.

—— 'Qumrân and the Interpolated Paragraph in II Cor. vi. 14–vii. 1', *C.B.Q.* XXIII (1961), 271–80.

—— 'The Use of Explicit Old Testament Quotations in Qumran Literature and in the New Testament', *N.T.S.* VII (1960–1), 297–333.

—— '"4Q Testimonia" and the New Testament', *Th.St.* XVIII (1957), 513–37.

Flusser, D. 'The Dead Sea Sect and Pre-Pauline Christianity', *Scripta Hierosolymitana* IV (1958), 215–66.

—— 'Two Notes on the Midrash on II Sam. vii', *I.E.J.* IX (1959), 99–109.

Foerster, W. Art. σέβομαι κτλ., *T.W.B.* VII, 168–95.

Fraeyman, M. 'La spiritualisation de l'idée du temple dans les épîtres pauliniennes', *Ephem. Theol. Lov.* XXIII (1947), 378–412.

Friedrich, G. Art. σάλπιγξ κτλ., *T.W.B.* VII, 71–88.

—— 'Beobachtungen zur messianischen Hohepriestererwartung in den Synoptikern', *Z.Th.K.* LIII (1956), 265–311.

Fuller, R. H. *The Mission and Achievement of Jesus. An Examination of the Presuppositions of New Testament Theology* (London, 1954).

Gärtner, B. 'Bakgrunden till Qumranförsamlingens krig (The Background of the Qumran War)', *Religion och Bibel*, XIX (1960), 35–72.

—— *Die rätselhaften Termini Nazoräer und Iskariot* (Horae Soederblomianae, 4; Uppsala–Lund, 1957).

—— *The Areopagus Speech and Natural Revelation* (Uppsala–Lund, 1955).

—— 'טליא als Messiasbezeichnung', *Sv. Exeget. Årsbok*, XVIII–XIX (1953–4), 98–108.

Gelin, A. Art. Messianisme, *Diction. de la Bible*, Suppl. V, 1165–1212.

Gerhardsson, B. *Memory and Manuscript. Oral Tradition and Written Transmission in Rabbinic Judaism and Early Christianity* (Uppsala–Lund, 1961).

Ginsberg, H. L. 'The Oldest Interpretation of the Suffering Servant', *V.T.* III (1953), 400–4.

Ginzberg, L. *The Legends of the Jews*, I–VII (Philadelphia, 1938–46).

Gnilka, J. 'Das Gemeinschaftsmahl der Essener', *B.Z.* V (1961), 39–55.

—— '2 Kor. 6, 14–7, 1, im Lichte der Qumranschriften und der

Zwölf-Patriarchen-Testamente', in *Festschrift J. Schmid* (Regensburg, 1963), 86–99.

Goguel, M. *Vie de Jésus* (Paris, 1932).

Haenchen, E. 'Johanneische Probleme', *Z.Th.K.* LVI (1959), 19–54.

Hanson, S. *The Unity of the Church in the New Testament. Colossians and Ephesians* (Uppsala, 1946).

Heaton, E. W. 'The Root שאר and the Doctrine of the Remnant', *J.T.S.* III (1952), 27–39.

Herntrich, V. Art. λεῖμμα κτλ., *T.W.B.* IV, 200–15.

Hochmuth, E. *Die Gebete der Kriegsrolle*, Inaug.-Diss., Karl-Marx-Univ. Leipzig (1959).

Holm-Nielsen, S. *Hodayot. Psalms from Qumran* (Aarhus, 1960).

Hvidberg, F. F. *Menigheden af den nye Pagt i Damascus* (Copenhagen, 1928).

Iersel, B. M. F. van. *'Der Sohn' in den synoptischen Jesusworten. Christusbezeichnung der Gemeinde oder Selbstbezeichnung Jesu?* (Nov. Test., Suppl. 3; Leiden, 1961).

Jeremias, J. Art. ἀκρογωνιαῖος κτλ., *T.W.B.* I, 792–3.

—— Art. Ἰωνᾶς, *T.W.B.* III, 410–13.

—— Art. λίθος κτλ., *T.W.B.* IV, 272–83.

—— Art. παῖς θεοῦ, *T.W.B.* V, 653–713.

—— 'Der Gedanke des "Heiligen Restes" im Spätjudentum und in der Verkündigung Jesu', *Z.N.T.W.* XLII (1949), 184–94.

—— *Golgotha* (Angelos, Arch. f. neutest. Zeitgesch. u. Kulturkunde. Beiheft 1; Leipzig, 1926).

—— *Jerusalem zur Zeit Jesu*, I–III² (Göttingen, 1958).

—— *Jesus als Weltvollender.* (Beiträge z. Förd. christl. Theol., 33; Gütersloh, 1930).

Johnson, A. R. *The One and the Many in the Israelite Conception of God* (Cardiff, 1942).

Klijn, A. F. J. 'Stephen's Speech—Acts vii. 2–53', *N.T.S.* IV (1957–8), 25–31.

Kosmala, H. *Hebräer–Essener–Christen. Studien zur Vorgeschichte der frühchristlichen Verkündigung* (Studia Post-Biblica, 1; Leiden, 1959).

Kuhn, K. G. 'Die beiden Messias Aarons und Israels', *N.T.S.* I (1954–5), 168–79.

—— 'Les rouleaux de cuivre de Qumrân', *R.B.* LXI (1954), 193–205.

—— 'The Lord's Supper and the Communal Meal at Qumran', in K. Stendahl, *The Scrolls and the New Testament* (New York, 1957), pp. 65–93.

Lane, W. R. 'A New Commentary Structure in 4QFlorilegium', *J.B.L.* LXXVIII (1959), 343–6.

Larsson, E. *Christus als Vorbild. Eine Untersuchung zu den paulinischen Tauf- und Eikontexten* (Uppsala–Lund, 1962).

Léon-Dufour, X. 'Le signe du Temple selon saint Jean', *Rech. S.R.* XXXIX (1951–2), 155–75.

Linton, O. *Das Problem der Urkirche in der neueren Forschung* (Uppsala, 1932).

Liver, J. 'The Doctrine of the Two Messiahs in Sectarian Literature in the Time of the Second Commonwealth', *H.T.R.* LII (1959), 149–85.

Lohmeyer, E.–Schmauch, W. *Das Evangelium des Matthäus* (Göttingen, 1956).

Lohse, E. *Märtyrer und Gottesknecht. Untersuchungen zur urchristlichen Verkündigung vom Sühntod Jesu Christi*, F.R.L.A.N.T.(N.F.), XLVI (Göttingen, 1955).

—— Art. Σιών κτλ., *T.W.B.* VII, 318–38.

Lövestam, E. *Son and Saviour. A Study of Acts 13, 32–37. With an Appendix: 'Son of God' in the Synoptic Gospels* (Coniect. neotest. 18; Lund, 1961).

McKelvey, R. J. 'Christ the Cornerstone', *N.T.S.* VIII (1961–2), 352–9.

Maier, J. 'Zum Begriff יחד in den Texten von Qumran', *Z.A.T.W.* LXXII (1960), 148–66.

Manson, T. W. 'The Son of Man in Daniel, Enoch and the Gospels', publ. in *Studies in the Gospels and Epistles* (Manchester, 1962), pp. 123–45.

Manson, W. *Jesus the Messiah. The Synoptic Tradition of the Revelation of God in Christ with Special Reference to Form-Criticism*[2] (London, 1952).

Mansoor, M. *The Thanksgiving Hymns* (Studies to the Texts of the Desert of Judah, 3; Leiden, 1961).

Mendner, S. 'Die Tempelreinigung', *Z.N.T.W.* XLVII (1956), 93–112.

Michaelis, W. Art. πρωτότοκος, *T.W.B.* VI, 872–83.

Michel, O. Art. ναός, *T.W.B.* IV, 884–95.

—— Art. οἶκος κτλ., *T.W.B.* V, 122–61.

—— *Der Brief an die Hebräer* (Göttingen, 1949).

—— *Der Brief an die Römer* (Göttingen, 1955).

Michl, J. Art. Engel, *R.A.C.* V, 60–97.

Milik, J. T. *Ten Years of Discovery in the Wilderness of Judaea* (London, 1959).

Moule, C. F. D. 'Sanctuary and Sacrifice in the Church of the New Testament', *J.T.S.* I (1950), 29–41.

Mowinckel, S. 'Some Remarks on *Hodayot* 39. 5–20', *J.B.L.* LXXV (1956), 265–76.

Nielsen, E.–Otzen, B. *Dødehavsteksterne. I oversaettelse og med noter* (Copenhagen, 1959).

Nötscher, F. 'Geist und Geister in den Texten von Qumran', in *Mélanges bibliques André Robert* (Paris, 1957), pp. 305–15.

—— *Gotteswege und Menschenwege in der Bibel und in Qumran* (Bonner Bibl. Beitr., 15; Bonn, 1958).

—— 'Heiligkeit in den Qumranschriften', *R.Q.* II (1959–60), 163–81, 315–44.

—— 'Himmlische Bücher und Schicksalsglaube in Qumran', *R.Q.* I (1958–9), 405–11.

Odeberg, H. *The Fourth Gospel. Interpreted in its Relation to Contemporaneous Religious Currents in Palestine and the Hellenistic–Oriental World* (Uppsala, 1929).

—— *Pauli brev till Korintierna* (Stockholm–Lund, 1944).

Pedersen, J. *Israel. Its Life and Culture*, I–IV (London–Copenhagen, 1926–40).

Pfammatter, J. *Die Kirche als Bau. Eine exegetisch-theologische Studie zur Ekklesiologie der Paulusbriefe* (Anal. Gregor., 110; Rome, 1961).

Ploeg, J. van der. *Le Rouleau de la Guerre* (Studies on the Texts of the Desert of Judah, 2; Leiden, 1959).

—— 'The Meals of the Essenes', *J.S.S.* II (1957), 163–75.

Rabin, C. *The Zadokite Documents* (Oxford, 1954).

Rad, G. von. *Theologie des Alten Testaments*, I (Munich, 1957).

Rengstorf, K. H. *Hirbet Qumrân und die Bibliothek vom Toten Meer* (Stuttgart, 1960).

Reuss, J. 'Die Kirche als "Leib Christi" und die Herkunft dieser Vorstellung bei dem Apostel Paulus', *B.Z.* II (1958), 103–27.

Riesenfeld, H. *Jésus transfiguré. L'arrière-plan du récit évangélique de la transfiguration de Notre-Seigneur* (Uppsala–Lund, 1947).

Ringgren, H. 'The Branch and the Plantation in the *Hodayot*', *Bibl. Research*, VI (1961), 3–9.

—— *Tro och liv enligt Döda-havsrullarna* (Stockholm, 1961).

Rost, L. 'Gruppenbildungen im Alten Testament', *T.L.Z.* LXXX (1955), 1–8.

Rowley, H. H. 'The Qumran Sect and Christian Origins', *B.J.R.L.* XLIV (1961), 119–56.

Schlatter, A. *Die Theologie des Judentums nach dem Bericht des Josefus* (Beiträge z. Förd. christl. Theol., 26; Gütersloh, 1932).

Schlier, H. *Der Brief an die Epheser* (Düsseldorf, 1957).

—— 'Vom Wesen der apostolischen Ermahnung. Nach Römerbrief 12, 1–2', in *Die Zeit der Kirche* (Freiburg, 1956), pp. 74–89.

Schmid, J. *Das Evangelium nach Markus*[4] (Regensburg, 1958).

Schmidt, K. L. Art. ἀγωγή κτλ., *T.W.B.* I, 128–34.

Schmidt, K. L. 'Jerusalem als Urbild und Abbild', *Eranos Jahrbuch*, XVIII (1950), 207–48.
—— K. L. and M. A. Art. πάροικος κτλ., *T.W.B.* V, 840–52.
Schnackenburg, R. *Die Kirche im Neuen Testament* (Freiburg–Basel–Vienna, 1961).
—— *La théologie du Nouveau Testament. État de question* (Stud. Neotest., Subsidia, 1; Bruges, 1961).
Schneider, J. Art. ἔρχομαι κτλ., *T.W.B.* II, 662–82.
Schrenk, G. Art. ἱερός κτλ., *T.W.B.* III, 221–84.
—— Art. λεῖμμα κτλ., *T.W.B.* IV, 198–200.
Schubert, K. 'Die Messiaslehre in den Texten von Chirbet Qumran', *B.Z.* I (1957), 177–97.
Schürer, E. *Geschichte des jüdischen Volkes im Zeitalter Jesu Christi*, I–III (Leipzig, 1901–9).
Schweizer, E. 'Die Kirche als Leib Christi in den paulinischen Homologumena', *T.L.Z.* LXXXVI (1961), 161–74.
Scott, E. F. *The Crisis in the Life of Jesus* (New York, 1952).
Seidelin, P. 'Das Jonaszeichen', *Stud. Theol.* V:2 (1952), 119–31.
Selwyn, E. G. *The First Epistle of St Peter. The Greek Text with Introduction, Notes and Essays* (London, 1952).
Silbermann, L. H. 'A Note on 4QFlorilegium', *J.B.L.* LXXVIII (1959), 158–9.
Simon, M. 'Retour du Christ et reconstruction du Temple dans la pensée chrétienne primitive', in *Mélanges M. Goguel* (Neuchâtel–Paris, 1950), pp. 247–57.
—— *Verus Israel. Étude sur les relations entre chrétiens et juifs dans l'empire romain* (Paris, 1948).
Smith, C. W. F. 'No Time for Figs', *J.B.L.* LXXIX (1960), 315–27.
Spicq, C. *L'Épître aux Hébreux*, I–II (Paris, 1952–3).
—— 'L'Épître aux Hébreux, Apollos, Jean-Baptiste, les Hellénistes et Qumrân', *R.Q.* I (1958–9), 365–90.
—— *Les Épîtres pastorales*[2] (Paris, 1947).
Stählin, G. Art. ξένος κτλ., *T.W.B.* V, 1–36.
Stauffer, E. 'Probleme der Priestertradition', *T.L.Z.* LXXXI (1956), 135–50.
Stendahl, K. Art. Kirche, *R.G.G.* III[3] (1959), 1297–304.
Strack, H. L.–Billerbeck, P. *Kommentar zum Neuen Testament aus Talmud und Midrasch*, I–IV (Munich, 1922–8).
Strathmann, H. Art. λατρεύω κτλ., *T.W.B.* IV, 58–66.
Strugnell, J. 'Flavius Josephus and the Essenes. *Antiquities* XVIII. 18–22', *J.B.L.* LXXVII (1958), 106–15.
—— 'The Angelic Liturgy at Qumrân—4Q serek širôt 'olat haššabāt', *V.T., Suppl.* VII (1960), 318–45.

Sutcliffe, E. F. *The Monks of Qumran as Depicted in the Dead Sea Scrolls. With Translations in English* (London, 1960).

Talmon, Sh. 'The Calendar Reckoning of the Sect from the Judaean Desert', *Scripta Hierosolymitana*, IV (1958), 162–99.

Teicher, J. L. 'Priests and Sacrifices in the Dead Sea Scrolls', *J.J.S.* V (1954), 93–9.

Vaux, R. de. *L'archéologie et les manuscrits de la Mer Morte* (Brit. Acad., Schweich Lectures 1959; London, 1961).

—— *Les institutions de l'Ancien Testament*, I–II (Paris, 1958–60).

Vermès, G. 'Car le Liban, c'est le Conseil de la Communauté', in *Mélanges bibliques André Robert* (Paris, 1957), pp. 316–25.

—— 'The Symbolical Interpretation of *Lebanon* in the Targums', *J.T.S.* IX (1958), 1–12.

Vielhauer, Ph. *Oikodome. Das Bild vom Bau in der christlichen Literatur vom Neuen Testament bis Clemens Alexandrinus* (Karlsruhe, 1940).

Volz, P. *Die Eschatologie der jüdischen Gemeinde im neutestamentlichen Zeitalter nach den Quellen der rabbinischen, apokalyptischen und apokryphen Literatur dargestellt* (Tübingen, 1934).

Wallace, D. H. 'The Essenes and Temple Sacrifice', *Theol. Zeitsch.* XIII (1957), 335–8.

Weber, F. *Jüdische Theologie auf Grund des Talmud und verwandter Schriften gemeinfaßlich dargestellt*[2] (Leipzig, 1897).

Weise, M. *Kultzeiten und kultischer Bundesschluß in der 'Ordensregel' vom Toten Meer* (Studia Post-Biblica, 3; Leiden, 1961).

Weiss, K. 'Paulus—Priester der christlichen Kultgemeinde', *T.L.Z.* LXXIX (1954), 355–64.

Wenschkewitz, H. *Die Spiritualisierung der Kultusbegriffe. Tempel, Priester und Opfer im Neuen Testament.* (Angelos, Arch. f. neutest. Zeitgesch. u. Kulturkunde. Beiheft 4; Leipzig, 1932).

Wernberg-Møller, P. *The Manual of Discipline* (Studies on the Texts of the Desert of Judah, 1; Leiden, 1957).

Widengren, G. *The King and the Tree of Life in Ancient Near Eastern Religion* (Uppsala Univ. Årsskrift; Uppsala, 1951).

Wolfson, H. A. *Philo. Foundations of Religious Philosophy in Judaism, Christianity and Islam*, I–II[2] (Cambridge, Mass., 1948).

Yadin, Y. 'A Midrash on II Sam. vii and Ps. i–ii (4QFlorilegium)', *I.E.J.* IX (1959), 95–8.

—— 'Some Notes on the newly published *Pesharim* of Isaiah', *I.E.J.* IX (1959), 39–42.

—— 'The Dead Sea Scrolls and the Epistle to the Hebrews', *Scripta Hierosolymitana*, IV (1958), 36–55.

INDEX OF AUTHORS

INDEX OF SUBJECTS

Jonah, 112f.
Judah, 24, 26, 38, 43

Law
  correct interpretation, 41
  exposition of, 69
  knowledge of, 8
  observance of, 4, 13, 17ff., 25, 27, 30,
    33f., 43ff., 67, 83ff., 99f., 108f.,
    115, 124ff.
Lebanon, 26, 43f.
Levites
  of Qumran, 5, 8, 10, 51, 81ff.
  of the temple, 1, 5ff.
Light–darkness, 49, 55, 102
  children of, 93

Maccabees, 14, 16, 18
Maskil, 128f.
Meal, the sacred, 10ff.
Members of the community
  age-limits, 7
  blemishes excluding from, 6f., 32, 62
  hierarchy, 8, 11
Messiah
  the coming, 14, 17, 48, 105, 109
  the corner-stone, 77f., 103, 133, 136
  of Righteousness, 38
Messianic self-consciousness, ix, 27, 47,
    91, 104, 106f., 111, 116, 118, 122f.,
    127, 137
Mišmarôt, 9
Moabite, 32, 62
Moses, 31, 67, 89
Mysteries of God, 29, 70, 140
  of Christ, 103

Nathan, 31f., 35, 39, 132

Paradise, 28
Pharisaism, 5, 81, 83
Pillar of the truth, 66, 68ff., 103
Plantation, 26, 28, 31, 37, 58, 64f., 77
Preacher of Lies, 24
Priests, the Christians as, 72, 79
Priests of Jerusalem, 1ff., 5ff., 12ff., 16,
    18f., 81, 107, 109, 113, 115, 123
  age-limits, 7
  duties, 9
  garments, 3, 9, 12
  hierarchy, 3, 8f.
  perfect sacrifices, 2, 27
  physical blemishes, 2, 6, 32

ritual bath, 2, 13
  table-fellowship, 10f., 13
Priests of Qumran, 4f., 8ff., 25, 32, 40,
    42, 73, 78, 81ff., 95
  priestly functions, 8ff., 51
  priests and laymen, 4, 23, 29, 78
Purification, 12f., 29, 44, 96, 124
Purity, 6, 10ff., 32f., 54f., 57, 59f.
  exhortation to, 50f., 55f., 59, 88, 91

Rabbis, rabbinic, 18f., 24, 45, 83
Remnant, the holy, 37, 39, 47f., 56, 126
Risen Lord, 100, 139
Rock, the holy, 24, 27f., 76f., 90

Sacrifices, 2, 9, 19ff., 25ff., 29f., 34,
    45ff., 61, 79, 83f., 86, 100, 108,
    115, 124
  see also Spiritual sacrifices
Saints of heaven (sons of heaven), 61,
    63f., 91, 94, 96ff., 100, 132
  of the most High, 47, 127ff.
Samaria, 24, 108, 119
Sanhedrin, 2
Scribes, 18
Seed of David, 37, 39, 40
Seleucids, 16
Servant of the Lord, *see* Ebed Yahweh
Shekinah of God (Presence of God), 2,
    16, 22f., 31, 33, 47, 50, 53f., 56,
    58, 64, 95, 100, 110, 114ff., 121,
    126, 129
Sheol, 113
Shiloh, 38
Shoot of David, 35, 37ff.
Sinai, 89f.
Son
  first-born, 37, 97f., 130ff.
  of God, 101, 123, 130, 138
  of man, 47, 118, 123, 125, 127ff.,
    137f.
Spirit, spirits, 29, 45, 56ff., 61, 64f., 69f.,
    73, 75, 85ff., 96, 98, 101, 103, 116ff.,
    121, 125, 132, 139ff.
Spiritual
  house, 68, 72ff., 84, 104
  priesthood, 79f., 83ff.
  sacrifices, 19, 29, 34, 44ff., 47, 72,
    80, 84ff., 100, 104
Stephen, 100, 112
Stone
  the corner-stone, 26f., 64, 69, 71ff.,
    75ff., 106, 133f., 136, 140

Stone (*cont.*)
  the living, 27, 66, 72, 75, 104, 133
  living stones, 43, 66, 75, 79, 104, 136
  rejected, 133f.
  tested, 71, 76ff., 133, 135
Stranger, 32f., 61ff., 76

Tabernacle, 17, 58
  of David, 35, 40ff.
Teacher of Righteousness, 4, 18, 23f.,
  37f., 42, 69, 73f., 101, 104, 125f.,
  135, 137f.
Temple of Jerusalem, 1, 8f., 13, 16, 18,
  21ff., 30, 32, 46, 50, 58, 68, 73, 81,
  84, 87, 94, 99, 119, 126
  altar of, 2, 20, 24, 46
  critics of, 14, 18ff., 24, 46, 84, 95,
  99f., 105, 109f., 112f., 116, 119ff.
  fall of, 33, 45
  holiness, 2, 13, 62
  Holy of holies, 2, 26f., 29, 53, 73,
  134
  liturgy, 8ff., 19f.
  profanation of, 14, 16, 19f., 46f.,
  190f., 139
  the holy rock, *see* Rock
  sacrifices, 2, 9, 19ff., 45, 99, 118

Yahweh's dwelling-place, 1, 7, 13, 16,
  22ff., 31f., 47f., 53f., 58f., 65, 90,
  92, 94f., 103, 108, 116, 140
Temple, the coming, 16f., 21, 25, 30,
  33, 35, 49, 54, 80f., 83, 91, 105,
  108, 110f.; *see also* Heavenly
  temple
Testimonia, 52, 54
Therapeutae, 11, 13
Tree of life, 28
Tribes, the twelve, 79
Truth, 23, 25f., 29, 69f., 76, 126, 129,
  135, 139

Wall, the high, 76, 135
  of Jerusalem, 76
  the tested, 26f., 68, 77f., 134f.
War, the eschatological, 93
  the holy, 10, 94, 102
Water of life, 28, 75
Wicked priest, 16, 18, 24, 43, 59

Zadok, sons of, 4f., 11, 14, 23, 40, 51f.,
  81ff.
Zion, the mount, 16, 23, 31, 35, 40, 44,
  48, 65, 71f., 76, 78, 89ff., 97f., 108,
  119, 126, 133

INDEX OF PASSAGES QUOTED

158

The Testaments of the Twelve Patriarchs
(*cont.*)
Levi
vii   3
xiv–xvi   20
xviii. 5 ff.   117 f.
Judah
xix. 4   59
Asher
vi. 3   67

Josephus
Antiquities
III, 7, 1 ff.   2
III, 12, 2   2
XVIII, 1, 5   20
Bellum
II, 8, 5   12
V, 5, 2   62
V, 5, 7   2, 12

Philo
De vita contemplativa
ix. 69 ff.   12

Targum Jonathan
Exod.
xv. 17 f.   31
Isa.
liii. 2 ff.   126
liii. 8 ff.   126

Targum
I Kings
iv. 33   43

Sifre
Deut.
i. 7   44
xxxiii. 12   33

Middot
v. 4c   12

C.D.
i. 3 ff.   22
i. 4   48
i. 4 ff.   38
i. 5 ff.   131
i. 7   23
i. 7 f.   37
i. 11   37
ii. 5   124

ii. 12 f.   30
ii. 17   67
iii. 12   5
iii. 18   124
iii. 19   73 f.
iii. 19 f.   22, 34
iii. 19 ff.   81, 83
iii. 20   5
iv. 1   5
iv. 1 ff.   5, 14
iv. 2 f.   82
iv. 18 ff.   19
v. 5   5
v. 6 f.   19
v. 18   23
vi. 6 ff.   37
vi. 7   37 f.
vi. 12 f.   19
vi. 15   59
vi. 20   45
vi. 21   62
vii. 4 f.   67
vii. 7 f.   67
vii. 14 ff.   41
vii. 15 f.   41
vii. 16 ff.   37
vii. 18   37
viii. 2   5
x. 5   23
x. 5 ff.   10
x. 6 f.   7
xi. 8   41
xi. 19 f.   20
xi. 20   46, 108
xi. 22   11
xii. 21 ff.   67
xiii. 3 f.   5
xiv. 2   73
xiv. 3 f.   5
xiv. 4   62
xv. 15 ff.   6
xvi. 13   20
xx. 7 f.   128
xx. 9 f.   51
xx. 22 f.   16

1QS
i. 8 f.   67
i. 18 ff.   10
i. 24   46
i. 25   67
ii. 11   51
ii. 17   51